Given in Memory of:
"Jim"
Louis A. DeCatur

by Carol DeCatur

MODERN HAMLETS

& THEIR SOLILOQUIES

STUDIES IN THEATRE

HISTORY & CULTURE

Edited by Thomas Postlewait

MARY Z. MAHER

Modern Hamlets

& THEIR SOLILOQUIES

AN EXPANDED EDITION

foreword by JOHN F. ANDREWS

UNIVERSITY OF IOWA PRESS Ψ *Iowa City*

University of Iowa Press, Iowa City 52242

Copyright © 2003 by the University of Iowa Press

Printed in the United States of America

Design by Richard Hendel

http://www.uiowa.edu/uiowapress

The publication of this book was generously supported by the
University of Iowa Foundation.

Printed on acid-free paper

Library of Congress Cataloging-in-Publication Data

Maher, Mary Zenet.

Modern Hamlets & their soliloquies / by Mary Z. Maher.—
Expanded ed.

p.   cm.—(Studies in theatre history and culture)

Includes bibliographical references.

ISBN 0-87745-826-X

1. Shakespeare, William, 1564–1616. Hamlet.

2. Shakespeare, William, 1564–1616—Stage history.

3. Hamlet (Legendary character).   4. Soliloquy.   5. Acting.

I. Title: Modern Hamlets and their soliloquies.   II. Series.

PR2807.M344 2002

792.9′5—dc21   2002067605

03   04   05   06   07   P   5   4   3   2   1

CONTENTS

Acknowledgments, vii

Foreword by John F. Andrews, ix

Introduction, xi

Hamlet's Soliloquies, xxxi

1. JOHN GIELGUD:
   The Glass of Fashion, 1

2. GUINNESS, OLIVIER, AND BURTON:
   The Mould of Form, 19

3. DAVID WARNER:
   The Rogue and Peasant Slave, 41

4. BEN KINGSLEY:
   In My Mind's Eye, 63

5. DEREK JACOBI:
   The Courtier, Soldier, Scholar, 92

6. ANTON LESSER:
   A Noble Mind, 121

7. DAVID RINTOUL:
   Th' Observ'd of All Observers, 135

8. RANDALL DUK KIM:
   Sir, a Whole History, 153

9. KEVIN KLINE:
   In Action How Like an Angel, 175

10. KENNETH BRANAGH:
   Speak, I Am Bound to Hear, 201

11. SIMON RUSSELL BEALE:
   The Motive and the Cue for Passion, 227

Notes, 247

ACKNOWLEDGMENTS
Expanded Edition

It is an odd quirk of the history of performance that so much of it leaves not a rack behind. We do not know what David Garrick's soliloquies looked and felt like, beyond a couple of scattered reports from witnesses, more precious because these are so rare. What the performer intended to convey and how he shaped his performance is simply irretrievable. Those lost gems of creativity continue to be my quest in this book.

So when Holly Carver, director of the University of Iowa Press, approached me about expanding *Modern Hamlets and Their Soliloquies*, I was intrigued with the idea of bringing the work into the present by selecting Hamlets that represent the best of the transition into the twenty-first century. I refer to those actors who, according to my opinion, taste, and experience, performed the role in a stellar and convincing way. For Hamlet is a role that not only requires discipline and stamina but also calls upon the deepest competencies in classical acting. It demands individuality and panache, that elusive stamp of personal style.

Kenneth Branagh first came to mind. His characterization carries many qualities of the man, providing the energy of someone who has produced the best of the late twentieth-century filmed Shakespeares with a sure knowledge of what delights and instructs a contemporary audience. Branagh's performance also has a sense of command, which he has exhibited in numerous ambitious projects: He is an idea man, a producer, a fund-raiser, a playwright, and a screenwriter as well as an actor and a director. Furthermore, he is a mover and a shaker, socially conscious, political, progressive. Of all the filmed versions of *Hamlet*, Branagh's is much more focused on textual integrity yet never lets go of the flexibility and capability of the film medium. He has prov'd most royal as both artist and entrepreneur.

Simon Russell Beale was another natural choice. I first met him when I was teaching in London in 1989. A colleague in Shakespeare studies, Susan Baker, invited him as a guest lecturer for her class. After class, he joined us for a beer and I found him not only gracious, but possessed of a sparkling wit and intelligence. His career has progressed quickly as he takes on role after role, displaying an astonishing range and capability. I remembered smiling with pleasure during three performances of his Hamlet, marveling at his mastery of craft, which never lost immediacy or naturalism. He is one of the few modern Hamlets who chose to address his solo speeches directly to the audience: They became his intimate companions and then his chief mourners at the end of the play.

I am pleased and gratified with these new offerings. Happily, both men are also friends and mutual admirers of each other's work.

Finally, I would like to express appreciation to Tamar Thomas, Lyn Haill, Trish Montemuro, and David Ira Goldstein, all of whom helped make these interviews possible.

Expanded Edition

Hamlet is widely considered to be the most demanding of Shakespearean challenges, and the majority of observers would identify it as the most complex and problematic role in the entire dramatic repertory. It should not surprise us, then, that the most enduring measure of a classical actor's stature in the theatrical pantheon tends to be the degree to which he—or she—has prevailed as the Prince of Denmark.

This is a consideration that has never been lost on those who have aspired to the highest laurels, and the reputations a noble heritage exalts with greatest reverence are almost inevitably associated with those performers who have left indelible marks upon our perception of this ever-evolving character. One consequence, perforce, is that anyone who attempts to portray Shakespeare's enigmatic protagonist, if only for the briefest of interludes in the span of a lengthy career, is confronted with all the ghosts of Hamlets past. And in no aspect of the part is this more intimidatingly the case than with the soliloquies, which have always been so integral to any depiction of the playwright's most celebrated title figure. How these famous passages are rendered in a particular sequence of defining moments is always the key to everything else in even the most richly nuanced of productions.

It is immensely to her credit that Mary Maher has focused upon this all-important topic, and it is even more to her praise that she has managed to persuade so many of the significant Hamlets of our era to revisit and talk about the anxieties, dilemmas, rhetorical strategies, staging techniques, and specific choices that even the most confident of professionals usually prefer to keep to themselves. The result is an engaging volume that has already established itself as a classic in its initial incarnation, the groundbreaking version of this ongoing exploration which was first published in 1992.

To have conceived and completed such a study—with its fascinating and frequently remarkable account of the ways in which a brilliant cadre of creative minds and sensibilities have confronted some of the most difficult acts of psychological and aesthetic interpretation imaginable—was an extraordinary achievement, and it was instantly recognized as such. Now I'm delighted to report that, in response to innumerable requests, Professor Maher is providing us an even more comprehensive collection, an expansion of the original anthology to incorporate fresh reflections from two of the Danes who have done so much in recent years to keep an august tradition vibrant: Kenneth Branagh and Simon Russell Beale.

Two additional Princes now grace the pages of this expanded edition of *Modern Hamlets and Their Soliloquies*. Kenneth Branagh's star-marked 1997 production of *Hamlet* has been hailed as one of a kind, merging an international cast with an epic rendering of the complete text directed by Branagh, who also plays the title role. Simon Russell Beale's 2000–2001 Hamlet at the Royal National Theatre, which bridges the cusp of the twenty-first century, brings us through the end of a millennium with a version lauded and applauded by London and New York critics. Our wisest and most compelling course is to relish this feast which has been set out for our enjoyment and edification. With that prospect in view, I hope you'll now join me in savoring the treats that are here displayed in so enticing a fashion.

John F. Andrews

INTRODUCTION

"*Hamlet*, in my opinion, is pound for pound the greatest play ever written," declared Laurence Olivier.[1] Indeed, the role of Hamlet is the quintessential feat for actors: to have achieved it with distinction is a mark of attainment in the profession. As Joseph Papp observed, "You haven't graduated until you've played Hamlet."[2] If Hamlet is the supreme acting challenge, then his soliloquies are the major performance challenge within the play. The role of Hamlet is dependent upon the soliloquies for completion—they are the hallmark of his persona.

Soliloquies are the actor's "big moments" for the evening. He analyzes and hones those passages more thoroughly, especially in the case of "To be, or not to be," which John Gielgud called "the famous purple patch which everybody in the audience waits for." This study approaches the soliloquies as a phenomenon of performance, an event which may absorb and project many different interpretative options under the pressures of actual theatrical production. It offers a detailed record of how various twentieth-century English and American actors, beginning with John Gielgud, have approached the challenges and problems of delivering the soliloquies in *Hamlet*. Had we this same information about Richard Burbage, much of our thinking about soliloquies would not be speculative.

I interviewed the following Hamlets: Derek Jacobi, Ben Kingsley, Kevin Kline, David Warner, Anton Lesser, David Rintoul, and Randall Duk Kim. John Gielgud chose to interline and emend a chapter I had drafted about him, a way in which he often works. Alec Guinness wrote a letter about the delivery of the soliloquies. Sadly, both Laurence Olivier and Richard Burton died before the writing of this book, but I hope that I have represented them accurately in chapter 2 by discussing their filmed performances.

The time span of *Hamlet* productions featured here covers a half century, from Gielgud's 1936 American production to Kevin Kline's 1990 *Hamlet*. I decided to interview established actors with a commitment to classical drama. Some have worked in British and American companies such as the Old Vic, the Royal Shakespeare Company, and Joseph Papp's New York Shakespeare Festival. Others have worked in commercial theatre and film as well (e.g., Gielgud, Burton, and Kline). Still others have performed primarily in regional theatres and traveling companies (e.g., Randall Duk Kim). I sought a representative balance of actors from a variety of backgrounds and levels of experience. I placed the Hamlets in chronological order because that sequence demonstrated a shift from following established acting conventions to freeing up the actor for a greater range of performance choices in the soliloquy mode.

Of course, availability for interview and consent to be interviewed factored into my list of actors—as did luck and serendipity. In a way, the actors who appear here actually chose me by answering affirmatively to my requests for interviews. Each saw performance of the role as an important achievement in his career. Other actors declined, and left me (I later saw) with a weeded garden, a shortened but quite representative list.

The interview process was somewhat complicated, as I suspect it always is with actors. I pursued Ben Kingsley, who had extensive film commitments on the Continent, and finally snared him when I was on a brief Easter holiday trip to London. We conversed in the lobby of the Lyric Theatre, Hammersmith, in the midst of one hundred shouting children who had come in for a Saturday drama workshop. I ignored all that and turned on my trusty tape recorder; Kingsley gave me his undivided attention and an unusually thorough interview. The responses that I collected from actors were insistently eclectic, in many ways unsystematic, and invariably pragmatic. Certainly, interpretative options multiplied.

I felt it necessary to contrast stage presentations with some discussion of media versions of Hamlet's soliloquies. The latter do not absolutely require an interview from the actor, partly because we can so clearly observe for ourselves how the actor performed the soliloquy on film or video and partly because in electronic media the decision-making process usually lies conclusively with the director.

On occasion, I interviewed other people who could offer inside information. For example, Tony Church was Polonius to Warner's Hamlet, Julian Glover was Claudius to Jacobi's Hamlet, Barry Edelstein was Kevin Kline's dramaturg. John Trewin, critic for the *London Observer* and author of *Five and Eighty Hamlets*, talked with me a few months before he died about the major twentieth-century British Hamlets that he had seen. These conversations were incidental, however, and I did not make a systematic effort to interview, say, each Hamlet and his director. That, I fear, would have taken more years and more resources than I had. Nevertheless, when certain people made themselves available, I took advantage of the opportunity.

I prepared two pages of interview questions for each actor. The queries clustered around four topics. I asked each actor to describe the overall production style or concept, the performance space, and the influence of these factors on the way he delivered the soliloquy. The second set of questions was designed to probe the relationship between the actor and the director in order to discover their working styles and their decision-making processes. The third set of questions sought to find out how each of the seven soliloquies was spoken regarding the conveyance of images and meaning, the intention of the actor, properties used, gestures and movement employed. The fourth area addressed matters of text—control of structure in performance, verse-speaking, cuts, editions used. Before I interviewed each actor, I prepared additional questions specifically tailored to his own particular production. My goal in each interview was to work through all of the questions; sometimes I succeeded and sometimes I didn't. So I added a kind of insurance policy wherein I provided each actor with a final draft of his chapter to add to or emend.

To prepare for each interview and to provide background for each essay, I checked a promptbook when one existed. A promptbook shows where an actor stood onstage to deliver a soliloquy and what blocking, scenery, and lighting effects were used.[3] I checked a sound recording (again, when one existed), such as those available at the National Sound Archives in London. I also read newspaper and journal reviews, program notes, directors' statements, interviews of actors and directors, journals of productions, and biographies and autobiographies as supporting material. Naturally, I grounded my work in the theoretical and literary-critical material that had been written about soliloquies as well. There were a few fine books available, but none treated soliloquies contextually—as speeches existing within an actual performance setting.

Perhaps this is about as structured as one can be when one works in performance studies. I make no claim to having done a scientific inquiry. Each essay, as I drafted it, was organic and emphasized the nature and the quality of the subject matter that the interview produced. Some interviews focused on text and meaning; others were more about the uniqueness of the production; sometimes the actor was strongest and most informative when describing his acting process or his method of working outward from rehearsal. My good friend and colleague Ralph Berry, who has written a number of books in performance studies, heartened me with this comment: "We are building a bird's nest, Mary—not a geodesic dome." A collection of talented and information-rich actors provided unusually intriguing insights about their art and craft. I hope that I have done them justice in attempting to give a flavor of the surge, movement, and complexities of performance.

In its strictest sense, the word "soliloquy" means "a speaking alone." Some scholars have refined this definition by saying that the speaker believes or perceives himself to be alone.[4] There are two general ways of managing each of Hamlet's soliloquies onstage: the actor can move toward the audience or the actor can allow the audience to move toward him. The latter choice I call an "internalized" method of delivery, in which the actor does not directly contact a theatre audience but speaks to himself; the theatre audience is in the position of overhearing him.[5] Internal soliloquies have been called "meditations," "confessionals," and "secret convictions." They are also labeled *psychomachia*, or "the war within." However, these terms are too narrow for the variety of content in each soliloquy and the range of performance choices available to an actor.

The alternative is the "externalized" method of performing the soliloquy, in which the actor clearly makes eye contact with members of the audience and interacts with them, allowing their laughter and other responses to overtly affect his delivery, perhaps to the extent of altering the timing he has rehearsed or causing him to gesture in a way he has suddenly "found" in the act of performance. Once he has made definite eye contact with the audience, the whole of that speech is perceived as externalized; consequently, an actor usually does so at the *beginning* of the speech for clarity.

Another option, of course, is that the actor may use any combination of the internalized and externalized modes within any given production of *Hamlet*. When combined modes are employed, usually one or another (internal or external) is *clearly dominant*:[6] it was not unusual for Hamlets who chose the direct-address mode to find that one of the soliloquies was best addressed inwardly even though he performed the other six outward. There was a tendency for most of the Hamlets I interviewed to internalize the second soliloquy, "O all you host of heaven." About the remainder, the actors took a great variety of options. I do not mean to champion one mode over the other. Neither is right or wrong, better or worse. Each mode of acting the soliloquy is a separate performance choice with an integrity of its own and needs to have a logic that fits into the aesthetic boundaries that the production creates.

Overall, a continuum of performance choices exists for the Shakespearean soliloquy. At one end are those most direct to the audience, as Edmund's soliloquies are traditionally spoken in productions of *King Lear*. Quite often, although not exclusively, comic soliloquies fall into this group. At the other end are soliloquies like Richard III's final "I am I" speech, which is almost always performed internally. In the middle is a series of soliloquies which offer various possible approaches: the actor or director can exercise a choice about how the speeches are performed. Hamlet's soliloquies fall decisively into this third category.

Very early on, I found that good productions had an aesthetic wholeness which precluded looking at a soliloquy in isolation from the rest of the production. A study about the performance of soliloquies should treat the production as a context for making decisions. Those maxims held here: every production of *Hamlet* that I researched created its own world and generated its own set of possibilities for performing the soliloquies. In each essay, I used as context what Michael Goldman called the three societies of the theatrical experience: the represented world onstage (metaworld), the acting ensemble (the cast), and the theatre audience.[7] Frequently, I discovered that a production had a story beyond the plot, a small society that the acting company created. This extratextual setting occasionally influenced the way the actor decided to perform his soliloquies.

The investigation of the soliloquy in this book is limited to the character of Hamlet partly because the word *soliloquy* is synonymous with the phrase "To be, or not to be." Indeed, Hamlet has 200 of the 280 lines of soliloquy in the play. He is a true soliloquizer because his role definition would be incomplete had he been provided with only dialogue. Soliloquizers are characters who invite us into the judgment process in an almost anatomical way—close to the bone. To the other characters, Hamlet speaks in riddles, obliquely, even confrontationally. In the soliloquies, his discourse is candid and genuine. Horatio is Hamlet's friend, but the audience can become his intimate companion. The soliloquizer takes advantage of that feature of our social lives, the difference between close friends and acquaintances. Close friends are permitted to see our true personalities—warts, insecurities, and inconsistencies. They sit outside the operating room and say, "Do you think he'll make it?" or in the courtoom and say, "Do you think he'll get off?" and hazard fascinating insider opinions. The audience never has quite this same relationship with Claudius and Ophelia, who also have soliloquies. These characters give solo speeches, but they remain apart from the familiarity and mutuality that Hamlet engenders.

Hamlet's soliloquies vary in length from eleven to fifty-seven lines. He delivers seven of them.[8] (They are printed for easy reference in their entirety at the beginning of this book.[9]) Finally, Hamlet's soliloquies encompass a great variety of forms which demonstrate many of the demands of classical acting: highly emotional tirades, thoughtful and contemplative speeches, "double" soliloquies, persuasive speeches, arias about acting.

Scholars speculate on what it is that influences the way an actor finally chooses to perform a soliloquy. A variety of forces are probable, since theatre production is a team effort, an attempt to draw disparate elements into a unified and artistic whole. The more the elements cohere and complement one another, the more successful the event. Here I have separated possible influences into categories in order to generalize about them.

Theatre Architecture and the Playing Space
According to received wisdom, the architecture of the theatre and the shape of the performance space should determine the way a soliloquy is performed. This idea has been under discussion since the Swan drawing was discovered and has been recently revived by excavations of the Rose and the Globe theatres in London. Unfortunately, we simply cannot be conclusive about another time and place, especially when the evidence is fragmentary. We are on far stronger ground to document and draw from

our own theatrical spaces and our own performance conventions. In our own time, an actor and a director do not simply walk into a theatre and announce, "Right. It's a thrust stage and we're stuck with that. We'll do the soliloquies direct address." Both actors and directors manipulate the performance space—building forestages, reconfiguring the actor-audience relationship, and even choosing to deliver very internalized soliloquies in theatres which seem to encourage maximum directness with an audience. In fact, if this study is any index, the shape of the theatre is one consideration, certainly, in determining how soliloquies will be performed, but it is not, in all cases, an overriding concern.

The Text

There is a popular assumption that somehow Shakespeare's text spells out, or *requires* to a great extent, how lines in a soliloquy ought to be delivered. Studies abound in which a scholar offers a "close reading" in a nontheatrical setting and concludes that certain lines have to be performed in a certain way.[10] Such readings assume that each Shakespearean speech has an inherent meaning that is present in the line and interpretable (read "actable") in only one appropriate way. However, stylistic elements in soliloquies, such as rhetorical questions ("Who calls me villain?") or first-person-plural speakers ("When we have shuffled off this mortal coil"), do not automatically dictate specific performance modes. To say so is to become so managerial as to determine how the actor must ply his art. We do know, from the history of performance, that Shakespeare's text is made of very malleable stuff. Actors constantly test its tensile strength by trying different performance options. Peter Brook strongly advised against textual interpretations set in concrete: "The Deadly Theatre approaches the classics from the viewpoint that somewhere, someone has found out and defined how the play should be done."[11]

At the turn of the century, the text was subordinate to scenic decor. So important (and so numerous) were the antiquarian settings of Tree and Irving on the picture-frame stage that the text was cut and rearranged to accommodate scene changes. Indeed, the "How all occasions" soliloquy was one of the traditional cuts in *Hamlet*. Text was the *last* concern of Victorian actors, many of whom simply borrowed wholesale the readings (and even the promptbook) of the actor who preceded them in the role.

Although William Poel's experiments in Elizabethan staging from the 1880s through the 1920s urged a return to textual fidelity, John Gielgud's full-text *Hamlet* in 1936 surprised audiences with its length—people joked that it was being done "in its eternity."

Respect for text as well as thorough exploration of the possibilities of textual interpretation was an idea that developed when Peter Hall took over the Royal Shakespeare Company in 1958. Although full-text productions were not the norm, scenes were not rearranged, and all texts were thoroughly researched. Verse classes were held for actors in order to train them in understanding the interaction of the text and its rhythms. Onetime university don John Barton and voice coach Cicely Berry emphasized textual exploration so much that a "house style" of directing the play outward began to take shape:

> What should [actors] do with a soliloquy? A situation in which a character is almost always alone and seems to be talking to himself. Should such a speech be done to oneself, or should it be shared with the audience? There are very few absolute rules with Shakespeare, but I personally believe that it's right ninety-nine times out of a hundred to share the speech with an audience and a grave distortion of Shakespeare's intention to do it to oneself. If the actor shares the speech, it'll work; if he doesn't, it'll be dissipated and the audience won't listen properly.[12]

In any case, the trend was set and the point was made: decisions about what a line means in performance should be made not in the quiet of the study but rather in the wider context of rehearsals, taking into consideration all the other pressures of production. A concern for textual fidelity carried over into the Time-Life British Broadcasting Corporation "Shakespeare Plays" series,[13] where the whole canon was videotaped in largely uncut texts. Shakespearean scholars responded with stage-oriented performance analyses that emphasized discovering all the possible staging clues in a text. New editions of Shakespeare were generated that claimed to be performance-oriented and usable in the theatre. More and more scholars documented productions, testing the aesthetic limits of performance choices.[14] It is important to note that theatre practitioners led this movement toward exploring and restoring text. The general goal was to open textual possibilities rather than to limit them. Twentieth-century actors have consequently inherited a duty to treat the text with care.

The Director

In the first third of the twentieth century, Shakespearean productions felt the emergence of the modern producer or director, who gradually replaced the actor-manager in companies like Frank Benson's. William Poel's ideas about the Elizabethan apron stage influenced Harley Granville Barker, who sought to project the play as far out into the audience as possible and to fuse spectator and actor in a new kind of theatrical experience.

Overshadowing all other Shakespearean directors during the first half of the twentieth century was, of course, Tyrone Guthrie, whose developing functionalism—that is, a relatively bare stage and acting areas— prompted a major reassessment of the director's role in Shakespearean productions. Guthrie strove to remove the demarcation line between audience and actor; although he did not abandon the proscenium stage, he came to believe that a strict realism was inappropriate for Shakespeare and to favor the open stage. Years after he directed his 1937 *Hamlet* (Olivier) and his 1938 *Hamlet* (Guinness) at the Old Vic, Guthrie developed some ideas about soliloquies:

> If you reflect that Shakespeare must have *known* that the speakers of his soliloquies could not face every member of the audience all the time, you are virtually forced to this conclusion: the soliloquies must have been spoken by the actor either on the move, or rotating on his own axis, so that at different moments everyone in the house could see his eyes and the expression of his face. When this idea first occurred to me, I tried speaking "To be or not to be"—a soliloquy which, in my opinion, demands repose and not movement—rotating slowly on my own axis. With a little practice I felt that I could have made my expression clear to everybody, if they had been in a circle around me, and still not seem to be fidgeting. The movements had, of course, to be carefully planned and executed very slowly and smoothly. I then tried to speak the speech sitting in a chair; and again I found that I could turn and direct my glance around a full circle without any fussy or fidgety movement. Technically, the trick

seemed to be to move the eyes first, then let the head follow, then let the shoulders slowly follow the head, and so on down to the feet.[15]

Guthrie experimented early on with stylized production concepts, whereby a director imposes his own vision on a play, selecting a particular period or idea which informs the entire production and its elements, including costuming, set design, characterization, and even textual cuts. Usually, a concept steers the interpretation of the play, drawing out one or two central themes which predominate over (and sometimes exclude) others. Such an overriding idea often influences many production decisions, including how the soliloquies might be performed.

Production concepts are a direct result of the power of the director in modern play production. One of the most influential was Peter Brook, who set the world of Shakespearean performance reeling with his saturnalian *A Midsummer Night's Dream*. Production concepts have become an imperative for the Royal Shakespeare Company. Directors like Peter Hall added to the forestage of the Royal Shakespeare Theatre[16] to facilitate a specific vision in his 1965 *Hamlet*, a concept so tightly built that only direct-address soliloquies made sense as a performance mode. During the Royal Shakespeare Company's "Peter Hall years" (c. 1958–67),[17] production concepts were justified because they promoted relevance, the philosophy that Shakespearean plays must speak to and relate to contemporary issues. They were widely imitated in the United States and on the Continent and are still the norm for Shakespearean production today.

After Peter Hall directed David Warner in *Hamlet* in 1965, more performance options opened up, not only for idiosyncratic and individualized ideas of Hamlet's character but also for performing the soliloquies: no actor could escape the shaping influence of the director in the twentieth century. Some actors, including Gielgud, Olivier, and Kline, knew that the only way to avoid being the victim (or hero) of a stylized concept was to direct oneself in *Hamlet*. They promptly created their own concepts, confirming Guthrie's belief that "an interpretative artist can only make his own comment upon the work which he endeavours to interpret,"[18] i.e., no production of Shakespeare, even if it is set in the time of the composition of the play, can be entirely concept*less*.

The Audience

The audience can indeed influence the way a soliloquy is spoken, and that leverage is exercised mostly in midperformance. In the case of the externalized soliloquy, for example, audiences often find themselves in very prescribed roles. Ralph Berry contends that Hamlet's soliloquies are seven sessions with the audience as psychiatrist, counselor, and analyst.[19] He also speaks of Hamlet's "wooing" the audience in the externalized soliloquy. The relationship has been described as one of juror, collaborator, or coconspirator. Some Hamlets have seen themselves as stage-manager prototypes, the audience within their power to manipulate. Laurence Olivier suggested just such a function in describing his stage performance of Richard III: "Halfway through I knew I was holding the reins. When I said, 'Can I do this and cannot get the crown' the audience made a sort of hhhaaaaa sound. The atmosphere was tingling. I had seduced Lady Anne and the audience as well."[20]

Here, Olivier was a direct soliloquizer, who was adept at channeling the sympathies of the audience and who managed, in one way or another, to bond with them. Clearly, many kinds of collusion can go on between performer and audience.

An audience can also affect the shape of a given performance. The topic of the stability and instability of performance, performance as an event which by its nature changes, is one that surfaces continually in the interviews. The actors' comments support what is widely acknowledged but largely inoperative in performance criticism: theatre productions change from night to night and even from moment to moment. Taken to an extreme, it could be argued that *performance* cannot be discussed at all, but only *performances*—that is, a series of shifting and imperfectly realized intentions, coupled with intended effects, that audiences grasp imperfectly and filter according to their individual tastes, values, and experiences.

Tradition

Tradition has more of an influence in the theatre than we like to admit. Three parallel legacies operate within this book: the tradition of Shakespearean acting, the tradition of acting Hamlet, and the tradition of acting the soliloquy. For much of the nineteenth century, acting in Shakespeare was characterized by declamatory delivery, statuesque poses, sweeping gestures, long pauses, and excessive stage business ("making points") invented to go along with the lines. Hamlets were thought of as dreamy and poetic. Later generations would consider that kind of acting "artificial," however, and Shakespearean sets in the late nineteenth century and through the early part of the twentieth century were highly realistic. In order for the soliloquies to be considered realistic as well, actors delivered them as "spoken thoughts." Sir Henry Irving and Johnston Forbes-Robertson each spoke out loud to himself but did not make eye contact with the audience. In fact, one of the reasons that we can speculate about the tradition at this time is that observers complained only when actors spoke too much to the audience.[21]

In the twenties and thirties, there was a move toward more psychological portrayals of Hamlet with John Barrymore. The trend was evident in Gielgud's highly emotional Hamlets, but more so in Olivier's conception of an Oedipal *Hamlet*. The size and scope of the acting remained large and actors still made points; performers were not, of course, completely free of the excesses of the previous age. Nevertheless, observers described Hamlets of this era as "more naturalistic," especially Olivier in his verse-speaking. Soliloquies continued to be internalized, although no longer performed in realistic sets but rather on stylized, antirealistic stages with acting areas and levels mounted, by and large, in proscenium theatres. By that time also, the play moved along in one long, flowing action rather than stopping for set changes.

Postwar Hamlets continued in the prewar image, either the honorable prince with the graceful profile or the Freudian prince with the hidden family secrets. The fifties and sixties brought an evolution to a mixture of two kinds of acting: parts of the text were highly rhetorical and versified and other parts were naturalistic and colloquial, and acting should reflect both. Guthrie spoke of Shakespeare's "intermittent realism" punctuated by highly operatic playing.[22] His ideas were later reinforced by Peter Brook, who, in *The Empty Space*, discussed Shakespeare's mix of Brechtian and Beckettian dramaturgy. Brook thought that Shakespeare's plays should be produced in a fluid alternation of illusion and nonillusion.[23]

David Warner's Hamlet in 1965 and Ben Kingsley's in 1975 announced a movement away from the romantic Hamlet to a more tough-minded prince. Warner's version spawned a few scruffy, lower-class princes who spoke the soliloquies directly to their audiences. Even though Richard Burton had played the film role of Jimmy Porter in *Look Back in Anger*, his 1964 Hamlet was on the cusp of change in the Hamlet tradition, a tough, virile character with an upper-class accent—directed, of course, by the leading romantic Hamlet of the thirties, John Gielgud.

After Warner, Hamlet did not have to be handsome or noble, and most actors knew that forty was pretty much the latest age at which they should attempt the role. In the late seventies, there was a periodic effort to restore the noble prince. After that time as well, it became difficult to categorize Hamlets. Warner's interpretation was clearly a turning point, breaking through a structured convention to offer many more performance options. His Hamlet opened the way not only for original ideas of character conception but also for the mode of performing the soliloquies. In this way, revolts which challenge tradition and help to reshape long-standing conventions are important.

Society and Culture

The political and economic conditions, the prevailing social values and attitudes, the general mentality of an age or generation—almost all are reflected in theatrical practice. When the sixties happened, replete with the shock and tumult of such historical events as the Vietnam War, it was logical that the change in social values would be reflected in theatre conventions and subsequently in the Hamlets of the era. Especially after John Osborne's *Look Back in Anger* at the Royal Court in 1956, theatre in Britain (where the Hamlet tradition was centered at the time) took a strong left turn. The plays of Noël Coward and J. B. Priestley, featuring genteel upper-class dilemmas in the drawing room, were brusquely shoved aside to showcase a struggle for self-assertion from the underclasses in Britain. The world was now ready and waiting for the ur-prince—or, as some critics labeled him, the *un*-prince—to rise from the ashes of social turmoil and to speak directly to audiences. It is significant that Warner emerged from the talents and energies of the leading classical Royal Shakespeare Company; despite its classical orientation, the RSC was particularly sensitive to and reflective of social change.

At this time as well, *Hamlet* productions on the Continent dealt with social and political concerns, often reflecting each individual country's postwar and cold-war atmospheres. In the United States, Shakespeare festivals (which began in the thirties) flourished at their highest level in the seventies and eighties, as America saw its theatre move to the regional areas of the country.[24] Although New York retained one of the largest Shakespeare festivals, a great deal of the "Shakespeare complex" was located in smaller, rural festivals.[25] Of the Hamlets represented here, Kevin Kline's was produced in the large, urban Shakespeare festival created by Joseph Papp, and Randall Duk Kim's took place in a smaller festival located in the woodlands of Wisconsin.

Earlier, the war and postwar years had produced a thriving assortment of media Shakespeares on radio, television, and film. Laurence Olivier launched his patriotic *Henry V*—generated from and funded by Britain's War Office as a propaganda film—and it was soon followed by his very influential 1948 *Hamlet*. Burton's 1964 *Hamlet* was simultaneously shown in movie theatres across the United States. The culmination of media Shakespeare was the massive seven-year (1979–85) series "The Shakespeare Plays," emanating from the BBC and coproduced with American corporations from Time-Life Television. Widely purchased by both American and British schools and universities, the series was influential in developing the "media soliloquy," experimenting with on-camera modes of performance.

The Actor

The most important influence on the soliloquy is the actor himself. I save him for last because, ironically, scholars do not focus on the performer. Instead, they concentrate on text and the shape of the theatre. But the actor who plays the role of Hamlet is the critical catalyst in the play. His gifts and capabilities determine, ultimately, how the soliloquies will be performed. Occasionally he has definite notions received from the text or from his training about how to perform solo speeches. Most important of all, he determines the character conception of Hamlet. He must match his personal traits and attributes with those of the character, determining which textual qualities to emphasize and which to downplay. Within that conceptual framework, he experiments to discover the most appropriate way to play the soliloquies—whether to deliver them internally or externally, the amount and quality of physicality to use, what vocal characteristics to employ, and how much business to invent.

Hamlet, more than any other part, is a "personality" role. Text meets personality and Hamlet is the product. The soliloquy must flow out-ward from each actor's character conception, and the actor's personality largely delivers that. The role requires that Hamlet be onstage for all except twenty minutes of the play. Consequently, the play is not about revenge or delay or murder but about how this actor's personality reacts to and experiences prescribed plot complications. Steven Berkoff dis-cussed the point in his book, *I Am Hamlet*:

> [Hamlet is] a quest for the most perfect we can make ourselves. So I *am* Hamlet since when you *play* Hamlet he becomes *you*. When you play Hamlet, you play yourself and play the instrument which is you. If you can make a good tune as an actor your best tunes will come out of Hamlet and if not then that does not matter but you will be a better actor for having played it, and been there.[26]

We can consider the actor a kind of critic, but we must understand that his initial context is rehearsal, a place for opening options rather than closing them. In modern theatre practice, the text is not a fait accompli but a springboard for performance solutions. How an actor chooses to express a line is part of what makes his profession a creative process; most actors like to open possibilities and are serious about justifying interpretative choices. Actors are entitled to their own reading of a line and, in fact, take a rather public punishment for being "wrong." Derek Jacobi generated critical outrage in his *Hamlet* when he decided not to play "To be, or not to be" as a soliloquy at all. There is overwhelming evidence in these chapters that certain Hamlets, especially those who have directed the play, are scholars and historians of the role.

An actor will often speak of his "journey" through a play, which means that he creates an inner biographical logic from the text to use as a per-formative undertext. His work is literary in some ways but pragmatic in others. He is pulled in both directions, endeavoring to be true to the dialogue while discovering his own emotional and physical potentialities in acting the script. John Russell Brown describes Paul Scofield in re-hearsal, "moving around and flexing his body as he spoke the words to himself,"[27] an actor in the act of interpretation, searching for the appro-priate theatrical metaphor, for the physical and vocal equivalent of speaking the speech that the playwright has offered him. Of course, in the soliloquy, the actor's freedom is considerable because he is alone onstage. In most cases, he has made concrete choices from the options he discovered during rehearsal.

The actors discussed in this book manifest a variety of reasons for making choices about delivering soliloquies. The stage space was influential for some, the fashion in playing for others, the production's concept for still others. There was a vigorous mixture of rationales, and very few unmixed motives. It is important that our assumptions be built on observing and recording, to the extent possible, the actual available information.

I will conclude with some generalizations that emerged as I interviewed these actors. First and foremost, there is no preordained way to perform a soliloquy or to deliver a given line in a soliloquy. Performance critics have been trying to administer this difficult truth for years, so I won't belabor the obvious. To a certain extent, the "meaning" of a soliloquy is lexically tied to its content; however, a different actor is performing that speech in each new production, from an individual personality set within a carefully manufactured theatrical context, so we must acknowledge that the "performed meaning" can contain additional layers of data. The meaning an actor intends to send (the meaning inside his head, what he is thinking about as he speaks the lines) may or may not be totally received by the audience member, who is perceiving sounds and sights through his or her own perceptual screen of experiences.

Generally speaking, direct-address soliloquies temper or even negate madness in a Hamlet. Direct-address soliloquies are perceived as more persuasive and objective, cooler and more rational than internalized soliloquies—Hamlet stepping outside the play and commenting upon it. Also, an actor is most convincing in delivering direct-address soliloquies if he has not developed close relationships with the other characters onstage, notably Horatio or Ophelia; thus it is logical for him to find support off the stage, with the theatre audience. Playing more humor in Hamlet's overall character conception aids an actor when he decides to speak to the audience. The wit of the character persuades spectators to be receptive to his direct-address speeches.

The converse is also generally true: an actor can move toward communicating full-blown insanity if he keeps his soliloquies inward. If he develops close relationships within the play's world, it is less logical for him to direct-address the soliloquies, to seek a support system outside the play.

The first and second soliloquies are definitional, serving as inciting incidents that propel the rest of the play. The first soliloquy gives a great deal of "casting" information; the audience sees what kind of person this Hamlet is, how his personality will be constructed. The second soliloquy is rarely directly addressed to an audience because almost all Hamlets are overwhelmed by the visit of the Ghost and look inward to find the appropriate emotional reaction. The burden of this soliloquy is self-expression and catharsis. The third soliloquy, with its sudden shifts of mood and intention, has the most histrionic potential for the actor. Its rhetorical pattern of asking questions cues some—but not all—actors to address it outward.[28] All the actors recognized the fourth soliloquy as much more contemplative and a strong contrast to the third. "To be, or not to be" often disperses an actor's concentration because the speech is so fatally famous and audience members are following along, sometimes out loud. The actor seeks the right performative pitch for the fourth soliloquy, resisting the tendency to flattening and trivializing it versus oversolemnizing and thus overstaging it. The fifth soliloquy expresses a renewal of Hamlet's determination to commit murder while also demonstrating that he intends to protect his mother from his revengeful objective; both beats have to be distinctly performed. The sixth, the "double soliloquy" (Claudius tries to pray, and Hamlet declines to kill him) requires complicated stage management because there is always someone in the audience who feels that Hamlet and Claudius can overhear one another. The seventh soliloquy was traditionally cut from turn-of-the-century productions.[29] In modern productions it has historical and political resonances. Fortinbras was, in the thirties, an admirable and noble prince, with whom Hamlet identified. After a series of brutal invasions of countries in the mid-twentieth century, Fortinbras took on the cast of a tyrant, and Hamlet, by identifying with him, would have been drawing inspiration from a marauder or despot. The performance meaning of the seventh soliloquy has changed over time in response to historical events.[30]

Having set forth these brief statements, I will now do what I set out to do: let the actors tell their own stories about the soliloquies. One of the most remarkable of their accounts is a fitting conclusion to these introductory comments because it testifies to the abiding power of the soliloquy from situation to situation and from age to age. The story is told by two well-known British actors, Richard Pasco and his wife, Barbara Leigh-Hunt, who toured with a production of *Hamlet* throughout the United States, Canada, Europe, and the Middle East. After receiving critical acclaim in the North American segment of the tour, the group prepared for the next stop:

RICHARD PASCO: It was so thrilling to have played the famous soliloquy all over the world—the sense of achievement, the sheer luck of doing it in incredible circumstances. And we had an amazing experience with it in Israel in 1967, literally days after the Six-Day War.

BARBARA LEIGH-HUNT: We'd been in Washington completing our U.S. tour when the war suddenly began. We were all glued to the television set—that one was able to watch a war, in that way, on television! And, of course, we were interested because we were due to fly to Israel. A cable came from the Foreign Office to say the visit to Israel was in balance, await further instructions. Another cable came to say that the war was completed, visit to go ahead as planned, and we couldn't believe it because we were convinced we wouldn't go! So we arrived four days after the war was over. You can imagine what the feeling in Israel was like—people's emotions were very, very near the surface. On a previous visit to Jerusalem, we'd not been able to get to the other side of the city because it was a divided city. There was an area called "no-man's-land," and there were pillboxes and sentries and rolls of barbed-wire fences. And on this trip there were huge signs on the wire that said, "This way to the wall." And someone had scrawled across it, "This WAS way to the wall." The wire had been cut and it was just rolled back and you could walk wherever you wanted to go. I remember going down to the Wailing Wall and walking back up to the gate where three coachloads of pilgrims had been deposited outside the gate. They ran down to the Wall—I've never seen such a large group of people so overwrought, all crying. We were all swept back by the tide of them as they passed. In England, people are so used to keeping their emotions buttoned down, so we were unused to seeing people publicly displaying grief or happiness in that way. Absolutely naked, unashamed, unalloyed—there for all to see. When we got to the kibbutz, we were all taken by different families to their homes. We were shown how the kibbutz ran and what they grew and how they lived their lives. And then we were taken to the dining hall to eat, and they put on this spontaneous entertainment for us.

RP: It was a wonderful evening in this huge canteen, a corrugated iron and steel building, with long, long tables and several hundred people there. A dinner, with wine and everything—and they entertained us with songs, poetry, dancing. It slowly percolated around us as a group that we would be expected to do something back to reciprocate. And someone said to me, "Dick, what are you gonna do? Charlie's doing something with his guitar."

BLH: And someone handed him a microphone and he stood on a table. And he told them how we'd been very involved in the war, having seen it blow by blow from the outside. And he told them how ill-prepared we were for the generosity of their welcome. He was always good at speaking what was in other people's hearts. He said that one of Hamlet's soliloquies seemed appropriate for the situation and then he just launched into "To be, or not to be." There was this momentary stunning silence—literally, you couldn't hear a sound. And then there was a storm of applause. It had gone right to their hearts.

RP: That was the best audience for that speech ever. It was an extraordinary experience!

HAMLET'S SOLILOQUIES

O that this too too sallied flesh would melt,
Thaw, and resolve itself into a dew!
Or that the Everlasting had not fix'd
His canon 'gainst self-slaughter! O God, God,
How weary, stale, flat, and unprofitable
Seem to me all the uses of this world!
Fie on't, ah fie! 'tis an unweeded garden
That grows to seed, things rank and gross in nature
Possess it merely. That it should come to this!
But two months dead, nay, not so much, not two.
So excellent a king, that was to this
Hyperion to a satyr, so loving to my mother
That he might not beteem the winds of heaven
Visit her face too roughly. Heaven and earth,
Must I remember? Why, she should hang on him
As if increase of appetite had grown
By what it fed on, and yet, within a month—
Let me not think on't! Frailty, thy name is woman!—
A little month, or ere those shoes were old
With which she followed my poor father's body,
Like Niobe, all tears—why, she, even she—
O God, a beast that wants discourse of reason

Would have mourn'd longer—married with my uncle,
My father's brother, but no more like my father
Than I to Hercules. Within a month,
Ere yet the salt of most unrighteous tears
Had left the flushing in her galled eyes,
She married—O most wicked speed: to post
With such dexterity to incestious sheets,
It is not, nor it cannot come to good,
But break my heart, for I must hold my tongue.

(I.ii.129–59)

SECOND SOLILOQUY

O all you host of heaven! O earth! What else?
And shall I couple hell? O fie, hold, hold, my heart,
And you, my sinows, grow not instant old,
But bear me stiffly up. Remember thee!
Ay, thou poor ghost, whiles memory holds a seat
In this distracted globe. Remember thee!
Yea, from the table of my memory
I'll wipe away all trivial fond records,
All saws of books, all forms, all pressures past
That youth and observation copied there,
And thy commandement all alone shall live
Within the book and volume of my brain,
Unmix'd with baser matter. Yes, by heaven!
O most pernicious woman!
O villain, villain, smiling, damned villain!
My tables—meet it is I set it down
That one may smile, and smile, and be a villain!
At least I am sure it may be so in Denmark.
So, uncle, there you are. Now to my word:
It is "Adieu, adieu! remember me."
I have sworn't.

(I.v.92–112)

O, what a rogue and peasant slave am I!
Is it not monstrous that this player here,
But in a fiction, in a dream of passion,
Could force his soul so to his own conceit
That from her working all the visage wann'd,
Tears in his eyes, distraction in his aspect,
A broken voice, an' his whole function suiting
With forms to his conceit? And all for nothing,
For Hecuba!
What's Hecuba to him, or he to Hecuba,
That he should weep for her? What would he do
Had he the motive and the cue for passion
That I have? He would drown the stage with tears,
And cleave the general ear with horrid speech,
Make mad the guilty, and appall the free,
Confound the ignorant, and amaze indeed
The very faculties of eyes and ears. Yet I,
A dull and muddy-mettled rascal, peak
Like John-a-dreams, unpregnant of my cause,
And can say nothing; no, not for a king,
Upon whose property and most dear life
A damn'd defeat was made. Am I a coward?
Who calls me villain, breaks my pate across,
Plucks off my beard and blows it in my face,
Tweaks me by the nose, gives me the lie i' th' throat
As deep as to the lungs? Who does me this?
Hah, 'swounds, I should take it; for it cannot be
But I am pigeon-liver'd, and lack gall
To make oppression bitter, or ere this
I should 'a' fatted all the region kites
With this slave's offal. Bloody, bawdy villain!
Remorseless, treacherous, lecherous, kindless villain!
[Oh Vengeance!] [1]
Why, what an ass am I! This is most brave,

That I, the son of a dear father murthered,
Prompted to my revenge by heaven and hell,
Must like a whore unpack my heart with words,
And fall a-cursing like a very drab,
A stallion. Fie upon't, foh!
About, my brains! Hum—I have heard
That guilty creatures sitting at a play
Have by the very cunning of the scene
Been strook so to the soul, that presently
They have proclaim'd their malefactions:
For murther, though it have no tongue, will speak
With most miraculous organ. I'll have these players
Play something like the murther of my father
Before mine uncle. I'll observe his looks,
I'll tent him to the quick. If 'a do blench,
I know my course. The spirit that I have seen
May be a dev'l, and the dev'l hath power
T'assume a pleasing shape, yea, and perhaps,
Out of my weakness and my melancholy,
As he is very potent with such spirits,
Abuses me to damn me. I'll have grounds
More relative than this—the play's the thing
Wherein I'll catch the conscience of the King.

(II.ii.550–605)

FOURTH SOLILOQUY

To be, or not to be, that is the question:
Whether 'tis nobler in the mind to suffer
The slings and arrows of outrageous fortune,
Or to take arms against a sea of troubles,
And by opposing, end them. To die, to sleep—
No more, and by a sleep to say we end
The heart-ache and the thousand natural shocks

That flesh is heir to; 'tis a consummation
Devoutly to be wish'd. To die, to sleep—
To sleep, perchance to dream—ay, there's the rub,
For in that sleep of death what dreams may come,
When we have shuffled off this mortal coil,
Must give us pause; there's the respect
That makes calamity of so long life:
For who would bear the whips and scorns of time,
Th' oppressor's wrong, the proud man's contumely,
The pangs of despis'd love, the law's delay,
The insolence of office, and the spurns
That patient merit of th' unworthy takes,
When he himself might his quietus make
With a bare bodkin; who would fardels bear,
To grunt and sweat under a weary life,
But that the dread of something after death,
The undiscover'd country, from whose bourn
No traveller returns, puzzles the will,
And makes us rather bear those ills we have,
Than fly to others that we know not of?
Thus conscience does make cowards of us all,
And thus the native hue of resolution
Is sicklied o'er with the pale cast of thought,
And enterprises of great pitch and moment
With this regard their currents turn awry,
And lose the name of action.—Soft you now,
The fair Ophelia. Nymph, in thy orisons
Be all my sins rememb'red.

(III.i.55–89)

FIFTH SOLILOQUY

'Tis now the very witching time of night,
When churchyards yawn and hell itself breathes out
Contagion to this world. Now could I drink hot blood,

And do such bitter business as the day
Would quake to look on. Soft, now to my mother.
O heart, lose not thy nature! let not ever
The soul of Nero enter this firm bosom,
Let me be cruel, not unnatural;
I will speak daggers to her, but use none.
My tongue and soul in this be hypocrites—
How in my words somever she be shent,
To give them seals never my soul consent!

(III.ii.388–99)

SIXTH SOLILOQUY

Now might I do it pat, now 'a is a-praying;
And now I'll do't—and so 'a goes to heaven,
And so am I reveng'd. That would be scann'd:
A villain kills my father, and for that
I, his sole son, do this same villain send
To heaven.
Why, this is hire and salary, not revenge.
'A took my father grossly, full of bread,
With all his crimes broad blown, as flush as May,
And how his audit stands who knows save heaven?
But in our circumstance and course of thought
'Tis heavy with him. And am I then revenged,
To take him in the purging of his soul,
When he is fit and season'd for his passage?
No!
Up, sword, and know thou a more horrid hent:
When he is drunk asleep, or in his rage,
Or in th' incestious pleasure of his bed,
At game a-swearing, or about some act
That has no relish of salvation in't—
Then trip him, that his heels may kick at heaven,
And that his soul may be as damn'd and black

As hell, whereto it goes. My mother stays,
This physic but prolongs thy sickly days.

(III.iii.73—96)

SEVENTH SOLILOQUY

How all occasions do inform against me,
And spur my dull revenge! What is a man,
If his chief good and market of his time
Be but to sleep and feed? a beast, no more.
Sure He that made us with such large discourse,
Looking before and after, gave us not
That capability and godlike reason
To fust in us unus'd. Now whether it be
Bestial oblivion, or some craven scruple
Of thinking too precisely on th' event—
A thought which quarter'd hath but one part wisdom
And ever three parts coward—I do not know
Why yet I live to say, "This thing's to do,"
Sith I have cause, and will, and strength, and means
To do't. Examples gross as earth exhort me:
Witness this army of such mass and charge,
Led by a delicate and tender prince,
Whose spirit with divine ambition puff'd
Makes mouths at the invisible event,
Exposing what is mortal and unsure
To all that fortune, death, and danger dare,
Even for an egg-shell. Rightly to be great
Is not to stir without great argument,
But greatly to find quarrel in a straw
When honor's at the stake. How stand I then,
That have a father kill'd, a mother stain'd,
Excitements of my reason and my blood,
And let all sleep, while to my shame I see
The imminent death of twenty thousand men,
That for a fantasy and trick of fame

Go to their graves like beds, fight for a plot
Whereon the numbers cannot try the cause,
Which is not tomb enough and continent
To hide the slain? O, from this time forth,
My thoughts be bloody, or be nothing worth!

(IV.iv.32–66)

MODERN HAMLETS

& THEIR SOLILOQUIES

John Gielgud in Hamlet, 1936. *Vandamm photo courtesy of the Billy Rose Theatre Collection, New York Public Library for the Performing Arts, Astor, Lenox, and Tilden Foundations.*

I

JOHN GIELGUD : *The Glass of Fashion*

Because of his extensive and varied experience with *Hamlet*, John Gielgud owned the role of the prince in a way that no other twentieth-century actor could. As James Agate wrote of Gielgud's 1944 production, "Mr. Gielgud is now completely and authoritatively master of this tremendous part. He is, we feel, this generation's rightful tenant of this 'monstrous Gothic castle of a poem' . . . I hold that this is, and is likely to remain, the best Hamlet of our time."[1] Gielgud played the role of Hamlet more than five hundred times in his long and distinguished career. He was one of the few modern actors who simultaneously performed in and directed himself as Hamlet. And in 1964 he was director of the play with yet another actor in the role, Richard Burton.

Gielgud read a draft of this essay before publication, adding his own insights, information, and commentary. His chart below delineates the places and occasions where his performances of Hamlet and his directorial involvement with the play occurred:

HAMLET

Director/Design

1. Old Vic, London, *1929–30*. Entirety and cut version. Production moved to Queens Theatre, Shaftesbury Avenue, for short season.

Harcourt Williams (Elizabethan dress)

2. New Theatre (now the Albery), London, *1934*. Then toured big provincial English cities.

John Gielgud (Durer-Cranach-Holbein design by Motley)

3. Empire Theatre, New York, *1936–37*. Moved to St. James's Theatre. Opened in Toronto, played also Rochester, Washington, Boston, Baltimore.[2]

Guthrie McClintic (Van Dyck design by Jo Mielziner)

4. Lyceum Theatre, London, *1939*. Kronberg Castle (for one week), Elsinore; open-air performances in courtyard.

John Gielgud

5. Tour of troop performances in the Far East, Karachi, Madras, Colombo, Rangoon, Singapore, Cairo, Delhi, *1944*.

John Gielgud

6. Haymarket Theatre, London, *1944–45*. In repertory with Congreve's *Love for Love*, *Midsummer Night's Dream*, Webster's *Duchess of Malfi*, Maugham's *The Circle*.

George Rylands, Cambridge Professor of English

7. Directed Burton in New York, *1964*, Lunt-Fontanne Theatre. Also Toronto, Boston, Washington.[3]

John Gielgud (Modern dress)

Gielgud's view of the chief character, his mode of playing, and much of his stage business set the fashion for Hamlets in the decades to come. In discussing the acting of a scene in the 1936 production, Bernard Grebanier asserted: "Because of the great prestige of Gielgud's wonderful production, *it has more or less become a tradition to play the scene . . . in the same way.*"[4] In a 1988 television documentary titled "John Gielgud: An Actor's Life," the narrator said, "His memorable assumption of some roles has stamped an impression so deep that other actors have found it difficult to erase."[5] As a model for others, Gielgud cannot be overestimated. Here, indeed, was a definitive Hamlet.

Gielgud came to the role steeped in its nuances and possessing an encyclopedic knowledge of past performances. A member of the famous theatrical family of Terrys, he "knew by heart the vivid description in

Ellen Terry's memoirs of how Irving played it."[6] But when asked if he had modeled his performance after anyone, he replied,

No, I didn't. I thought I had. I thought I would copy all the actors I'd ever seen, in turn, and by then I'd seen about a dozen or fifteen Hamlets [including H. B. Irving (Sir Henry's son), Ernest Milton, Henry Baynton, Arthur Phillips, Colin Keith-Johnston, and John Barrymore].[7] Of course, [the elder, Sir Henry] Irving was my god, although I'd never seen him. . . . I didn't try to copy, I only took note of all the things he'd done and looked at the pictures of him and so on. But when it came to the Vic, the play moved so fast and there was so much of it that I suddenly felt, "Well, I've just got to be myself," and I really played it absolutely straight as far as I could. Of course, I was fortunate in that . . . Hamlet had never been allowed to be given to a very young actor until I played it. It was the kind of prize that an actor, when he went into management at the age of forty or fifty, H. B. Irving, for instance . . . allowed himself.[8]

Gielgud seldom borrowed performance ideas from other actors for his Hamlet and only rarely from what he knew of Irving. He knew what other actors had done because that was the norm for actors, as well as theatre critics, in his age. But he felt that his portrayal was based on his own personality rather than anyone else's version.

Gielgud played his first Hamlet in 1929, at the age of twenty-six, and his last in 1945. This essay will focus on his 1936 production because it was the best-documented. In that production, Gielgud's acting of the role was neither as melodramatic and passionate as Barrymore's, nor as bloodless and delicate as Leslie Howard's. Howard's *Hamlet* opened in New York within a month of Gielgud's. The press created a "War of the Hamlets," thus generating publicity and box office sales for Gielgud's, which the critics preferred.[9] Indeed, he was in top form for this second shot at it:

The most thrilling Hamlet for me was the production in New York in 1936, because I felt I was on my mettle. It was my first big chance in America, and I was presented by an American management with an all-American cast. . . . Rehearsals were thrilling because everyone seemed so excited about my performance.[10]

Critics reviewing the production spoke of his restraint from bellowing and ranting, his intellectualism, and his "modernizing" of the role, which appears to mean not only a simplicity and a spontaneity in the acting of it but also a retention of the doubleness of Hamlet's character.[11] Gielgud kept the sardonic humor and the occasionally violent language;[12] he remained noble, still very much the prince, yet he did not lack fire. Certainly, his performance choices suggest a volatile Hamlet. The play-within-the-play scene was unusually active: He actually held a manu-script (presumably the "dozen or sixteen lines" he asked the First Player to insert) and thumped out the meter of the lines as the players spoke. He also walked around during the performance of "The Mouse-trap," drop-ping pointed phrases into the ears of both king and queen. As the playlet closed, he leaped onto the king's empty throne, shouting triumphantly, waving the manuscript in the air and ultimately tearing it to tiny pieces, which he threw like confetti.[13] He even took snuff from a silver box and then offered some to the gravedigger in that comic scene.[14] The combi-nation of melodramatic and realistic effects accounts for his being labeled both traditional and nontraditional. The public admired the perfor-mance, and the play ran for more than four months. He was feted lav-ishly in New York and afterwards on tour.

The production had opened at the Empire Theatre in New York and then transferred to the St. James's Theatre. It ran from October 8, 1936, to January 30, 1937. The 132 performances were produced by Guthrie McClintic and designed by Jo Mielziner. The design was "in the period," meaning Renaissance in style. It is the most thoroughly documented of the actor's portrayals because of Rosamond Gilder's book *John Gielgud's "Hamlet,"* in which she attempted to create a "verbal portrait"[15] of the production, a scene-by-scene description of both gestures and blocking as he played the role. The opening chapter discussed character concep-tion in a generalized way and was followed with notes from the actor himself.[16] Gilder's descriptions were a compiled account of what Gielgud most often did during each segment of the play. Although parts of it wax poetic in admiration of Gielgud, the book is nevertheless a remarkable endeavor in the annals of theatre history.

Gilder's account provides a sense of the actor's journey through the play. In the first "act" of the play (the production was divided into two acts, or nineteen scenes with one intermission[17]), Gielgud was manic but never totally mad, and within the second half he presented an integrated personality who had come to terms with what he had to do.[18] Gielgud mapped out certain "shocks," histrionic moments of realization, such as the Ghost's revelation of murder, which built to the firm resolution in the seventh soliloquy, "How all occasions do inform against me" (IV.iv.32–36).

Gielgud performed the first soliloquy ("O that this too too sallied flesh," I.ii.129–59),[19] as if anguish were its chief tonal quality. It followed a court scene which was rendered intimate and domestic since the courtiers and attendants exited at I.i.63 once the official business concluded. Consequently, Hamlet's discussion with Claudius and Gertrude was decorously private, yet he clearly indicated that he disliked his uncle. After the king and queen exited, he began his soliloquy by making an important transition for the audience, effecting a change between the character's outer persona as presented to Gertrude and Claudius and the private self, who suffered from events. Gilder observed: "As the doors close behind them, the mask of manners that has protected Hamlet's face drops."[20]

Gielgud continued the soliloquy by walking slowly upstage and coming to rest at the end of the council table. Finally, he turned and looked outward but did not make contact with the audience. On "weary, stale, flat, and unprofitable," each word dropped a note lower than the one before. As he began "so loving to my mother," the tempo accelerated as nausea about the recent marriage filled him. On the beat that ended "Let me not think on't," he covered his face with his hands. Unable to still his mind, he surged on obsessively: "a little month" began a build to the climax of "incestious sheets." On the final two lines, he sank back "into apathy and hopeless sorrow."[21] The soliloquy was delivered with two major vocal builds, some general slow movement about the set, and variety in emotion using horror and growing disgust as sizzling punctuation marks within a context of depression or "dull bitterness."[22]

In this soliloquy, Gielgud felt that pauses should be omitted except at the "natural places" marked for breath or when there were "full stops" (i.e., end-stopped lines).[23] A short pause was needed before "Frailty, thy name is woman" and a more definite break required before the summarizing couplet at the end. Nevertheless, there should be a drive through the speech at an unswerving speed as "thoughts and exclamations succeed each other."[24]

Gielgud wrote about the first soliloquy as one of the most exciting for the actor because it "seem[ed] to set the character once and for all in the audience's minds."[25] His actor's instincts told him that its position of primacy made it extremely important in establishing the audience-actor relationship. Once he had spoken, the actor could not make major changes in the character conception. Gielgud described the speech as a reaction to the first of a series of "shocks and surprises" that accumulate in the play. He felt that Hamlet, placed in an impossible predicament, found his way to his fate through episodes like this one.[26] Since the actor spoke to himself (avoiding eye contact with individuals), he had no other need than to be truthful. The audience was eavesdropping on his agonies.

The second soliloquy (at I.v.92–112) was clearly the second major shock in Hamlet's Denmark. It followed a very dramatic appearance by the Ghost, which ended with Hamlet's body lying on the ground racked with sobs. Gilder described the atmosphere: "The quick step and harsh quick words are the outward sign of all that has been growing in him since he heard of the Ghost, the tension that rises steadily, notch by notch, like a tightened violin string till it cracks at the Ghost's departure."[27]

Gielgud was aided by scenic effects here. The stage was darkened, and there was the eerie sound of wind blowing as Hamlet appeared on the ramparts. After the exchange between Ghost and son, Gielgud fell to his knees, his hand extended to the departing creature as lights blacked out for a hushed pause. Soon lights came up again faintly, and the soliloquy began with an "animal wail of pain":

He turns on himself, self-lacerating, driving unpityingly . . . little by little, he raises himself on one knee. He is bruised, beaten; only his will remains and forces him up, governing even the "distracted globe" which is indeed overburdened to the verge of frenzy.

"Ay, thou poor ghost" brings again the note of tenderness and pity, pity for the dead and for his father in his torment. The second "Remember thee" is an oath. The words that follow come quickly, rising in a swift crescendo of dedication to the final "yes, by heaven" which brings him to his feet. A pause, and then the infamy sweeps over him. "O most pernicious woman!" His first thought, even before Claudius and murder, is of her. Then his mind turns to Claudius—to the morning scene of flattery and smug smiles, to the laughter and revelry below at this very moment. His voice breaks with anger at such villainy. He moves to the right, almost to the spot where the Ghost had stood. On the tablet from which he has just wiped all "trivial fond records," on his brain seared by the Ghost's revelations, he will register this shame. The phrase ends on a high, hard challenge: "So, uncle, there you are," as he strikes his forehead with his hand.

Then, deep and very quiet, the oath of consecration, "Now to my word." Both hands clasp the sword-hilt. The blade gleams in an arc as he raises it to his lips. He stands straight as a lance, the silver line above his head piercing heavenward in salute. Slowly, with finality, with full and weary prescience, he lowers the sword, "I have sworn 't."[28]

Gilder's description of the soliloquy and her use of the word "frenzy" indicates that Gielgud enacted a total collapse, a physical shattering as well as mental chaos. The soliloquy was as personal as a nervous breakdown. It was therefore not shared with the theatre audience. He was deeply shaken but managed to restore his equilibrium through the ritual resolve of the final vow.

Gielgud's notes mention two pieces of business. To record in the "table of my memory," he "banged [his] head" at "So, uncle, there you are," since that phrase marked the conclusion of a long beat. Gielgud wanted his hands and body free from notebooks or other properties throughout the speech in order to use gestures which demonstrated the full physicality of the moment. He had earlier contrived to relieve himself of his cloak at the beginning of the scene, just in case it should hamper expression.[29]

For the third soliloquy ("O, what a rogue and peasant slave am I!" II.ii.550–605), Gielgud followed a through-line of action which began in the previous scene with the players. He had read and been convinced of the appropriateness of Harley Granville Barker's logic that references like "the unnerved father falls" as well as the mention of Hecuba and the "mobled Queen" (Gertrude, he felt) should explicitly be reacted to by

Hamlet. After the Hecuba speech, he took a very long pause to study the player's face as if he saw within the man a reflection of his own dilemma. This set the audience up for the forthcoming comparison of the player's emotions to Hamlet's emotions, a major propellant in the thrust of the third soliloquy. Hamlet reprimanded Polonius in telling him how to treat the players, making his rebuke an "explosion"[30] rather than advice, since tension had mounted under his skin during the player's speech. All of the players exited, and Hamlet drew one of them aside to ask for some "dozen or sixteen lines" to be inserted into the Gonzago play.[31]

Then followed a piece of business which helped Gielgud make the transition into the soliloquy. Rosencrantz and Guildenstern remained onstage to continue talking with Hamlet; however, "with a swift, repelling gesture, he dismisses them."[32] He then took a long pause, his back turned to the audience, and leaned on his hands on the table. This gesture endowed the first line "Now I am alone," with special meaning: in his desolation, he shared his anguish with no one. This also gave him preparation time for the burst of bottled anger that launched the whole first section of the soliloquy.

"O, what a rogue" began a torrent of self-deprecation, and Gielgud continued a vocal build to "damn'd defeat was made," whereupon he fell on a stool. But the battering of self had not stopped. He plunged into the short questions with vehement speed, rising quickly on "Who does me this?" There was a third build; this time his body shook with anger, the pitch of his voice rose up on "treacherous, *lecherous, kindless villain!*"[33] On the famous climactic "Oh Vengeance!" he grabbed his dagger and smashed it into the doorway; the dagger fell from his raised arm, and his body melted onto the top step with a pitiful bleat, "Fie upon it! Foh!" A long pause ensued in which only sobbing could be heard.[34]

Finally, there was a slow movement: he raised his head tentatively on "About, my brains." Soon an idea was seen registering on his face, his voice hoarse and whispery. Once he had begun, the details of the plan were important and accumulated quickly. Gielgud added to this speed a bit of madness: "the look of one loosed out of hell." He took a long pause before the final two lines in order to consider once more whether he was led by the devil or an honest ghost; his plan would ensure "grounds more relative." The scene closed with feverish business: "Gielgud throws himself into a chair beside the table and begins to write wildly on a piece of paper. There is a blackout."[35]

Gielgud divided the soliloquy into two distinct performance beats. The first half built to near-climax and a culminating peak at "Oh Vengeance!" Then followed six lines of transition, with Gielgud on his knees. The second section, played downstage and closer to the audience, was about plotting, where Hamlet posed the play-within-the-play solution. The business at the end, scribbling wildly, was an idea borrowed from Irving, an epilogue in which the actor begged for favor. For Gielgud confessed that early on in his career, he felt the final couplet should provide the logical moment for the greatest applause in the play.[36] If an intermission was taken at this point, there was great argument for playing for these effects; the break also allowed a space between the third and fourth soliloquies, the former a great aria, the latter so like a philosophical dissertation. The difficulty, for the actor, came in starting up again so near "To be, or not to be" while latecomers were seating themselves for the second half of the play. In this production, in fact, the interval break was taken later on, after the nunnery scene. Nevertheless, Gielgud insisted, "When I have played the part on first nights I have never been able to believe that I could succeed in it until this applause has come."[37]

The fourth soliloquy ("To be, or not to be," III.i.55–89) followed a mere fifty-five lines later. The scene was in the great hall of the castle, a huge room with two flights of stairs. The business of stowing Ophelia had been dispatched by Polonius and Claudius. Hamlet came in defiantly, stage right. He saw that no one was there and continued to the stage left platform, where he began the famous lines thoughtfully and inwardly; there was no attempt to speak to the audience. Gielgud reported that it was occasionally difficult to ignore them because "frequently one can hear words and phrases being whispered by people in the front rows, just before one is going to speak them."[38]

This soliloquy was clearly more cerebral than the others; Gilder calls it "mystic contemplation."[39] She recounts that each successive idea registered on Gielgud's face as Hamlet mentally shuffled the thoughts for consideration. The possibility and the longing toward death were balanced against the fear of what it means to no longer be alive. He seemed to be moving toward one concept particularly, a mind magnetized by the need to examine the void: perhaps it was like sleeping; perhaps it was like sleeping *no more*, and so Gielgud emphasized those words.[40]

Gielgud used few gestures and little movement in delivering the speech. On "bare bodkin," he omitted the actual knife but suggested it with a pantomimic movement of the left hand, as though a dagger lay point inward in his palm. On the phrase "puzzles the will," he began to pace about the stage.[41] His restless movement at this juncture indicated that he had returned from his trance to the world of action. He needed to get on with the task. Ophelia entered, and the spell of the speech was broken.

Gielgud carefully connected this speech with the big soliloquy which preceded it: "I now realize that the effect of despondency in 'To be, or not to be' is a natural and brilliant psychological reaction from the violent and hopeless rage of the earlier speech."[42] Closely juxtaposed as they are, the two soliloquies provide differing but perfectly legitimate responses for a passionate and intelligent man: "Rogue and peasant slave" effectively purges, and "To be" theorizes, philosophizes, contemplates. Gielgud also noted that "various directors have changed the order of the scenes and placed the two soliloquies in an exchanged sequence. I can see no excuse for this theory."[43]

Gielgud believed that "To be, or not to be" was so arresting, so filled with images and intricate mental cul-de-sacs that it tended to lure the performer. However, it must not be delivered as a set piece or "turn":

> This particular speech in itself is such a perfect thing that if you have executed it correctly you are apt to feel complete and satisfied at the end of it, but not ready to go straight into the rest of the scene. Like so many other great speeches in this play, it has to be studied, spoken, re-studied and re-spoken until one can combine in it a perfect and complete form of poetry and spontaneous thought and at the same time use it only as a part of the action. The character and value of the speech lie in the fact that it leads on to the next part of the scene, just as it must grow out of the previous action. Of course, the better one speaks it and the more completely one can win the audience by a good delivery of it, the more difficult it is to join it to the subsequent conversation and interplay with other characters.[44]

He attempted what he thought was a "great innovation by walking about in this speech," but Mrs. Patrick Campbell came to the play one night and implored him to cut out the movement as it distracted from the lines.[45] He later added, "She was quite right and I never did it again."[46]

Both the third and the fourth soliloquies end in irresolution toward carrying out the deed. This Hamlet wanted resolution or he would not have chastised himself so caustically during the third soliloquy. "To be" showed that he had serious cause to consider the weighty consequences: once Hamlet decides to act, many people's lives are irrevocably altered.

The Gilder account reveals that the fifth soliloquy ("'Tis now the very witching time of night," III.ii.388–99) was omitted entirely. In the text, it follows closely upon a quite exciting rendering of the scene with Rosencrantz and Guildenstern and the recorder, which Gielgud elected to play as follows:

> As Rosencrantz and Guildenstern move forward to follow [Hamlet], he turns on them with the crack of a whip. A flash of upraised hands holding the recorder between them. A downward stroke and a sharp report as the recorder breaks in two across his knee. Then with a flourish, he hands a piece to each of the King's hounds. "Leave me friends!" high and hard. The spiral snaps off at its apex. The lights black out.[47]

Gielgud explains the omission. Here was a place where he profited from the stage history of a former Hamlet:

> The recorder scene [which precedes the "witching hour" soliloquy] was one of Irving's greatest triumphs, but many subsequent Hamlets cut it out. Personally, I would rather sacrifice almost anything else in the play, while admitting frankly that the breaking of the recorder at the end of it—taken also, I think, from Irving, though I am not sure—is pure theatrical business and not justified by the text. . . . I soccumbed [*sic*] to it at the Queen's Theatre [in his first Hamlet] . . . and found the resulting applause, and the chance of cutting several seconds playing time in a version that was inclined to run too long, too strong a combination to resist. When I played the soliloquy that followed, "'Tis now the very witching time of night," the scene would pass entirely without applause. This soliloquy, with its curious references to Nero and Hamlet's thought of matricide (never touched on anywhere else in the play), is one that does not go with

an audience. . . . Perhaps the speeches are too frankly Elizabethan[48] in feeling, or it may be that they have less poetic appeal than
others. In any case they are very difficult to deliver and unrewarding
to play.[49]

Gielgud's choice to cut the fifth soliloquy is defensible from a theatrical
point of view. First, he was performing his Hamlet at a time when to be
ignorant of what other actors had done with this role was tantamount to
not doing one's homework; certainly the critics were aware of traditional
business, and the actor was also. Here, he chose to include business that
was part of the performance tradition of *Hamlet*. Second, to deliver the
soliloquy might have destroyed the moment in a scene that was carefully
designed to reach a theatrical peak. Finally, the major point of the soliloquy, Hamlet's intention to "do such bitter business as the day / Would
quake to look on" had been aptly made without speaking those lines.
The actor had made a performance choice—to act the intention of the
lines rather than to say them. In a production where very few textual cuts
were made, this one was perhaps justifiable.

The sixth soliloquy ("Now might I do it pat," III.iii.73−96) took place
in Claudius' "dressing room."[50] Preparation for the scene was very intricate. The room contained a prie-dieu slightly to the left of a doorway
draped in green; there was a chair to the right. As the king knelt to pray,
he heard a noise, so he got up and swung the drapery back with his
sword. Seeing nothing amiss, he laid the sword on the chair and returned
to his praying. The audience was now fully anticipating an intruder, and
when the drapery next shivered, Hamlet appeared and approached only
so far as the chair, which he grasped. He saw the sword and announced,
"Now might I do it pat," as he snatched it and pulled his sword arm back
to strike.[51] All of this took place behind and out of sight of the king. As
Hamlet spoke, the mental image of sending Claudius to heaven while his
father's shade wandered in hell arrested his sword. On "Up, sword," he
cradled the long blade in his left arm and "crouching forward he pours
out the venomous words, enunciating the plan he determines to carry
out: then with a swift stealthy swing he is at the doorway again. One last
glance, a flash, and he is gone."[52] The king looked up quickly at his
empty chair, sensing a narrow escape as he saw that the sword had disappeared entirely and then heard Hamlet's cry to Gertrude offstage. It

was one brief, illumined movement for Gielgud: an appearance, a quick judgment, a retreat—certainly not a moment for contemplation.[53]

Gielgud was proud of the stage business with the sword, partly because he considered it to be his own invention. The sword had hampered physical action for Hamlet within the play scene, so it was arranged that Claudius carry it from there. Hamlet then collected it in Claudius' chamber and carried it off to Gertrude's closet: "Hamlet must, of course, enter [her chamber] with drawn sword in order to threaten his mother and kill Polonius."[54] Property details of this kind had to have a logic for Gielgud because he felt the first obligation of the actor was to make the plot believable to the audience.

Furthermore, he felt that in his production, as well as in most productions, the prayer scene stretched truth extraordinarily. Like the fifth soliloquy, this speech "is one that does not go with an audience."[55] Unless an elaborate staging plan was used to physically separate Claudius and Hamlet, the audience would simply not believe that the two characters could not overhear one another's soliloquies.

The last soliloquy ("How all occasions do inform against me," IV.iv.32–66) is described by Gilder thus:

Scene 13. A plain in Denmark.
A backdrop suggests a barren stretch of plain with gnarled trees breaking the grey expanse. Fortinbras talks with one of his captains and there is a sound of martial music in the distance. As the two soldiers are leaving, right, Hamlet comes in from the opposite side with Rosencrantz, Guildenstern and an attendant. He recalls the captain for a moment's colloquy on the subject of Fortinbras' expedition against Poland. The spectacle of this army of men ready to do battle, to die, for a "straw" arrests his attention. Shading his eyes with his hand he looks out toward the distant encampment. For a long moment he stands lost in thought and then dismisses the soldier. A word from Rosencrantz reminds him of the presence of his associates—and he sends them on ahead remaining alone in contemplation of his obsessing problem; thought and action in eternal conflict.[56]

There was a distinct change of tone in the delivery of this soliloquy, which Gilder describes as "an inner assurance." The self-deprecation was still present but seemed somehow more clear-eyed, more in perspective. The acting reflected this: "His tone is firm, the timbre of his voice strong and resonant, his few gestures clear-cut, decisive."[57]

As Hamlet described Fortinbras, he compared himself with the Norwegian prince. Fortinbras would endanger others' lives for a straw, an eggshell: one's motivations need not be overjustified if honor is the issue. Gielgud's Hamlet drew strength from the image of soldiers plunging to their deaths, and his eyes and face shone with rededication, his voice vibrated with purpose. "How stand I then" began a final vocal build to the end of the speech where the closing couplet rang out: "From this time forth, / My thoughts be bloody, or be nothing worth!" Gielgud's pose reflected readiness: "His hands strike downward, holding the edge of his cloak, his head is up and back, his whole movement vigorous."[58] Via a process of self-communion, the actor "builds a nobler mansion for his self-accusation"[59] and emerges more decided than he has been in previous soliloquies. Now he saw an opportunity and embraced it. Gielgud viewed "How all occasions" as a "very *important* soliloquy" that showed Hamlet's state of mind as "clear, noble, and resolved" before he went to England, with a "clear understanding of his destiny and desire."[60] Here was an assertion of the Victorian notion of the noble prince who valued honor above "the death of twenty thousand men." After World War II and Vietnam, it would become less and less popular to find inspiration in Fortinbras, and, in fact, his portrayal on the stage would become more and more brutal and dictatorial.

Most of Gielgud's discussions of the soliloquies are rendered from the point of view of what must have been going on in Hamlet's mind as Hamlet *talked with his inner self.* It is important to note that the production emphasized Hamlet's friendlessness. Gielgud described him as lonely but betrayed and disappointed by his friends constantly. The relationship with Horatio never got developed, didn't give Hamlet support or comfort, and the character never quite "makes himself coherent."[61] Horatio remained a foil and a shadow. Ophelia didn't quite count as a confidante, either. Consequently, Hamlet was his own audience, and the theatre audience was in the position of overhearing very personal matters. The actor never violated decorum nor attempted to interact with the audience. In turn, the spectators did not become his sounding board or his support system. This self-communing Hamlet reflected the twentieth-century preoccupation with psychological realism. The performance choice to speak the soliloquies inwardly was consistent with the ideas of the decade.

In many ways, Gielgud's *Hamlet* was a product of the transition that theatre practice underwent in the first part of the twentieth century. The period of architectural realism that dominated the stage in the late 1800s—epitomized by Beerbohm Tree's live rabbits roaming the forests of *A Midsummer Night's Dream*—was only beginning to decline when Gielgud was a youth. Since the very first Hamlet he saw, at age twelve in 1916, had been H. B. Irving, son of his idol Sir Henry Irving, his early models came from a stage tradition that favored "authentic" scenic decor and broad, heavily gestural acting in which actors made "points," dramatic bits of physical and vocal business that drew admiration and applause from the audience. G. B. Shaw complained that Barrymore had cut one-third of the text of *Hamlet* only to replace those minutes with extensive interpolated stage business.[62]

However, Gielgud was also aware of reactions to and rebellions against an excess of stage ornamentation and of "artificial" acting. He was acquainted with the work of William Poel, who advocated a return to the continuous staging of Elizabethan practice, where scene followed scene in quick progression via the actors' entrances and exits without long waits and elaborate backstage scene changes. Gielgud's first performance of Hamlet (in 1929 at the Old Vic, directed by Harcourt Williams, a disciple of Poel's) harked back to Poel in its use of period costumes and settings, circa 1520.[63] The 1936 Hamlet dealt with here was a solid combination of old elements and new. It was set in 1620, used a fuller text than usual (approximately 250 lines were cut, but not one scene was completely omitted), and featured a young Hamlet. The proscenium arch stage was dressed for realism and employed small finishing touches in hand props; however, the overall visual sweep of the scene design was highly reminiscent of Gordon Craig and Robert Edmond Jones, whose futuristic styles created acting areas via arches, stairs, and levels in almost modular sets. Furthermore, the play flowed unhampered, and act curtains were replaced by blackouts; only slight changes were made on the permanent set between scenes by minimal shifting and redraping of existing set pieces. In the preface to Gilder's book, Gielgud acknowledged the influence of Gordon Craig's "unlocalized settings" and mentioned the "violent reaction against the old-fashioned realistic settings," adding that "the necessity of using drop curtains, near the front of the stage . . . for short scenes during which furniture is being moved on the main stage, is most unsatisfactory." Clearly, he saw himself as part of the new style of scenic decor.[64]

Within this blend of styles, which looked backward to pictorial realism but forward to "the New Stagecraft," only the internalized soliloquy would suffice, because the acting style continued to pay homage to realistic playing and the soliloquies needed to obey, as far as possible, the laws of realism. Great care was taken to aid audience members and to treat them as if this was the first time they had seen the play, a murder mystery which needed emphasis on certain phrases and specific non-verbal action to underline important plot information. Effort was made to link images within soliloquies to actual events the audience had witnessed: a given phrase was concretely joined to a scene which had just taken place or was about to take place. The scenes were simple and straightforward, with little transposing or rearranging of Shakespeare's original sequence. Moreover, there were no strewn properties, no excess of objects. The gestural scheme was spare, with Gielgud making sure at all times that his hands and body were free to express plot essentials and to complement the words with appropriate movement. Such perspicacity revealed an interest in the realistic elements of the plot—a notion that there must be a logic of language and action at work if onlookers were to comprehend and to perceive stage effects accurately. Gielgud himself spoke often of whether or not an audience made a connection between stage activity and the dialogue. Furthermore, Gielgud insisted that the soliloquies be organic to the whole play. Each one was carefully motivated so as to relieve it of a "set piece" quality. There was a great deal of emphasis on preparing for each soliloquy and integrating it into the action so that it was not treated as a declamation which became in and of itself a complete scene.

Although Gielgud clearly still "made points" in very physical dramatic actions, his primary concern was the coherent flow of the play. His audience peered through the fourth wall of the set and overheard the actor speak. He never once acknowledged their presence with direct eye contact. Although it is possible that the angle of vision changed somewhat as he moved from one theatre to another, he nevertheless described most of the houses he performed in as proscenium arch theatres, "all except

Elsinore, and one performance extemporized in a senate house in Madras during a monsoon!"[65] When directly asked about the matter, he explained:

It is impossible to describe one's method of acting in details of eye contact and changes of movement, etc. I have never bothered to examine them myself, feeling that it would make me unduly self-conscious. One tries to assess every new audience according to the way they seem to respond, and works to gauge their reactions as the play proceeds, but in Shakespeare one does certainly play outwards quite deliberately towards the audience. The few times I played away from a proscenium—Elsinore and Madras—I found the proximity of the audience stimulating but also distracting, especially if one has good eyesight as I have, and cannot keep [from] noticing individual faces or odd clothes.[66]

Gielgud strongly advised that "the soliloquy is most easily spoken close to the footlights,"[67] "always as far downstage as possible"[68]—references to that trough of lights so often present in proscenium arch theatres. A Hamlet would have been deterred from addressing the theatre audience because the lights in his eyes would have prevented him from seeing them and thus would have worked to separate actor and audience. We can rest assured that this actor would have made eyes and face visible and available to the audience, and he also would have been distinctly and precisely tuned to stirrings and responses from them. However, he never described himself as the ultimate sharer with the audience nor did he make specific efforts to contact them.

The inward soliloquy elicited a certain kind of performance from the actor. In this production, Gielgud's movements were large, flowing, and melodramatic. Although some of this was due to the *façon* of acting, there was another reason. If the actor does not step forward onto the apron and "say" his feelings to an audience, i.e., articulate the depth of his emotions directly, then he can be granted license to more broadly *en*-act them, to increase the physical size and scope of his performance. Stepping forward to address the audience is a step nearer to bringing the camera in closer; it is the stage analogue of a close-up shot. And stepping back from the camera (from the audience) allows the actor larger physical manifestations of his inner emotion.

Interestingly enough, Gielgud still gained sympathy from his audience. His Hamlet suffered great angst totally alone, without support from the cast or sustenance from the theatre audience. There was, inside the fourth wall of realism and inside the world of this production, no one to talk to. The interaction and energies the actor might otherwise have shared with an audience were channeled into the performance he was giving. The inward soliloquy bypassed direct persuasion of an audience and worked toward enthralling it via the force of the actor's charisma. Gielgud's acting made this clear. It was a performance which combined highlighted theatrical moments with the psychological realism of an internally tormented man trapped in a web of circumstantial events. His tears, though not in the tradition of the Victorian "manly man," elicited pity and secured the compassion of his audience.

It was of major importance that Gielgud's soliloquies were not delivered using direct eye contact with the audience. This tradition remained strong in the theatre up through the middle of the twentieth century. Although Gielgud did not set the fashion, and although his presentation did not take place on a "realistic set," his model was enormously influential in perpetuating the tradition of performing the world's most famous speeches during the first half of the twentieth century, a period when the basic actor-audience relationship in theatre structures was changing. It was not until the sixties that other actors began to experiment with the performance mode of the soliloquies within theatre spaces. Gielgud truly was "the glass of fashion and the mould of form" through which modern Hamlets mirrored themselves.

2

GUINNESS, OLIVIER, AND BURTON :

The Mould of Form

Each time a newcomer undertook the role of *Hamlet*, he was shadowed by the force of tradition. Hamlets in the middle decades of the twentieth century were still influenced by what Gielgud had epitomized in the role, especially in the performance of the soliloquies.

This chapter considers three Hamlets who followed in that path. The first, Alec Guinness, performed two Hamlets, one in 1938 and another in 1951. In answer to my request for an interview, Guinness replied in a letter, which is reprinted here and followed by a brief discussion.[1] The second, Laurence Olivier, performed a Hamlet on the stage in 1937 and then both acted in and directed his powerful award-winning film in 1948. I have focused on the film because so many people, including actors and directors, have used it as a reference point for *Hamlet*. Although a renegade and innovator in most matters of staging, Olivier based his film presentation of Hamlet's soliloquies on the traditional method of delivery. The third Hamlet, Richard Burton, was directed by Gielgud as he undertook the role for the second time in 1964. Burton most certainly did not model his interpretation after Gielgud's, but he followed the convention of performing very theatrical yet internalized soliloquies. In fact, Burton nearly outdid turn-of-the-century actors in flamboyance, seeming to "play for points" in a display of vocal tricks and physical action. Gielgud, Guinness, Olivier, Burton, and Tyrone Guthrie—who produced Olivier's 1937 and Guinness' 1938 *Hamlet*—were all part of the Shakespeare heritage at the Old Vic from 1930 to 1960. Neither Richard Burton nor Laurence Olivier was alive when this study was written; fortunately, both left viewable records of how they approached Hamlet's soliloquies.

ALEC GUINNESS

Alec Guinness debuted in Shakespearean roles as Osric in Gielgud's 1934 *Hamlet* at the New Theatre and also played Osric in Olivier's 1937 *Hamlet*, directed by Tyrone Guthrie at the Old Vic. Guthrie produced Guinness' first Hamlet, which was in modern dress, in 1938–39 at the Old Vic, and Guinness directed himself in a traditional production of *Hamlet* at the New Theatre in 1951.

Guinness' letter reveals information about the soliloquies:

> I am afraid it would be wasting your time to meet to discuss the Hamlet soliloquies. I haven't a thought in my head about them and doubt if I ever had. Both in Guthrie's modern dress production at the Old Vic in 1938 and again in my own disastrous production in 1951 the soliloquies were delivered in the conventional way—as introspective speeches, as if the character was thinking aloud to himself and not as [if he was] explaining his situation to an audience, as is sometimes now the case. Certainly Gielgud and all actors I had seen either before him or around that time, did the same. In fact, I suppose one could say that the soliloquies were treated as *part of the play* and not [as a] comment on it. But right or wrong I don't see it makes a great deal of difference.
>
> With both Hamlets I played I dismissed the idea that Hamlet was aware he was being spied on either before or after the "To be or not to be." I took the line that there was something odd about Ophelia being alone and reading (or at her orisons) when he first spots her—in the 1938 production I followed Prof. Dover Wilson's reading of "sullied" rather than "solid" in the first soliloquy. In 1951, I reverted to "solid." (In 1938 I also used—I think—Dover Wilson's punctuation of "What a piece of work" speech). Guthrie, at that time, was rather influenced by Prof. Ernest Jones and some of it may

Alec Guinness in Hamlet, *1938. Photo courtesy of the Raymond Mander and Joe Mitchenson Theatre Collection.*

have brushed off on me—largely unawares. Guthrie persuaded me to tackle the soliloquies at break-neck speed. My diction was good enough in those days to do so. I think we had in mind the "celerity of thought." When I came to do it in 1951 I had been impressed, in the previous few years, by the Madariaga book on this play. I think, also, that Granville Barker spoke for most of my generation of actors (and the previous one) with his *Prefaces to Shakespeare*. However, I think Granville Barker's "Hamlet" Preface is, possibly, the least satisfactory of his commentaries.

. . . *Of course* every young actor wants to play Hamlet. 1) It's a smashing part in a great play. 2) Whatever his future holds, by way of success or failure, he can always claim it as one of his roles, and one that everyone has heard of. 3) It can be a marvelous ego trip—something to which very few actors are averse. 4) With the soliloquies you have the stage to yourself. Given reasonably "princely" qualities, a mordant wit and a measure of sweetness of nature very few actors fail to make a mark in the part. And for *someone* in the audience they will always be the first Hamlet to have been seen— and that is a big asset. Most people's favourite Hamlets are their first experiences of the play—which means they are probably young and it is to the young (with questioning minds) that the character appeals.

Yours sincerely,
Alec Guinness

A number of soliloquy issues are raised here. First and foremost, from the late thirties through the fifties, a certain way of performing soliloquies continued to hold the stage: soliloquies ought to be inwardly addressed. Additionally, they ought to be integrated into the performance and not performed as set pieces where the production halts for the actor to do a turn.

Also, Guinness acknowledged that Gielgud was a primary model. In fact, Guinness' entire involvement with *Hamlet* was unwittingly bound to John Gielgud's acting of the role. Since Guinness played Osric in Gielgud's 1934 production, he professed to having watched his idol from the wings "for about 170 performances." [2] Gielgud also recommended to the young actor his first acting teacher and subsequently offered Guinness a number of his early roles. Guinness explained, "My own . . . feebleness was in being a bit *ersatz Gielgud*. I wasn't trying to be him, but I was so imbued with his production [of 1934], and mine was only four years later." [3] Guinness describes Gielgud as "my actor-hero, my patron, and later my very good friend." [4] He declared that "every young actor in London was wearing hats like Gielgud and throwing their head back or trying to get into his productions. . . . Everything from my generation stems back to Gielgud or to Guthrie." [5]

There are hints in the letter of the relationship between actors and directors in the thirties, a period when directors were still an emergent phenomenon. At this time, the actor did his own homework and made his preparations. Guinness' homework included scholars Harley Granville Barker and Salvador de Madariaga. [6] Ernest Jones' book *Hamlet and Oedipus* appeared to influence Guthrie more than it did Guinness, [7] who seemed uninterested in Freudian approaches. However, he did assume the authority of scholars in certain line readings. Madariaga was rarely read after the forties. Only Granville Barker remains a heavyweight in Shakespearean scholarship, in part because his book is founded on several years of practical experience in the theatre. In any case, Guinness announced just after his second *Hamlet*:

> I admit I have read a lot about *Hamlet*—the usual stuff—but I must confess that I have never found anything that appealed to me. . . . Granville-Barker I took gravely and steadily over a period of years, but he never fired me. When Madariaga appeared with his bombshell I was thrilled and appalled for a week, but came to the conclusion that I hardly agreed with a word he said.[8]

Typically in the thirties, the director did not shape the character conception of each Hamlet, nor did he take an authoritarian position regarding interpretation: he simply hired the type of personality he wanted and assumed that casting would take care of interpretative decisions. However, he would certainly offer suggestions about the pace of the production, and in the 1938 *Hamlet* Guthrie conceived a somewhat unconventional production in modern dress. Later classified as controversial and intriguing rather than commercially notable, the costuming had Guinness in a fisherman's sweater and rubber boots in the graveyard scene where mourners stood around Ophelia's grave in a cluster of black umbrellas. However, audiences had difficulty accepting Guinness' low-key and naturalistic portrayal of Hamlet. Guthrie explained: "His youth, combined with rare intelligence, humour and pathos, realized a great deal of the part. He had not yet quite the authority to support, as Hamlet must, a whole evening, or to give the tragedy its full stature. The performance demanded that the public reach out and take what was offered. To this demand the public is rarely equal."[9]

Nevertheless, the 1938 production offered some innovative stage business in the soliloquies, which suggested naturalistic (rather than heroic) acting. In the first soliloquy, "O that this too too sallied flesh," Guinness recounted,

> I wore a uniform for that and was kind of sitting on a stool or chair. And then to take a pocket handkerchief out and blow your nose and put it away again! I mean, maybe now I might find that vulgar, but at the time, it did wonders for me because now they [the audience]

know that I've been in an emotional state, but controlling it. Well, you can't do that in [romantic, Elizabethan period] costumes . . . it's those sorts of things that made it fascinating to work on.[10]

Guinness also closed the third soliloquy, "O, what a rogue and peasant slave," by squatting on the ground and tapping on a drum that the players had left onstage. The curtain fell on this lovely, metatheatrical gesture.[11]

Guinness did not give up on the role. His second production of *Hamlet* in 1951, which he directed himself, was troubled with myriad problems, some technical, some administrative, and some aesthetic. Kenneth Tynan[12] claimed that there was a clear-cut image of Hamlet inside Guinness but that he wasn't yet ready to assert it. Guinness knew that he did not want to portray a romantic hero, but he also retreated from projecting a full-fledged antihero. Later on, Guinness explained:

To the best of my ability, I'm *real*. I try to follow Shakespeare's own advice to players. The critics wanted Hamlet as "the sweet gentle prince." He *isn't* sweet or gentle. Look at the viciousness of his colloquy with Ophelia. They wanted him young and romantic. He's 30. He *isn't* romantic. I don't think Shakespeare meant him to be. That is a false tradition.[13]

Alec Guinness was a Hamlet trapped in the stage tradition of the noble prince when his personality was not suited for it. His actor's instincts told him there was another admissible character concept within the text, but he did not find it. Had he done so, he might have changed his opinion about the performance of the soliloquies. Neither mode is right or wrong, but it does indeed make a difference which one an actor chooses.

LAURENCE OLIVIER

Laurence Olivier played *Hamlet* in his first season at the Old Vic in 1937 at the age of twenty-nine. The production ran for only six weeks, and scant historical traces remain, not even a promptbook. Both the director, Tyrone Guthrie, and Olivier were influenced by the Freudian interpretation of Professor Ernest Jones, spelled out in his *Hamlet and Oedipus*.

Laurence Olivier in his 1948 film of Hamlet.
Photo courtesy of the Rank Organisation.

Oddly enough, reviewers hardly noticed Hamlet's unusual relationship with his mother nor indeed any significant Freudian overtones. Two other characteristics of the production captured attention instead. First of all, critics remarked on the way that the actor spoke Shakespearean dialogue. There ensued from this performance a long-standing preoccupation with comparing Gielgud's more classical and rather musical mode of speaking the verse with Olivier's novel and more naturalistic mode, an argument which endures today.[14] Second, critics focused on Olivier's athleticism and virility, both of which made it difficult to believe that this particular Hamlet could have possibly delayed Claudius' death as long as he did.[15]

Much better known to a world audience is the black-and-white film version of *Hamlet*, both directed and acted by Olivier in 1948. This project, which took place at the end of a decade of his work at the Old Vic, won four Academy Awards.[16] The movie was enormously influential, and many of the actors in this book admired it. Eventually, after wide distribution and re-viewing by the public, Olivier surpassed Gielgud as the ideal cultural image of Hamlet.

The film was in part a response to critics of the 1937 production who questioned Hamlet's ability to delay. Accurately described as "an Oedipal cinepoem,"[17] the film posited a sexual attraction between mother and son, showing erotic kisses between Hamlet and Gertrude as well as suggestive camera shots of her bed. Olivier and his text editor, Alan Dent, rearranged scenes and liberally cut dialogue and characters. Only about half of the original text was used, Fortinbras—as well as Rosencrantz and Guildenstern—disappeared, and difficult words were glossed and modernized. These changes were made partly to clarify the logic of the story for viewers and partly to support Olivier's interpretation.

In the film, the Hamlet presented was a thinker and only belatedly a doer. The interpretation was spelled out in a prologue printed on the screen and read in a voice-over by the actor, a cutting from the "vicious mole of nature" speech (I.iv.24–33). The voice added that Hamlet was "a man who could not make up his mind." The dreamlike, shadowy movie made use of dissolves and a constantly moving camera to reveal the inner Hamlet. The interpretation was heavily reinforced by the handling of the soliloquies, which slowed plot action and focused on the thought processes of the major character.

Two soliloquies disappeared. Only the last couplet of the third soliloquy was retained: "The play's the thing / Wherein I'll catch the conscience of the King," shouted quickly following the players' scene. Since the player's speech was cut and the play-within-the-play retained in pantomime only, there was no point in keeping the third soliloquy. The seventh soliloquy ("How all occasions") existed in the shooting script (Olivier gave it on horseback at the seashore) but was ultimately omitted from the film.[18]

The first soliloquy, "O that this too too *sullied*[19] flesh," followed the first court scene (just after Gertrude leaned closely over Hamlet and delivered a lengthy kiss). As courtiers exited, Hamlet stood alone. The camera panned over a table of state papers and rested in a tight close-up on Hamlet's face. Olivier was very careful to make no eye contact with the camera. He looked to the right of frame and to the left but never at the viewer, thus never acknowledging the audience outside the play's world. The close-up itself served as an establishing shot indicating that what followed was happening inside Hamlet's head. Most of the soliloquy came "voice-over," with Hamlet saying aloud only those lines which were literary links and tag phrases such as "not so much, not two" and "within a month." However, "Frailty, thy name is woman!" *was* spoken aloud. The character was clearly in a dialogue with an inner self. Hamlet was a despondent character—his physical movement was slow and limited, his steps measured and leaden as he walked around the council chamber.

The second soliloquy (after the Ghost's appearance) was set on the smoke-filled ramparts. Hamlet spoke from the floor, where he had fallen. He did a kind of push-up on "And you, my sinows, grow not instant old / But bear me stiffly up," as if trying to get his muscles to work. Olivier was impassioned for the first time in the film, his voice rising in pitch as he shouted the ending of the soliloquy. During it, he brandished a sword, then threw it down, a gesture repeated in the film and throughout the soliloquies, perhaps an effort to throw the instrument of revenge from himself rather than commit the crime. He then retrieved the weapon and made his closing vow upon it. Finally, he went to the edge of the ramparts and looked down, an activity also repeated later in the "To be, or not to be" soliloquy. All of the soliloquy was spoken aloud but never into the camera.

"To be, or not to be" had been moved to follow the nunnery scene,[20] which concluded with Ophelia weeping and distraught on the stairs. The camera made a long transition by panning upward over three sets of stairs and out a doorway (accompanied by William Walton's "elevating" music) to a cloud-filled sky on the ramparts of the castle. Placing this well-known soliloquy outdoors was itself a departure from stage tradition, but Olivier obviously wanted a clear separation from the nunnery scene.

Next, there was an overhead shot of waves breaking, and suddenly the back of Olivier's head loomed into sight—the camera drew closer and closer, as if probing into his mind. More sea waves followed, and then an image looking like the classical medical-book picture of a human brain was superimposed very briefly on the screen. Hamlet was in communion with an audience that was a literal inner self, a cortex-looking object. "To be, or not to be," began voice-over against clouds juxtaposed on waves in the sea, perhaps simulating waves of thought. Olivier sat on the edge of the precipice and leaned over, dangerously punctuating the temptation of suicide. He spoke aloud "Whether 'tis nobler," and on "by opposing, end them," he drew a dagger. Then, the soliloquy continued voice-over and Hamlet closed his eyes until "perchance to dream," when he awoke from the trance and the speech continued, spoken by the actor aloud. On "might his quietus make" he looked at the dagger. The next lines were very direct, with Olivier speaking almost but not quite into the camera eye. On "that we know not of" he tossed the dagger into the sea; he had given up the notion of suicide as a result of speaking the soliloquy. He stood near the edge of the precipice, but on "turn awry" literally turned away from the danger of falling, walking into safety on "lose the name of action."

The soliloquy had been a dialogue with self, the "out-loud" or more conscious voice taking precedence. The outer self had dominated over the inner temptation. The whole sequence was another demonstration of a man who could not make up his mind. At the end of it, at least suicide was ruled out.

The fifth soliloquy, "'Tis now the very witching time of night," began with Olivier facing away from the camera, the first lines spoken into shadows and to himself. The remainder of the lines were articulated out loud as he made his deliberate way through light and dark shafts of light, as if vacillating between good and evil intentions as he progressed. The soliloquy was used as a transition for Hamlet to make his way to his mother's bedroom.[21]

The final soliloquy used was the double soliloquy, where Claudius attempted to pray and then Hamlet spoke. Claudius agonized over his (much-edited) entreaty, clutching his "bosom black as death" and kneeling in front of a lighted candle, head on his hands. Hamlet approached from behind, the suspense aided by stirring music. *All* of the "Now might I do it pat" speech was presented voice-over. Since it is much more important to play scenes for realism on film, Olivier was, with the voice-over technique, preserving the convention that Claudius didn't hear him speak the lines, even though the two men were no more than two feet apart. Olivier was also separated from Claudius for the viewer because he was foregrounded in the frame. As Hamlet neared the decision, "And now I'll do't," he saw an icon of Jesus, which the candle illumined, and arrested his drawn sword. Halfway through the speech (at "No!") he turned away from the king. The act of rationalizing deterred him, but the visual image of the religious statue added weight to the argument. He then exited up a long flight of stairs, the same action that concluded the second soliloquy.

Olivier had not only employed the method of internalized soliloquies, he clarified it unequivocally through the medium of film. The alternation of voice-over with actor-spoken voice clearly demonstrated "spoken thoughts" in a way that stage technique never quite could. The device that was *not* employed, "in-camera" soliloquies, would have signaled direct address to an audience outside the play. None of Olivier's film soliloquies established that bond.

This choice was completely logical for the production Olivier crafted, which featured a ratiocinative prince who had numerous interior duologues as he tried to settle a dark and sexually forbidding conflict—the turmoil that was posited as a reason for his delay. Since Olivier had excised the two soliloquies that showed Hamlet chastising himself thoroughly for delaying, he had to hone the acting to show a character who could *believably* delay. Even the physical movement of the actor was limited within the soliloquies—in fact, all of the physicality of the actor was downplayed except in traditionally very active scenes such as the duel, where the delay was clearly over. Furthermore, the character was presented as dour and humorless, with much of Hamlet's natural wit cut from the dialogue or muted. The actor's vocal quality throughout most of the soliloquies was hushed, secretive, and soft. Olivier's was not a sociable Hamlet. His only firm relationships in the play were with Horatio, who hovered about protectively and, of course, with that "mind's eye," that inner self that Hamlet continually consulted. There was no attempt to contact an audience outside the play's metaworld. The interior audience was so well established that the viewer almost felt the presence of a second Hamlet. Perhaps it was the camera itself, roving, following, peering, persuading.

RICHARD BURTON

Richard Burton played his first Hamlet at the Old Vic in 1953.[22] However, the performance that people remember was directed by John Gielgud in 1964 and ran for 138 performances.[23] It previewed in Boston and Toronto and opened in New York. Filmed at the Lunt-Fontanne Theatre and edited for performance via a process called Electronovision, it was subsequently screened (in black and white) for just two showings on June 30 and July 1, 1964, in nearly a thousand movie houses throughout the United States.[24] After that, almost all copies were destroyed.[25]

This is one of the better-documented Hamlets available because two companion books about the production exist. *John Gielgud Directs Richard Burton in "Hamlet": A Journal of Rehearsals* (1967) was written and edited by a young actor in the cast, Richard L. Sterne, who smuggled a tape recorder into the sessions and consequently salvaged directorial notes between Gielgud and the players. William Redfield's *Letters from an Actor* (1966) is an epistolary account from the man cast as Rosencrantz.[26] Used together, these records give us a balanced account of the rehearsal negotiations, complete with gossip about the movie star atmosphere that drew fans in droves and caused police cordons to be set up on opening nights of the tour. Richard Burton and Elizabeth Taylor were first married during the Canadian engagement, and that event served to whet the public's interest in the play.

Gielgud and Burton represented such a great difference in playing styles that one wonders why they chose to collaborate. Burton's acting

Richard Burton in Hamlet, *1964. Photo courtesy of the Raymond Mander and Joe Mitchenson Theatre Collection.*

was "natural," complete with the grunts and groans of "the Method" school of acting mostly associated with American performers. However, he could also be "a bardic actor . . . crooning, humorous, and exotic,"[27] with rhetorical flourishes and a tendency to intone Shakespearean verse. By 1964, Gielgud's performances of the role belonged, in the public's eye, to the more romantic and mellifluous style of verse-speaking—the graceful prince with the classic profile.

Gielgud and Burton respected one another despite the occasionally blunt notes the director gave. He could be charming, democratic, and autocratic, all in one rehearsal. The accounts show a great deal of flexibility and good humor during rehearsals. Many of Gielgud's ideas were freely used by Burton and even became his favorite bits of business.[28] It is difficult to pinpoint which moments of business or speech belonged to which person. Both Burton and the supporting cast recognized the "cornucopias filled with forty years of reading, studying, considering, and analyzing Shakespearean verse"[29] in their leader:[30]

> Burton wants Gielgud's discipline. Gielgud wants Burton's spontaneity. Both are men of strong conviction and large accomplishment. Both are men of exceptional capacity but neither is so arrogant as to believe that he alone has all the answers. They balance because of their differences. It is most ingratiating to watch them in operation together. The thrilling bad boy and the watchful don.[31]

> Burton had seen other actors in the role: "About twenty . . . Redgrave, Gielgud, Scofield twice, Robert Helpmann twice, Alan Badel, John Neville, Griffith . . . Olivier's film . . . Maurice Evans."[32] He felt that Gielgud's was the best, yet he had no intention of modeling his own characterization after Gielgud's. Unknown to Gielgud, Burton's lifelong acting coach, Philip Burton, who worried that "Gielgud would be trying to get *his* Hamlet out of Richard,"[33] was called in to help Burton out with the role.[34]

Gielgud's concept of the production first drew Burton into the enterprise—the unusual idea to stage the play as one of the rehearsals that preceded the final dress rehearsal. The stage set looked like the inside of a theatre not yet outfitted for the performance, with simulated red-brick walls, a raised platform, and sliding back doors at the rear. The playing space, flat and long, widened into a rectangular opening. The costumes were modern rehearsal clothes; actors brought in their own clothes from day to day until Gielgud settled on something he liked.[35] One day Burton wore a dark V-neck sweater and dark trousers; Gielgud noticed it and had five such outfits duplicated.[36] After much experimentation, Gielgud decided to use his own voice as that of the Ghost, over a huge shadow of an Elizabethan warrior thrown on the back wall. Actors faced out front to see its entrance, as if a specter were placed between themselves and the spotlights. Critics were agreed about the production concept: It was bothersome at first, but one got used to it. It was a device, rather than an attempt to rethink the play. Gielgud made little of the rehearsal idea beyond Polonius' being stabbed through a wardrobe rack and an occasional cloak thrown over modern clothes.

Gielgud's preference for "entirety" texts emerged: a virtually uncut version, the production ran for just over three and a quarter hours in length. The director used a conflation of Quarto and Folio texts, retaining the final "How all occasions" soliloquy.

Critics were divided on the issue of Burton's characterization. Those who lauded his acting of the role felt it had "a certain vigor and compulsion,"[37] was "forceful, direct, unpretentiously eloquent,"[38] "a brilliant Hamlet,"[39] "the quicksilver Hamlet,"[40] who "[became] my image of Hamlet and I can't imagine his being supplanted."[41] Other reviewers held mixed opinions, and Walter Kerr wrote an unfavorable critique declaring, "Mr. Burton is without feeling."[42]

The critics attempted to describe the character that Burton offered, citing his intelligence, his ironic humor, his decisiveness and strength, his manliness, and his princeliness (or lack of it). The actor's voice was both revered and razored. On the credit side, Martin Gottfried proclaimed: "This man has no human voice! It is an instrument of infinitely variable qualities. Bouncing sharply with rocklike steeliness, it suddenly blossoms into mahogany. Vowels burgeon into widening circles and then contract to scratch against ice."[43] Others disagreed: "He is speaking his lines too trippingly, hurdling consonants and vaulting vowels, especially in his soliloquies, which start out eloquently and deteriorate into so fast a pace that you feel that it is indeed a rehearsal and he is hurrying through to get to the next piece of business."[44]

The vocal techniques are noticeably dated, especially in the first three soliloquies and some of the longer monologues. The actor uses naturalistic speech as well as a poetry-reading voice. His bizarre tonal changes, odd contrasts in pitch, and unusual elisions in the verse would be called "chanting" or "intoning" today. He also had sharp contrasts in volume, with a word suddenly being yelled out. Many of the pauses were laboriously long, resulting in a kind of speechifying. Although Burton's voice had a rotund beauty and was eminently well trained, the technique often sounded like an exercise by a voice-virtuoso—one who occasionally strove for the sense of the line but just as often worked against it. Ultimately, the method calls attention to itself. Interaction scenes, in contrast, were very conversational and realistic.

Gielgud paid close attention to Burton's verse-speaking and warned against "shouting" the lines:

> GIELGUD: Sometimes, Richard, you're inclined to shout out very loudly on one word, rather than to build a speech to a climax of a shout on three or four lines, which is to me more effective. You keep one word high and all the rest are lost to it. And if you do this too often, it becomes dull and coarse. . . .
>
> BURTON: I do have a tendency, as you tell me, John, to shout.
>
> GIELGUD: It's very dangerous—as dangerous as speaking too beautifully.[45]
>
> . . . Have a care as to shouting. You shout brilliantly; both you and Larry Olivier do—two splendid cornets. I am a violin, I'm afraid, not too good at shouting. But these hunting calls you do so well can be tiresome when sounded too often.[46]

The performance of the third and the fourth soliloquies will serve as examples of the kinds of delivery Burton used. He regarded these as his two biggest challenges:

> Some nights I like doing "To be or not to be" more than I like doing "O, what a rogue and peasant slave." But it depends on whether I feel in good fettle or not. You can sort of sit back on "To be or not to be," and you can't on "O what a rogue."[47]

Before "O, what a rogue," Burton had dismissed Rosencrantz and Guildenstern by shouting them off the stage, making each word of the dismissal a further push: "AYE——so——God——be——with——(malicious chuckle)——you!" He followed this with a pause of over ten seconds. On "Now I am alone," he walked to a chair and sat, but he was up and shouting swiftly by the time he reached "DREAM of passion." On "And all for nothing, / For "Heck——Yew——Bah," he divided the name and drew it out with pauses. He then raced through the next few lines, emphasizing "DROWN" and not pausing after "amaze indeed / The very faculty of eyes and ears. Yet I"—and this "Aiiii" is drawn out in a bizarre, yodeled falsetto—while the next phrase, "a dull," was nearly swallowed but then choked out in a Donald Duck voice. He hurled himself toward "and can say NOTHING; NO," at which point the remainder was ranted at tremendous speed. The questions beginning at "Am I a coward?" went far too quickly for him to contact the audience, and indeed, Burton turned his body completely around in a kind of spiral twirl onstage, ending with an electrifying yell, "WHO DOES ME THIS HAH?"

Although the climax of the speech was yet to come, Burton ended "fatted all the region kites with this slave's OFFAL" on an unusually high note. He then began the classic build on that same upper note, bellowing each word through "TREACHEROUS, LECHEROUS, KINDLESS VILLAIN!" after which the "O" was drawn out in a glissando which went from a high pitch to a low and sounded more like "Oh-ho-ho." "Vengeance" was sobbed out with both hands upraised in the air and a full ten-second stop after it. Then he looked at his lifted hand as if he'd caught himself sleepwalking on "What an ass am I!" The remainder of the speech was quieter as he evolved his plan to catch the conscience of the king. Of course, Burton exited to a strong round of applause.

The speed of the speech, the way of bending and spinning the voice against the sense of the line, the prerehearsed, mechanical gestures—all these things make the execution of the soliloquy operatic and artificial, a set piece. Burton had suggested to Gielgud the raised-arm gesture at the climax: "I did a thing in *Henry the Fifth* which got an enormous laugh but would not be funny in this play . . . my arms went right up in the air, like this . . . and then I just simply dropped them. Perhaps we could do that with 'Oh Vengeance!'⁴⁸ An interviewer asked him later on:

Q: You deliberately play for a laugh on "Why, what an ass am I"?
A: Sometimes I do, sometimes I don't. . . . I discovered that I was raising the wrong arm on "Oh, vengeance." I was using the up-

stage arm, but it seemed the audience couldn't see my face when I looked up at the hand on "What an ass am I." So I changed to the downstage arm and it worked. Purely a technical thing. It seems that unless they can see your face when you make fun of yourself they don't get the joke.[49]

These vocal and physical theatrics caused Walter Kerr to react negatively and accounted for his charges of passionless and mechanical acting: "Now the words spill and spin and seem to spit at themselves in a fury, but it is an automated fury, a high-jump that has had no running start to prepare it. Indeed it is very like pressing the next highest button on an electric stove. We believe factually that there has been some alteration in temperature, but we see no flame."[50]

Gielgud and Burton had agreed on what the famous fourth soliloquy meant. Burton said:

I've read critics who say he's not saying "Shall I kill myself or not?" He's rather saying "Shall I be King or not?", or "Shall I kill the King or not?" In other words, "to be" the boss, "or not to be" the boss. But that, it seems to me, is a bit far fetched, because everything else [in the context] applies to death and heaven and hell, and so on. An actor friend of mine has always wanted to cut "To be or not to be" as being a hold-up of the play. But it would be like . . . cutting your knee off and still walking.[51]

For this speech, Burton walked onto the raised platform, stumbling slightly. He looked all around the set, making no effort to contact the audience. His eyes were glazed, his mind distant. He gave the soliloquy quietly, in a contemplative way. He even sat down on a stool on "enterprises of great pitch and moment." Occasionally a word was shouted, but vocal acrobatics were rare. This soliloquy was most cited by critics: "The 'To be, or not to be' soliloquy presentation—casual, introspective, and recited with few flourishes—makes sense."[52] Perhaps Burton was parodying the Player King in the previous soliloquy, "O, what a rogue." However, the first three soliloquies were given in a declamatory style, whereas the remaining four were given in the restrained mode of "To be."

The records suggest that Gielgud determined to whom the soliloquies would be spoken. Burton made himself completely available to the audience, but he did not contact them directly. The discussion came up during rehearsals for "O, what a rogue and peasant slave":

> BURTON: Do you think I'm too far from the audience? I'd like to speak it to them.
>
> GIELGUD: It's such a phony Shakespearean technique to come out on the apron in a proscenium theatre. It seems to me it's more realistic to keep it within the scene.[53]

At another point, Gielgud suggested that Burton underplay his directness to the audience:

> Richard, don't play full front so much in the "too, too solid flesh" soliloquy. Give us your profile and use the stage more. That will bring it into the scene and relate it so that it's more natural and less like a speech.[54]

> When you said "What would *he* do—" [it was] as if you were asking somebody really there. You're alone; you needn't take it so outwardly. Then it won't seem as if you are talking to the audience. Try to conceal the fact that it's soliloquy by making it more to yourself. Don't use quite so much voice, because the moment you shout, we feel "Who's he talking to? Is somebody up [onstage or above stage] there?" It's coming very well, though.[55]

Gielgud's views about the soliloquies emerge fairly clearly. He felt that if the soliloquies were audience-addressed, they would be perceived as set speeches, and *that* was to be avoided. He seemed to think that only an internalized soliloquy should be permitted in a proscenium arch theatre such as the Lunt-Fontanne. Obviously, there was still no tradition of audience address as an integral part of the play and a necessary technique for certain kinds of production concepts as well as for certain characterizations of Hamlet. For Gielgud, the direct-address soliloquy was a device that jarred audiences out of the illusion.

There are numerous signs that this production was on the cusp of changing styles in theatrical performance. First of all, there were two distinct acting styles represented onstage. Claudius, Gertrude, Laertes, and Ophelia belonged to a school of acting characterized by statuesque body stances, declaimed lines, very little intimacy or eye contact between characters, and enormous pauses after speeches of any length. In contrast, Hume Cronyn, much acclaimed for his Polonius, was very "naturalistic" in body and speech: One was never sure when he was speaking verse or prose, and he took all of the dialogue at a good clip. He brought out comedy in the character that other actors have overlooked. He was very interactive with fellow players.[56] On the other hand, audiences applauded long and loud after every single scene and every major speech in the play, a convention seen only in opera performances in the late twentieth century.[57] The Warner *Hamlet*, staged just a year later, does not exhibit this convention.

Richard Burton's performance fluctuated radically from night to night. In a 1988 biography, Melvyn Bragg concluded:

> He was bored with *Hamlet* by the time he left it. To amuse himself he had tried out several different interpretations during the run, including a homosexual Hamlet. He would also insert lines from Marlowe or in German to see if anybody noticed. It was always hard for him to sustain an interest once he had cracked a problem. He went out to conquer, did so, and was then often indifferent.[58]

Burton wrote in one of his private journals:

> After, shall we say, 10 weeks of playing Hamlet on the stage one's soul staggers with tedium and one's mind rejects the series of quotations that Hamlet now is. Has there ever been a more boring speech, after 400 years of constant repetition, than "To be or not to be?" I have never played that particular speech, and I've played the part hundreds and hundreds of times, without knowing that everybody settles down to a nice old nap the minute the first fatal words start.[59]

It is difficult to determine whether Burton's variations upon the theme of Hamlet were due to a certain Welsh feyness or became more pronounced with the embroidery of a Welsh imagination. Unpredictable he was—in life as well as in art—and these changes from performance to performance were a characteristic of his playing style throughout his career.

Burton was a Hamlet pulled in two directions. He was in rebellion against a strong director who was grounded in, indeed even personified, the traditional Hamlet. Gielgud's ideas were perfect for his own time, but they did not fit Burton's personality nor his decade. I believe that Burton was strongly inclined toward the option of the direct-address soliloquy, but Gielgud was so strong a representative of the accepted tradition that Burton did not challenge it. The performance mode he used kept verging on that technique anyway, perhaps a subconscious expression of his true inclinations. He faced full front and occasionally came very close to contacting the audience, but he held himself just inside the line of doing so, aloof from them. This avoidance mode probably accounts for the strange twirl of his body during the questions in the third soliloquy ("Am I a coward? Who calls me villain?" etc.), which are easily audience-addressed. Burton's peculiar solution to this dilemma was to show off by indulging himself in an even older tradition of elocutionary display. Perhaps his boredom factored in as well, and he felt he had conquered the role of Hamlet. Other models of Hamlet had not emerged to convince him that classical roles are never conquered but always open to fresh interpretation—although David Warner would appear soon to "show . . . the very age and body of the time his form and pressure." How interesting the Gielgud-Burton collaboration would have been had they decided to shatter the glass of fashion and become the mould of form.

David Warner in Hamlet, *1966 (revival of Royal Shakespeare Theatre's 1965 version). Photo courtesy of Tom Holte Theatre Photographic Collection in the Shakespeare Centre Library, Shakespeare Birthplace Trust.*

3

DAVID WARNER : *The Rogue and Peasant Slave*

When David Warner was performing *Hamlet* at the Royal Shakespeare Theatre one evening, a member of the audience actually entered into the play. It was near the end of the second act, just after Hamlet dismisses Rosencrantz and Guildenstern. With a sigh of relief, Warner breathed, "Now I am alone." He raked the stalls with his eyes, scooping in the balcony with a wide look, and then began the soliloquy: "O, what a rogue and peasant slave am I . . ." The audience followed him closely. He gave the natural builds in the speech, moving through "What's Hecuba to him, or he to Hecuba, / That he should weep for her?" At the series of short questions, beginning with "Am I a coward?" Warner paused, just to think about what he'd said. Surprisingly, one of the spectators shouted, "Yes!" Warner responded, "Who calls me villain, breaks my pate across, / Plucks off my beard and blows it in my face, / Tweaks me by the nose, gives me the lie i' th' throat / As deep as to the lungs? Who does me this?" And now a name was shouted out from the audience! Warner was excited and responded with some vehemence, "Hah, 'swounds, I should take it; for it cannot be / But I am pigeon-liver'd . . ." Warner remembered this as one of the most exhilarating nights of his acting career. He was stunned with the rightness of feeling and the naturalness of speaking these soliloquy lines directly to the theatre audience. The text supported him absolutely. No adjustments in timing, motivation, or thought needed to be made. He was still making discoveries inside the act of performance, and it filled him with a sense of awe about Shakespeare's dramaturgy.[1]

This *Hamlet* was director Peter Hall's contribution to the social revolution of the sixties. Scruffy, antiheroic, powerless in the sweep of the military-industrial complex of Denmark, Hamlet was recycled and reconstituted to adapt to the needs of the emergent theatre audience for the new Royal Shakespeare Company. Ralph Berry details the way in which the character interpretation in this 1965–66 production broke the mould: First of all, Warner was not shown as attractive. He did not fit the matinee-idol image of the Leslie Howards or the John Nevilles of the past, with their flowing hair, romantic profiles, and gently rhythmic verse. In fact, he was downright unprincely. The production did not offer a delicately costumed and obviously wronged heir to the throne of Denmark.[2] Newspaper headlines announced a clear departure from tradition: "AN EXISTENTIALIST PRINCE,"[3] "THE UNFINISHED HERO,"[4] "MIDDLE-CLASS HAMLET,"[5] "PRINCE OF DENMARK STREET."[6]

Warner said that the critics took Ophelia's soliloquy too literally: they demanded, "Where IS 'the glass of fashion and the mould of form' that she speaks about, where IS the courtier, where is the soldier, where is the scholar, where is the *prince*?" Furthermore, Warner's Hamlet was not middle-aged. Up to this juncture in the twentieth century, it was not unusual to see an actor of fifty playing the part. Only Gielgud and Guinness had dared to be so young, both attempting the most difficult of classical roles for the first time in their early twenties. Warner was barely twenty-four. Berry sums up the audience appeal: "The *éclat* of David Warner's Hamlet sprang from the fact that he looked like, and was, a contemporary of a heavy proportion of the audience."[7] Critics emphasized the youthful flavor of the character conception: "He shelters in childishness, seeking to appear not merely too insane to be responsible for his actions, but too young. His disguise is . . . the willful untidiness of an undergraduate, the half-baked impertinence of the adolescent who would test his parents' love to the limit of tolerance."[8] "He imprints an image of a pale, defiant boy, immensely tall and thin, trying to live with some sort of honest sense of dimension."[9]

Hall's pre-production ideas were spelled out in a presentation to Royal Shakespeare Company actors at the start of rehearsals for the production in the summer of 1965.[10] He began with a discussion of Hamlet's "trembling on the point of full maturity."[11] Hall emphasized his isolation in a court where Claudius was a "master of appearances"[12] and Polonius "the kind of shrewd, tough establishment figure you can still meet in St. James's."[13] What Hall saw as a contemporary political dilemma guided his notions about the tragedy:

> For our decade I think the play will be about the disillusionment which produces an apathy of the will so deep that commitment to politics, to religion or to life is impossible. For a man said to do nothing, Hamlet does a great deal. For a man said to refuse experience, he experiences a great deal. He is always on the brink of action, but something inside him, this disease of disillusionment, stops the final, committed action.[14]

Hall was alarmed by the apathy he saw in the youth of the sixties, and his production explored the reasons for their political inaction. These young people and the sympathetic liberal elite of Britain were Hall's target audience in two important ways: indeed, he wanted them to become regular theatregoers, but he also wanted them to judge, rather than merely be entertained, once they got to the theatre: "[Hamlet sees that] politicians . . . have to lie and cheat. And Hamlet refuses this. The young must feel this about their rulers even when there is no crime in question. They must believe that the millennium could come tomorrow if power were in the right hands."[15]

Tony Church, who played Polonius in the production, recalled Hall's ideas:

> Peter's lecture was about a Hamlet fighting an establishment so well oiled that it was actually impenetrable . . . it would eat people and just go on. It was very much based on the British establishment. We'd only just escaped thirteen years of very strong conservative rule, and there was a feeling that it was still very much about.
>
> . . . I based Polonius on Harold Macmillan, who was a sort of Lord Burleigh of his time. The whole thing about the English establishment was that it was extraordinarily good-humored and bland; you couldn't get past it. It would be very difficult for a young man to rebel because you couldn't actually find the points to hit at. As Harold Hobson once said in an article, "What the English establishment does well is buy people in."[16]

It was the impenetrability of the bureaucracy that was suggested within the production, rather than any benign qualities. As Church stated, "Our world was designed to work *without* David Warner." Contemporary events as influences in Hall's production may have been based on Jan Kott's notions about re-creating Shakespeare's plays so that they appealed to the modern consciousness.[17] Church added that another influence was Martin Holmes' *The Guns of Elsinore*, which described Hamlet within the context of war articulated in Horatio's I.i speech about battle preparations. These notions had already filtered into Hall's previous work on the Royal Shakespeare Company's *Wars of the Roses* production, where a predominant militarism overshadowed the events of the *Henry VI* plays.

The first sight that confronted an audience as this *Hamlet* began was a cannon pointed straight at them. The stage set itself, as Stanley Wells described it, "was permanent in some respects, but it could be rapidly rearranged. Beyond a black false-proscenium arch . . . two great black walls slanted inwards, their further ends separated by two massive doors."[18] The rear panels could be changed to represent designs, bookshelves, frescoes, gravestones, in order to effect changes of scene. Critic Ronald Bryden called the design "a superb inferno of bitumen ramparts and lakes of black marble."[19] Designer John Bury used unusual textures, which he made particularly heavy and overpowering to reflect "the enclosed world and stifling politics of Elsinore."[20] Photographs of the set show the upstage area filled with panels which angled inward and severely weakened most of that area for acting. This was indeed a claustrophobic kingdom which sought to enmesh Hamlet. It is no wonder that he escaped so frequently to the forestage to be free of the confinement of the set.

Tony Church as Polonius and the other bureaucrats wore "compact costumes, the square, powerful Holbein line but Victorian materials, grays and silvers and maroons and lots and lots of black pin-stripe to suggest court and officialdom." The design concept reflected the director's idea of an efficient political machine, founded on financial stability and reeking of power and old money. Even the accents used projected an overbearing sense of upperclassness ("Hamlet" became "Hemlet"). Church concluded that Hamlet was the grit that finally stopped the workings of this vast combine.

Other stage icons that critics noted were Hamlet hemmed in by officials at the council table in I.ii, an image that reinforced the confined quality of the court, and also the huge contraption that represented the Ghost, Hamlet's father. The twelve-foot puppetlike machine was operated by other actors and, at one point, cradled Warner like a baby in its arms and punctuated Hamlet's youth within the surrounds of an oppressive and impersonal court. Tony Church felt that the closing moments of the play were the most shocking and foreboding, since they suggested that an even more malign force might replace Claudius:

> In the end when Fortinbras arrived, the wicket gate was punched in, a man came in and took the huge grate bars off the door, and an army appeared—total occupation. The beautiful ice-cold figure of Fortinbras was absolutely the sense of realpolitik. . . . At the end everybody on the stage regards Hamlet's killing of the king as treason. There is no indication that anyone [onstage] ever supports Hamlet. Hamlet was a troublesome madman, a deranged student who spoke totally unacceptable things at the wrong time . . . and had to go.

Ideally, the actor-director relationship produces ideas which complement the production. Hall appeared to have been Warner's mentor; he was, after all, ten years older than Warner and had been director of the Royal Shakespeare Company for five years. Nevertheless, the collaboration between the two men was close and fruitful. Church felt that Hall's casting of Warner was especially propitious:

> Warner was, in a sense, plastic material in [Hall's] hands. Warner didn't know the play, had never seen anyone play it before. [He had seen the Kozintsev film and the Olivier film.] You couldn't find an actor that naive now. . . . This was the brilliant thing Peter had done in that he was able to take someone who had no preconceptions at all and point him in the right direction. He knew what [Warner] could do, what the boy represented, and what his charisma meant—and he knew Warner didn't have any hang-ups. . . . Warner was picking his way through this extraordinary territory for the first time. I don't think it will ever happen again.

David Warner was trained at the Royal Academy of Dramatic Art when he was eighteen and nineteen. He vividly remembers the day that, at age twenty-one, he was asked to go to Stratford:

> I was working at a small theatre run by the Royal Shakespeare Company called the Arts Theatre in London that did experimental plays. I had seven lines in a play. . . . Peter Hall saw that and came round to the dressing room to talk to the other actors and he said congratulations to me and that he hoped one day I might like to join the company. Lo and behold, a year later I was invited to audition for this *Henry VI*, and I went back and back and back for six years.

As he began working on *Hamlet*, he was taken through the play by Robin Phillips, then Peter Hall's associate director: "I was asking for extra time and . . . he helped me learn the lines." Warner felt he could ask Phillips to help him with meaning in the dialogue. But it was inside the rehearsal process that Warner and Hall forged their working relationship and mutually agreed on actual technique:

> It was either Peter suggested to me or I suggested to him, or it may have been a mutual moment . . . I wouldn't claim credit, and certainly I was given enough of a stick on the way to do things. He would always assemble the whole cast and have models of the sets and have this whole concept of the piece. He didn't say to you, "You will play it in this way. You will do this and you will do that," but he laid it out in a pretty pertinent way which way he wanted to go.

Warner describes the working environment:

> Also, Peter Hall's speech to the company would be one thing, but, you know, I sort of stayed within the house [the theatre] with him and we'd talk away from the other people, so what was the rehearsal process and what was friendship we developed while we talked things over? It wasn't a question of a student and a teacher, I honestly believe, because when I left, I did three movies with him. He would never turn to me in my wildest imagination and ask me for advice about how to direct it nor would I ask him for advice about how to act it. But I think that we would have a fair amount of instinct going. He'd say, "This time, David, would you mind—" and

I'd say *okay* because I could just tell by the inflection of his voice what he was going to ask me to do on the next little run-through. So, I think it would be fair to say that I *put in*. For me to say it was Peter Hall's idea to do the soliloquies [a certain way], I don't think it *worked that way*. I may have turned around and just said it, or maybe one day because I was always trying something new, I just did it.

Despite the original and very coherent concept behind this production, the critical reception to Warner's Hamlet was decidedly mixed—as Berry says, "This was a much-loved and much-attacked *Hamlet*."[21] Some reviewers took pains to announce their biases: "Ideally speaking, the critic should walk into a theatre with his mind a virgin surface, a wax tablet from which all previous markings have been smoothed away. . . . I was far from any such state when I entered the Royal Shakespeare Theatre. . . . the tablet was full of scratches made by preconceptions and speculations."[22] Robert Speaight in *Shakespeare Quarterly* warned that "most of the critics and many of the spectators came to Mr. Peter Hall's production of *Hamlet* with their memories of Sir John Gielgud concealed like a hand grenade in their pockets" and then declared that "this is undoubtedly the most important theatrical statement on the play which has been made for a long time."[23]

Ronald Bryden wrote a thoughtful piece which eventually declared, "In other words, against all expectation and professional habit, I have to say that the new Stratford *Hamlet* seems to be a great and historic production."[24] Most of the reviews were cautious and balanced: "This is a powerful and disquieting production, and one that promises to grow in stature and authority with its hero . . . a good *Hamlet* but not yet a great one."[25] However, the critic for *The Spectator* was clearly offended: "It won't do. *Hamlet* as an existential tract will not do. . . . he is anti-heroic, anti-romantic and very suitably the subject of the shrill pre-pubescent ecstasy in the gallery."[26] John Trewin was regretful but direct: "I could imagine Horatio looking down on the dead Hamlet and saying, 'Goodnight, sweet Prince, and flights of angels sing thee to thy rest from the problems of commitment in life and politics.'"[27] John Gardner summed up the wariness of the press: "As soon as young prince Hamlet stops being predictably beautiful, like Bach, and starts sounding like Bartok, there is trouble."[28] And the chairman of the Royal Shakespeare Company's Board of Governors, Sir Fordham Flower, concluded that the "criticisms you have read are just about calculated to fill the house for years."[29]

Articles began to appear in the local papers asserting that Hall and Warner were unabashed by the critical reception. On its return to Stratford, the RSC program printed, at Warner's insistence, a page of press clippings titled "FOR" and "AGAINST," with the added comment that "this production of Hamlet, an immense success, provoked strong feelings amongst the critics."

Warner said that his verse-speaking was also the subject of critical turmoil. He had eschewed formal training in verse-speaking at drama school and did not attend Cicely Berry's verse classes at the Royal Shakespeare Company because he found the production itself to be very exhausting. When asked about verse structure and image patterns, he declared that *the meaning* is the most important thing: "The critics who liked the production never mentioned the verse. The ones who didn't went for the jugular and said I was like a schoolmaster lecturing the audience." In actual fact, there was a wide variety of responses. Although generally positive, Hugh Leonard professed ambivalence: "Mr. Warner has a habit of pausing irrelevantly in the middle of lines; and more importantly, his soliloquies were disposed of almost shamefacedly in the manner of an atheist reading the *Song of Solomon*. A grievous fault, but here let me seem to contradict myself and say that this was the most exciting *Hamlet* I have seen."[30]

In the midst of an overwhelmingly favorable review, one critic added, "I had the impression, through much of the evening, either that Mr. Warner was ignoring the beat, or that the conductor was giving him the wrong one. I also thought that he shouted far too much, and sometimes in odd places."[31] And in the act of razoring most of the production, another critic eulogized: "It is refreshing to hear verse taken at such a clip (as he takes 'To be or not to be,' for instance) and receive its overall shape instead of being seduced by passing phrases en route."[32] Warner himself accepted most of the remarks philosophically by forgiving critics who condemned him and held him personally responsible for the sins of an entire evening. He also felt that it was much easier to play nightly against mixed reviews because people's expectations were more normalized. If the reviews are too positive, the actor has to top himself each night to hold the audience, and if the reviews are too negative, one has the opportunity to improve the production and turn audience opinion around. This is especially true of the repertory situation in Stratford, when the play is scheduled to run for a set period of time no matter what.

Though the critics fluttered and fanned, the response of the youth of Great Britain was unilateral. Word got around that this was the "young" *Hamlet,* and teachers in the area brought busloads of school students to the production. The production also drew in college students. Tony Church describes them as "not rebels but they would have liked to have been." They brought sleeping bags and slept in long queues which extended around the back of the theatre and across the street, just in order to hold a place in the ticket line. From the beginning of the run, they had found their Hamlet: "The response, especially among the younger members of the first night audience, was sustained cheering,"[33] giving Warner eight curtain calls.[34] That the youth of the nation had been shaken from apathy seemed to be evidenced in this letter from a student who took a critic to task in the local papers:

As for Mr. Warner's performance—"small" Mr. Trewin called it. My comment is that Mr. Warner's was one of the "largest" Hamlets I have seen—and I have seen many despite my tender years. . . . He was a true Shakespearian tragic-hero. . . . [Trewin's] criticism seems to be based upon the fact that Mr. Warner was given a long ovation but that this response was not an accurate comment on his performance because it was predominantly youthful applause. For some unaccountable reason this exuberance seems to count for little in Mr. Trewin's estimation—indeed his opinion of young people generally seems to be pretty low.[35]

Overstated, perhaps, but it showed no lack of courage. There was a tendency among critics to compare Warner to a rock star: "It is painstakingly intelligent in conception, as contemporary as the Rolling Stones. And, finally, just about as attractive."[36] Church stated that there has been nothing like this interest in a play before or since that time. Actors in Britain now in their mid-forties claim that this was the most important *Hamlet* of all time. The nostalgia for it has not diminished today.

Warner himself completed the circle of identification. He had a special relationship to and a deep compassion for young people coming to see this play for the first time. Church described it as a mutual act of discovering, with Warner "picking his way through the mine field of this extraordinary text" and the young out front helping him to do it.

Warner had more than his own youthfulness to account for his interest in "kids." He'd had a troubled childhood and didn't do well in the usual subjects like math or sports. However, one person greatly influenced his life and offered a rescue:

> My saving grace was that I lived about twenty miles from Stratford-upon-Avon. A wonderful English literature teacher in my last of eight schools saw that I was in difficulty academically because of domestic problems—I couldn't concentrate on my lessons while I was in school—I couldn't get it together at all. It was she that got me interested in theatre at school because I played Lady Macbeth and Shylock in a tiny little production. It gave me an identity where I managed to get to the last class, the top class. She tried to encourage me to go to Stratford to see theatre with a school party and I went, but I couldn't understand it, I couldn't understand what anyone was talking about . . . because my brain wouldn't do it. Although I did have the kind of feeling that maybe someday it would be lovely to be a sort of actor.

Warner felt that part of his not comprehending what was happening onstage could be attributed to an artificial mode of playing: "I couldn't understand the Bard not only because of my lack of academic training but also because there was a lot of declaiming onstage, a lot of 'the voice' and a kind of posturing that got in the way of understanding." These early experiences were a seed that lay dormant for a long time. Even at the Royal Academy of Dramatic Art, where Warner had taken a medal for his performances in class, there was a feeling that Shakespeare was somehow not relevant:

> In drama school, we used to go to Shakespeare classes, and we'd say, "What are we doing THIS for? When are WE gonna do Shakespeare—run off and join the Royal Shakespeare Company? What for—to do Starveling!!" I mean, there were Shakespeare buffs in the class, yes, but by and large we never thought we were gonna DO this

---

Shakespeare stuff. What USE was it to us . . . like algebra or geometry or trigonometry!

Once Warner was at Stratford as an actor, Shakespeare's text unfolded to him: "When I was asked to play it, I could actually understand it. When I read it, I understood it for the first time!" His excitement and elation were passed on to the audience, and it became his mission to bring them the classics:

> Having been a member of a schools audience at Stratford and think-ing about how even many of my contemporaries found it difficult and uninteresting to watch, it was my job as a twenty-three-year-old up on that stage, playing one of my best parts—to make it *under-stood.* Bearing in mind that a vast proportion of that audience *were required* to go, I wanted to make it as interesting as possible. I had to approach it by trying to understand the play as much as possible and then to communicate it so that they understood it, which gave Hamlet a kind of humanity instead of its being the famous solilo-quies and the famous scenes just *presented.* As if Hamlet was saying all this for the first time and sharing it with them. . . . One thing I DON'T want to do is bore the pants off these kids—I mean, this is just something I'd want NOT to do.

Warner was so careful of the young people that he persuaded Hall to take the act interval right after the second entrance of the Ghost (forty-five minutes into the play) rather than after "How all occasions" (two and one-half hours into the play):

> Peter Hall said that every ten years a play like *Hamlet* will mean something different to a generation—this particular one meant a lot to the kids. And nothing was *changed*—we didn't do a kind of glitzy production or anything. So that was very gratifying—*to be told that young people might like this.* Both Peter and I felt that the *kids there* needed to be involved in order to sit in that theatre. Now the best way to involve them is to be *with* them.

Warner's sense of being with them showed most strongly in the solilo-quies. Here was an instinctual actor who did not even know what the stage convention of the soliloquy was, that in the twentieth century it was primarily played in front of an audience but not necessarily *to* them. There was a rush of critical commentary regarding the performance mode that he chose:

> This is a Hamlet desperately in need of counsel, help, experience, and he actually seeks it from the audience in his soliloquies. That is probably the greatest triumph of the production: using the Elizabethan convention with total literalness. Hamlet communes not with himself but with you. For the first time in my experience, *the rhetoric spoken as it was intended to be*, comes brilliantly to life.[37]

> In the soliloquies, he had a special gift for involving the audience.[38]

> In this way, he builds carefully, using the soliloquies not so much for thinking aloud as for taking the audience into his confidence and seeking silent support.[39]

> He delivers the soliloquies as though he were dictating to the literary pirates, jotting down the First Quarto version of the play.[40]

> To gauge how close this production gets to contemporary truth one has but to watch the way in which David Warner slams out the soliloquies directly to the audience—as though pleading for their aid—and finding only himself reflected in the rows of upturned faces.[41]

> His agonies of mind are most strongly communicated naturally enough in the soliloquies, which have the tone of desperate appeals.[42]

> . . . a telling quietness of delivery that invests the soliloquies in particular with an extraordinary air of spontaneity.[43]

> How fresh and meaningful he makes the familiar lines of the soliloquies sound.[44]

> When Mr. Warner speaks the great soliloquies, he comes to the front of the stage and rakes the first few rows of the stalls with ravaged eyes, searching distractedly for a comfort that is not there or anywhere.[45]

To have them [soliloquies] spoken directly to the audience as at a public meeting ensures that we listen closely and attentively to the argument. They are appeals for our support and understanding and establish a rapport which is rarely obtained by more fluent and sonorous Hamlets. It creates an atmosphere like a teach-in.[46]

He speaks the great soliloquies direct to the audience, downstage, as if demanding immediate answers.[47]

He subtly displaces the rhythm of the verse so that the soliloquies become direct while remaining poetic. Only Olivier has steered so true a middle course between reciting and turning Shakespeare into Noel Coward. . . . [Warner] makes you feel, not like a spectator at a spectacle, but like yourself sitting late at night in a coffee bar while your best friend explains his problems.[48]

But what will annoy many Shakespeare lovers is the way Warner speaks the soliloquies.[49]

The comments indicate how thoroughly established was the convention of the inner-directed soliloquy in *Hamlet*. People were so accustomed to the notion of the actor's executing this stage convention as if he were totally unaware of the audience that some actually objected to his performing them in a way Elizabethans may have found "natural."[50] An examination of each of the speeches will show how Warner integrated his character conception with the requisites of the production concept.

In the council scene of act I, scene ii, the king, the queen, Polonius, and Hamlet (Hamlet hemmed in by the others) were trucked in on a platform to center stage, looked down upon by a tapestry bearing two giant horses caparisoned for battle.[51] Despite the closeness of sitting side by side throughout the proceedings, Warner showed unconcealed rancor toward the king and queen by literally shouting what is usually played as an aside, "A little more than kin, and less than kind" (I.ii.65), at them. On "I shall in all my best obey *you*, madam" (I.ii.120), the audience hummed in response, indicating their awareness of his impertinence.[52] The scene was overpopulated with trumpeters, drummers, halberdiers, counselors, and secretaries, all of whom ministered to Claudius and, of course, none to Hamlet.[53]

Warner said that this soliloquy "was the most difficult to get into," not only because it was the first one but because Hamlet had to break free of the vast, efficient organization which had just left the stage. He needed to find supporters, and he virtually located them out of the play, within the theatre audience. From an acting point of view, the performance energies now had to be channeled off the stage, and eye contact had to be spread across the audience, requiring a great push of force in a new direction. The way Warner decided to do this soliloquy set the precedent for the way that he did most of the rest.

The first soliloquy ("O that this too too solid flesh," I.ii.129–59)[54] began with Warner sitting upstage center, having been released from his imprisonment at the council tables by the exit of the group. Projecting his reticence, he did not rise and move toward the audience until "Fie on't" (six lines into the speech). On "Possess it merely" he crossed to downstage center to establish further contact. The pace of the soliloquy was gunshot. Very fast, furiously angry, he slammed it out as if pounding on things and gnashing his teeth. There was little attention to rhythm or verse, with few pauses, some in odd places. There was a slowing down on "galled eyes" and his voice dropped to a whisper on "post with such dexterity to incestious sheets." He concluded the soliloquy on "it cannot come to good" and crossed downstage right to sit on a chair. Robert Speaight found the sitting posture a reflection of "an unsettled mind in a seemingly settled society."[55] Warner's intention here was to finally express the bottled anger that had accumulated throughout the council scene. He did not use the soliloquy to bond with the audience, slowing down and wooing them with eye contact; he rather assumed their collusion and let off steam. The character established was a rebellious prince who did not respect authority.

Before the second soliloquy, the stage picture revealed the powerful image of a young child cradled in the giant metal arms of the elder Hamlet,[56] giving a feeling, as Warner says, of "total love and belief in the father." Warner reacted quite violently to the Ghost's request for revenge, even to shouting "WHAT!" (not in text) and then sobbing throughout the Ghost's long speech. The Ghost exited upstage center, and Hamlet (positioned in stage center) fell onto his back, facing upward. Warner explained his reactions in the soliloquy as "the soul coming out of him" and "the nearest he was to any kind of concentrated nervous breakdown." He felt that there wasn't much logic to the speech that an actor

---

could follow. Warner took a particularly long pause after "O most pernicious woman!" and then overemphasized "damned villain" in the next line. He rose later and again fell to his knees, using a prop on the last six lines: "In 'meet it is I set it down,' I had a kind of little notebook. I had a cape on and a kind of coat and it was in one of the pockets. [I] took notes. . . . I think the production where people do the motions with their hands is the best way to do it actually." Perhaps most interesting of all, this soliloquy was not direct address: "I didn't do that *to* the audience, because it simply wasn't a discussion with them—it was coming out of a swoon." The passage was too personal and too emotional to be shared.

Warner began the third soliloquy ("O, what a rogue and peasant slave am I!" II.ii.550–605) after Rosencrantz and Guildenstern had left by crossing to upstage center and sitting on a table. In this speech, he began his most direct and most intimate communication with the audience. He rose and crossed to downstage center, the very edge of the forestage, to pose the question "What would he do / Had he the motive and the cue for passion / That I have?" "Who calls me villain . . . " had a sustained pause following it. The whole series of ensuing questions were then asked point-blank of the audience.

When asked if he "set the lines up" each night for that one bold challenger to answer him, Warner replied, "You mean warming them up? No, no, that would have unbalanced the thing. All I could think was that I was *prepared* for it to happen every night." He reiterated how astonished he was to find that speech perfectly orchestrated for audience participation: "It all fitted in so perfectly with this person who ostensibly was trying to heckle me," and it gave a huge boost to the line " 'swounds, I should take it," which played with an absolute logic after the dialogue with the audience member.

On "Bloody, bawdy villain!" he broke contact with them and suddenly darted upstage to hurl the lines to the king's empty chair. After the climactic "Oh Vengeance!" he sat down on the table again. He began a fresh burst of hostility on "And fall a-cursing like a very drab, / A scullion" where he grabbed a chair and kicked it over with an angry bang. On "Fie upon't, foh!" Warner crossed to upstage center, facing toward the rear of the set, as if to collect himself and regain his temper. With the relationship that he had established, it would have been inappropriate to intimate displeasure with the audience. When he began his plan about the play within the play, he returned to downstage center to resume his duologue with them. The closing couplet was delivered after a laconic laugh, very directly to the audience as he exited at stage left near the proscenium. The actor handled huge twists of emotion, guilt, self-anger, and wrath, but still retained the connection he had made with the audience. He didn't nurture an attachment—he merely assumed it and they followed his bidding. He was, however, specific and careful about which emotions were directed where. He had to be because much of the speech was loud and energized, not pleading or persuading.

Warner recalled that there was an agreement to play the nunnery scene as if Ophelia were up to something and Hamlet had a feeling that people were hiding behind the arras. But first came the fourth soliloquy ("To be, or not to be," III.i.55–89), performed in its usual location, shortly after the third soliloquy. Ophelia had gone off the stage. Hamlet entered upstage center through the left door. He crossed to down center, stopped, and then turned downstage to face the audience, contacting them immediately with a searching look which created a very theatrical pause before the opening phrase. On "Devoutly to be wish'd" he went to the very edge of the forestage and stayed there for most of the speech, until "lose the name of action," when Ophelia reentered.

Although the content of this speech was very contemplative and personal, Warner never questioned that it should be given to the audience. Indeed, he felt that this soliloquy was the *most* direct of all of them. He saw it as sharing his dilemma with them ("after all, he'd shared everything else!") and "debating gently" the very serious options. Hamlet was in a terrible situation and was having great difficulty resolving it. He turned over solutions in his mind, wishing that one answer would stand out as the most logical. One critic commented that by emphasizing the "insolence of office" he "seems to be speaking for a whole debunking generation."[57] Warner said, "I don't think they should come up on the stage and shake Hamlet and say, 'Pull yourself together!'" However, "there's absolutely no reason why one shouldn't use the audience as the one you're speaking to instead of yourself." It is notable that he was considerably quieter and more low-key in speaking, a distinct change of delivery from the soliloquy before: "First of all, absolutely everybody knows this speech, especially the first two lines of it. That's the killer. It wasn't a question of saying it beautifully, it was just a question of trying to make it clear."

At the end Warner spoke the transition lines, "Soft you now / The fair Ophelia" in a highly conspiratory whisper, which indicated how closely he and the audience had bonded. However, he shouted alarmingly, "Nymph, in thy orisons / Be all my sins remem'bred," suddenly changing the mood and whirling away from her. There was no attempt in this production to show a close relationship with Ophelia;[58] in fact, at one point Hamlet slapped her. This action reduced even more the possibility of onstage confidants for Hamlet.

The fifth soliloquy ("'Tis now the very witching time of night," III.ii.388–99) was notable for its speed. However, Warner did take great care to emphasize that he intended no harm to his mother by unbuckling his sword belt along with the pledge "I will *speak* daggers to her, but *use none.*"[59] Everything that happened after the play scene was angry and fast, as if Hamlet were filled with renewed determination.

The prayer scene at III.iii contains the double soliloquies—the first from Claudius and then Hamlet's. Critics complained that it was difficult for them to believe in Claudius' remorse, given the decisive and resolute character that had been built. However, Robert Speaight disagreed and felt that Brewster Mason gave the soliloquy a "calm argument of his desperate case."[60] Claudius' soliloquy was positioned within an enclosed area, a private chamber with a council table and seats and a prie-dieu located slightly down left. He spoke to himself.

In contrast to this, Warner sought to enlist the audience as his ally, his objective being collusion through intimacy, not belief through cool rationality. He began the sixth soliloquy ("Now might I do it pat," III.iii.73–96) by entering from upstage right, crossed through the chamber unseen by Claudius, and made his way free from the chamber. He soon crossed to down center, level with the proscenium, and after "And so am I reveng'd?" (the third line), he went downstage right, to the very edge of the forestage and worked that section of the audience. On "know thou a more horrid hent" (about two-thirds of the way through), he broke upstage and took his exit at left upstage center.

His purpose was highly persuasive: he wanted all the support for himself; none should go to Claudius. The soliloquy was delivered with three major pauses. The first was after "And so am I reveng'd," which was a natural place for Hamlet to make a major realization. The second was after "this same villain send / To heaven" as he continued his train of thought. The third was after "No," where there is only one word on an entire line; here the actor made the ultimate decision not to murder the king and to resheathe his sword. His physical movements toward the onlookers roughly coincided with these textual beats.

The final soliloquy ("How all occasions do inform against me," IV.iv.32–66) was prepared for with a great show of militarism as act IV, scene iv opened with a powerful parade of weaponry and soldiers which marked the entrance of Fortinbras. In contrast, Hamlet was brought in by one guard. Warner intended that the speech be mostly a commentary on soldiers who fight unnecessary wars. He neither saw any particular inspiration in Fortinbras nor thought him admirable. The seventh soliloquy was Warner's favorite because it had a great deal of personal meaning for him as well. It represented the end of a beat where "all these things are ending, there is some kind of future there, he's come to terms with some kind of peace with that phase of his life." Although it was his last soliloquy to the audience (the second and final interval followed) and nowhere did he have the opportunity to talk to the audience again, it felt good to him to speak some of the sentiments expressed. Warner explained,

> There was a lot going on then in the sixties, Vietnam and everything, and although this production was not commenting on that, David [Warner, the actor, as opposed to Hamlet, the character], I think, was feeling something there about that particular situation, "The imminent death of twenty thousand men . . . Go to their graves. . . . " I grew to like this speech, and it began to mean more things as one just played with it. Perhaps some of this was purely personal.

Tony Church said that the closing line, "My thoughts be bloody, or be nothing worth!" although very direct to the audience and very calmly reasoned, threw a gauntlet down to Claudius. Hamlet was now determined and ready to act.

In summing up the performance, a number of points emerge. First of all, the production was engineered to have Hamlet remain almost friendless and without allies. Seventy-five of Horatio's lines were cut, thus weakening his role. Ophelia's and Hamlet's relationship was not presented as an intimate one. The supernumeraries in the cast were often increased to emphasize "officialdom"; the larger the cast, the lonelier and more isolated was the character of Hamlet. Warner found his closest companions to be the theatre audience, and to reinforce this decision, none of the soliloquy lines were cut. Second, the blocking pattern on this particular stage set almost always put Warner far downstage or actually on the forestage to deliver the soliloquies.[61] It is to be emphasized that he took the initiative in establishing contact with his audience, feeling obliged to do so from the viewpoint of the persona. Third, Warner says that the production grew; the difference between the way he did the soliloquies at the beginning of the run and at the end was that he gained more confidence in technique and increased his affinity with the audience. He felt that the soliloquies got most intimate at the Aldwych Theatre; there was no change in the basic blocking or the production concept, however. Fourth, Warner truly relished audience contact, a mode some actors are distinctly uncomfortable with in performance:

> Given the fact that Shakespeare wrote lines when nobody else was onstage, it's quite logical that it gets said to the audience because the audience is THERE. I'm not saying that the way I did it was *right*, but it was certainly right for me to do it that way at that time. The point was to involve them. You cannot depend on how good-looking you are or your sexuality or a gimmick as such—you've got these words and a sense of contact. . . . it was a wonderful feeling to be able to bring them into me.

If Warner had elected to do the soliloquies inwardly, it would have been a serious violation of his character conception as well as of the aesthetic coherence of the production design.

About delivery of the soliloquies, Warner said:

> It wasn't a question of moving the whole head in an arc or moving the head up and down. It was looking up into the audience and acknowledging them and then down below, but it was not a great

big circular movement of the head to the stalls and back or anything. Occasionally, the eyes would flicker. You just do it so that they KNOW that you mean to include them. This is something to do with technique.

The sound recording of this production provides additional insights about the performance. It was taken halfway through the Aldwych season, during a matinee on March 9, 1966, at a time when the play was "set" and in a good, working groove. The most obvious feature was the lively rapport between the audience and the chief performer. There were bursts of reaction and small murmurs of engagement throughout. The recording microphone was located near two younger students, and from time to time one could hear them discussing what had happened onstage in enthralled voices. The power and energy of David Warner was manifest. He played very strong anger and considerably more comedy than was revealed in reading the reviews of the production. He was cynical and very much the wisecracker. The joking was often at the expense of authority figures, like Polonius, who did not play his own lines for laughs. The spectators responded very favorably to Warner and spurred him onward. There was an exchange of energy which they gave and he fed upon. The audience was very lively and picked up on nuances of text—small puns, emphasized words, pauses. One can almost feel the heat of the group as one listens to it.

Conclusively, the form and pressure of the age had conspired to create a rogue-and-peasant-slave Hamlet. In exploring why these soliloquies were performed direct-address, a convergence of answers emerges. First and foremost, director Peter Hall was a driving force in devising a production concept in which no other way of performing the speeches seemed appropriate. He began with his reaction to a particular political climate, as Church described it, "the corrupted end of a long conservative administration . . . sex scandals [Profumo] and all that going on," the oppressiveness of which produced a profound disaffection in the youth of Great Britain. On the surface, then, Hall wanted to make a production that was "relevant" and spoke to the audience of the sixties, a unique and eventful decade. However, no matter how political Shakespeare can get (as Alan Sinfield has pointed out), "in the work of the Royal Shakespeare Company we may perceive a strain of opportunism, or at least a wish to sustain the company itself."[62] Critics reacted with a huge flap of attention, and the play sold tickets with amazing constancy. It became such an important play in the Royal Shakespeare Company's repertory that after it was performed for the first season in Stratford (August 19–December 11, 1965, 46 performances), it was transferred to the Aldwych Theatre in London for a season (December 22–February 12, 1966, 29 performances) and then *returned* to Stratford for a third season (April 28–November 12, 68 performances), totaling 143 performances.[63] This was a procedure rarely accorded any other production—at best, most plays phase out after the London run. Obviously the critical controversy had done no harm at the box office. The revenues from *Hamlet* were sorely needed by a company unsure of its next subsidy from the Arts Council.[64]

The production reinforced the new image Hall sought for the company that he had taken over in 1960, that of a "popular theatre" that appealed to a dissident and leftist intelligentsia and drew in politically well-tuned audiences. Hall had a strong sense of the readiness being all. He had found the right actor, he had accurately felt the pulse of this tumultuous era, and he had an obligation to sell this dramatist. Shakespeare's dramaturgy permitted both a direct confrontation and a direct dialogue with the audience because the mode of delivery of the soliloquy is *optional*. What had once been an inward and internalized *psychomachia* Hall turned outward, to a more political and more engaging stance. Even the set design, non-Elizabethan and heavy in its execution, facilitated audience contact. The old rhetoric, Renaissance in origin, had suddenly become the new: forget the tropes and schemes of the early seventeenth century and concentrate on the arguments and strategies used to persuade. Shakespeare in performance had suddenly abandoned the beautiful man speaking well and introduced a Hamlet bent upon swaying an audience. Warner's role was that of a lone dissenter who elicited its overwhelming sympathies.

Lastly, the production initiated a brief resurgence of soliloquies addressed to the audience. Nicol Williamson's 1969 *Hamlet* at the Roundhouse, directed by Tony Richardson, saw him talking to the audience on all four sides in a theatre-in-the-round situation. Hall also directed Albert Finney in a 1970 *Hamlet*, where Finney reached out to the offstage audience in the vast auditorium of the Olivier Theatre.

David Warner felt that it was all completely natural:

If we were accused of talking to the audience and nobody had done that before, then I guess . . . we broke a bit of ground. During the Restoration, actors were talking AT the audience. As far as I was concerned, I was talking WITH the audience. . . . And sometimes one might be a bit curt with them. Maybe one was looking for a parent figure or a father figure or trying to talk to a young brother or a sister he didn't have. But that would be up to some analyst trying to analyze what was going on. As far as I was concerned, it was the most personal thing in the world. Sharing Hamlet's words with strangers—we weren't strangers by the end of the evening! After that, they may know something about the play and something about you. A lot of actors say there are moments, maybe just once in a split second in your career, you get next to God. There is this ONE-NESS—one moment where every single member of the audience is THERE, together with yourself, where you feel everybody is in tune, one split second. I don't mean chatting together, I mean being quiet together. I don't mean being lifted off the ground or anything—just a moment of total understanding. It's a spirit or something . . .

4

BEN KINGSLEY : *In My Mind's Eye*

Reviews of Ben Kingsley's 1975 *Hamlet* were shrouded in the news of the death of its director, twenty-eight-year-old Mary Ann ("Buzz") Goodbody. Four days after its opening, she took her life by overdosing on barbiturates. The newspaper headlines documented her demise in graphic detail and expressed the shock of the arts community in Britain. She was, at the time, the first and only woman director at the Royal Shakespeare Company. At the age of twenty-four, she had been singled out for a national drama prize while at Sussex University, caught the attention of John Barton, and was added to the ranks of the company. Her early interest was experimental theatre, and she had a strong involvement in Theatregoround, the Royal Shakespeare Company's touring group that aimed at taking Shakespeare to the people. This assignment was fitting because she was interested in the class struggle, a member of the Communist party, and active in the women's liberation movement. She had won her directorial spurs on a production of *King Lear* after being appointed artistic director of The Other Place in 1974 and had just opened a fascinating *Hamlet* with Ben Kingsley, who remembered:

> When I last saw her on that Thursday night, she said, now our next phase of work is to go back to the text and use all of the energy of the cast, which was terrific, she said, a great release of energy, and pin those words down just a bit so we can hear more. There is a lot of emotion, but we want now to make the words like daggers, clear

Ben Kingsley in Hamlet, *1975.*
Photo courtesy of Joe Cocks Studio, Stratford-upon-Avon.

and incisive. All the music is there, I just want to conduct it a bit more and sharpen it up, she said. So I thought that the next phase of work would be something to look forward to. And then on Saturday, two days later, she was dead and I was astonished. But she left a note, she bought her pills, the doctors gave her a prescription. A very considered act.[1]

Both she and Kingsley were in those early proving-ground years of their careers. Buzz Goodbody's work showed strong promise, and distinct artistic and practical philosophies had begun to take shape. Not one of the university-educated breed of actors, Kingsley had begun his career on a schools tour in 1964 and performed in regional repertory in England before joining the Royal Shakespeare Company in 1967. He played supporting roles for a long period of time, including Demetrius in Peter Brook's famous 1970 production of *A Midsummer Night's Dream*. This *Hamlet* was one of his early hefty parts. The honor and glory of starring roles such as the Oscar he won for Best Actor in *Gandhi* were yet to come.

Kingsley is known for his incisive intelligence and his ability to be articulate about his craft. The famous dark eyes shone as he recalled his director, Goodbody. He spared no praise in describing a mutually productive alliance:

It was the relationship of two people who were not only able to befriend each other but to love each other. We had a great, very intimate rapport, very close—we told each other practically everything. I remember I arrived in Stratford one morning from London. I had a lot of major choices to make in my life at that time. I was in the middle of a terrible dilemma. She met me at the theatre—very funny, I had the same kind of breakfast, a coffee and a sticky bun, just like I bought now. And she asked me how I was and I told her that I felt tired and old and burnt out. At thirty-two! [he laughs]. An hour later, I felt marvelous. And I told her, it's wonderful being with you, because you can come in and you make everyone else feel great. She was very loving, very kind to me, but also projected onto me, no—*allowed* me to enjoy a profound sense of responsibility to my craft, to the audience, to fellow actors, to the very dangerous and wonderful story that we were telling—the dynamite of this play and its realpolitik—youth, old age, death, suicide—to be aware of all these responsibilities.

She did this by example, of course, because she worked a fourteen-hour day, three rehearsal sessions every day. We were called for two of them, the actors for *Hamlet*. She would do all of them, all day, all afternoon, in the evening. And then drink, smoke, chain-smoking Players No. 6, listening to very loud pop music in the morning with her hair in rollers and her hair dryer going. Everything, everything. You thought, what does she do when she goes home to bed—lies there going like that [he stares upward] until she goes into the rehearsal room again with her friends? So she was dependent on me and I was dependent on her. Mutually dependent. I wanted very much to be *her* Hamlet. I wanted her to say, you've got it—for your generation, for me, for us, for your friends, in the middle of the seventies, you've hit it. I wanted her to say that so much. [Pause] And she finally did.

She would earnestly provoke and provoke until we'd all got there. One day, after one really good dress rehearsal, she said, "Right, thank you very much. Excuse me a minute." She left through the doors and came back with a trolley of drinks and food and said, "I think that was very good and I've decided to give you all a party." She'd brought all that and set it up beforehand. She had known we would be good and then she wheeled in our presents. She thought that far ahead: "I'm going to have a run-through Monday. What can I do to make them all feel good. I know—I'll buy drinks and crisps and peanuts and paper hats and I'll bring a party into the room." That kind of childish, beautiful, naive, innocent thoughtfulness. To want to please people. At the same time, this stainless-steel, rapier-like intellect.

Kingsley talked about what happened in the rehearsal room, the beginning search for style and the honing of technical details. The cast worked very democratically, with open observation and discussion:

We were wondering what style to use, linguistically, whether we should break the text down into spoken idiom and do the lines with more colloquial grunts. To give you a terrible example, not that we would have ever done this outside of a rehearsal tactic, but we were being lulled into the area of "To be or not to be, I mean, you know, that's the question. You know what I mean, whether or not it is, like, sort of nobler in the mind . . ." There were the beginnings of that sort of thing from some of the more minor players in rehearsal who because they were in modern dress and so close to the audience didn't feel that the artifice of the language would be appropriate. But then, of course, the artifice disappeared and the *art* of the language became more prominent. And you realized that you could play with it much more easily than you could with any modern colloquial stuff. Polonius was doing it from the first week in rehearsal. The oldest actor in the company was word-perfect before any other actor and speaking at twice the rate and getting laughs from his fellow actors, the younger actors, in rehearsal! They'd look at one another and say, "Hey, what's going on? Old Andre [Van Gyseghem], he's brilliant. I like this, what he's doing?" They were slightly jealous. And then all that calmed down and we all listened to him and all discussed the acting style and I said, "Well, he's got it. Andre's got it." Bob Peck agreed, "He's the only one who's doing it, whatever he's doing." And then that's what Buzz said: "Don't hammer the emotion. Follow the line of the text and let the words work for you."

This, then, was the kind of guidance she interjected as a director. Rehearsals were free, explorational, relaxed, and when a discovery was made, she would articulate and punctuate it. Nevertheless, she was not hesitant to make demands, as Kingsley recalled:

We searched for a style of delivery for the soliloquies for the first two weeks. She would sit there in the auditorium and say, "I'd like for you today to do all your soliloquies to me." Fabulous, to do them to that face. That was a direct order. But that was not an immediate frozen choice. I had felt that the audience was going to be very close in that theatre and that if we didn't allow ourselves to connect with them that we would lose out on a lot of energy.

This, too, was one of the director's basic tenets. She felt that the play should be accessible to all of the audience at all times. The idea grew out of her early beginnings and her insistence that Shakespeare not be reserved for the upper classes or the intellectual elite. Her political consciousness, which coincided with the Royal Shakespeare Company's proclivity for socially relevant Shakespeare, spilled over into the rehearsal chambers. Moreover, her ideas worked. This particular production was uniformly acclaimed by critics. They called it "bold, trendy, and imaginative,"[2] "marvelous and exhilarating,"[3] "never a moment's dullness," and "riveting."[4] The usually restrained *Financial Times* tagged it "immensely exciting," with "melodramatic sparks" and "an unusual glow." Clearly, Goodbody's tabloid epitaph was erased by brilliant performances from the actors.

One of the consequences the cast had to live with was responsive ticketholders:

> We had a lot of people in the audience afterwards who stayed behind. But not as a memorial to Buzz, that became an integrated point of anger; it [the production] wasn't in memoriam, it wasn't a wake. We had to get beyond that, for her sake and for ours. Yet there were people, women her age, and men a little older saying, "That was for us. Thank you very much." One woman even stopped me in the street and said, "You did that play for me, you know."

The cast also became a repository of speculation about why the suicide had taken place. Many reasons were hinted at, but no one cause seemed preeminent. Terry Hands, acting director of the Royal Shakespeare Company at the time, issued a statement: "We are all shattered. She was somebody for whom we had the deepest admiration as a colleague and loved as a person. On both counts she is irreplaceable."[5] Everyone agreed that had Buzz Goodbody continued her career, she would have been brilliant. Kingsley added, "Yes, yes. And that's what they say about Hamlet—that's what Fortinbras says about Hamlet at the end of the play."

Hamlet opened on April 8, 1975, at the (then) second house of the Royal Shakespeare Company, called The Other Place, a tin-roofed Quonset hut transformed into a theatre space for low-budget projects, up the hill on Bridge Street in Stratford-upon-Avon.[6] The production ran for forty-six performances, then transferred to the Roundhouse in London on January 27, 1976, and ran for thirty-nine[7] more performances. The basic oblong shape and capacity of the two theatres were very similar (The Other Place seated 150, the Roundhouse 180). Designer Chris Dyer created an environment for presentation that adapted easily to either of the theatres. At the front of the "auditorium," he put the main playing area, on which most of the attention was focused. The critic for *Drama* magazine described it as "a platform-stage at one of the space's narrow ends [raised about three feet], but the action spilled out into the auditorium, both down the centre gangway and along narrow raised ramps down each side. A white back wall of sliding [stiff paper] panels and a red carpet [down the central gangway] augmented by occasional furniture, were all the set required."[8] Props and set pieces were sparsely used as the "sliding screens across the back of the stage could form a continuous neutral-coloured wall or . . . open to provide a central entrance or recess. . . . There was, too, the fore-edge of the stage to sit on . . . and a trap-grave."[9] It was colorfully labeled as a "disinfected school gym . . . white concrete bunker,"[10] a "wraparound acting area . . . a Kabuki bridge along one of the walls."[11] The newspaper reviews reflected a sense of jubilation and even a hunger for the directness of contact between the audience and the play:

> For sheer acting ability and audience manipulation I have not seen a better production. If the seats were rock-hard, the pleasure of the players' close contact and action around the audience was a massive compensation.[12]

> [The playing area offers] . . . a huge gain in tonal variety from nuances of conversation to full heroic delivery . . . asides can fall to cryptic undertone . . . giving the closest possible identification with the characters.[13]

> The proximity of the actors results not only in real physical involvement, but also in the chance to enjoy to the full details both gestural and environmental.[14]

> The four-hour text was delivered with tremendous vigor and great speed. . . . the graveyard scene uproarious . . . and the entire evening great fun.[15]

> Full use is made of the small auditorium: the players walk and run along ramps on either side of the stage and up and down the centre aisle. Hamlet's Ghost appears and vanishes near the Exit. All this encircling activity conveys the intimacy of a Theatre in the Round.[16]

The performance arena was transformed beyond a *set* into an *atmosphere*. "Spareness" and "paucity" were juxtaposed with adjectives like "oriental," "Brechtian," "Strindbergian" in describing it. An environment that permitted strong interaction between performer and audience was created from a place where people originally sat quietly and obediently as detached observers. Within this modern dress production of no specific decade or nationality, the actors wore costumes which suggested their status: "Gentlemen wore lounge suits . . . black coat and striped trousers . . . Fortinbras was in camouflaged battle-dress."[17] Hamlet himself wore a tweed overcoat and "well-cut business suit."[18] There was extensive use of doubled roles: thirteen actors played twenty-five characters. Critics continually singled out favorites among the supporting roles, for example, the "genial" Claudius, like a "company director at a shareholders' meeting" as well as his "cocktail-circuit queen."[19] The quality of the playing was applauded by critics: "a commendable ensemble effort," "the company displays a marvelous flexibility,"[20] and "the renaissance remoteness is completely subdued."[21]

Although the major soliloquies were left intact, there was considerable pruning of the text; smaller characters (Voltemand and Cornelius) were excised, but not Reynaldo or the gravediggers. These cuts seemed appropriate, given the emphasis on domestic relationships within the interpretation and in keeping with the production concept. Two intervals were taken, the first after Hamlet's initial meeting with the Ghost, and the second after the final soliloquy, "How all occasions do inform against me."

Despite the critical appreciation of the ensemble, the night belonged, as it should, to Ben Kingsley. A production with Albert Finney was running at the National Theatre simultaneously, but the Royal Shakespeare Company's production garnered all the praise. Kingsley was compared to a gangster, a pushy salesman,[22] "an excitable foreign delegate at a riotous UN session,"[23] "a mature, grim semitic Hamlet,"[24] having put on a "frantic disposition."[25] His character conception was certainly not one of the traditional romantic renditions of the past. The acting qualities appreciated were various but consistent. Nearly every critic mentioned the intelligence of the actor and his skill in handling the lines. Kingsley's favorite epithet was "a paratrooper of the intelligence." He indicated that he tried for as many laughs as he could "because there is great comedy and great wit in the role. I think I got every one there was to get," and Benedict Nightingale confirmed, "I can't remember a prince who found more humour in *Hamlet*."[26] There was unanimity about Hamlet's energy and versatility; the actor seemed to have struck many chords in the play, keyed out several of the major themes. That Kingsley was a "chilling alternation of rigid control and loose-limbed despair"[27] illustrated this view.

There was a running debate among critics about whether or not Kingsley's Hamlet had actually gone mad. Several wanted to place him on the brink of insanity, describing "burning eyes, darting gestures, satanic vehemence,"[28] and "an unfeigned madness never far behind that long, fine, greenish-white face of his, with its stark, strange eyes."[29] Another found him "neurotic if not psychotic,"[30] and one settled on "that kind of desperate grandeur of which the great Hamlets are made, of the tension between feigned and real madness."[31] Still another writer spent several paragraphs proving that this Hamlet was "utterly sane at all times."[32] Kingsley asserted, "He [Hamlet] wasn't mad. As he says, I am feigning madness. But in feigning madness, he gives himself so much license that he began to erode his own limits." Kingsley chose to interpret his Hamlet as if he were mad north by northwest but still knew a hawk from a handsaw, as if he had moments of madness but had not gone over into insanity.

Kingsley worked for direct audience contact and used the "juices" that flowed between audience and actor:

They were so close they were almost hanging off my nose, and I thought that if we didn't allow ourselves to connect with them we would lose out. There was so much energy pouring in from the audience. It is like tennis. The ball goes out to them and they react and then the ball goes back to the actor. But it also includes them, the essence of the play moves through the actors like a flame, a blazing torch which is passed around. You had to hand it back to the audience, but very delicately.

Recently I acted with somebody in a film. He was giving a huge amount of energy to his performance. But every actor who played with him was aghast—and he did it to me, too—he acted about three inches above my eyes! I thought, how are you going to get all the energy I'm giving you. I was acting *with* him and pushing energy into him but he wasn't getting it. What a terrible waste—all that pouring in that he could be using.

Eerily consonant with these descriptions, one critic maintained, "Ben Kingsley's Hamlet flickered like an imprisoned flame." Given this emphasis on communication, it was not at all unusual that the choice was made to give most of the soliloquies with maximum directness:

> I had terrific contact with the audience. . . . With my eyes, I create who the audience is and what they are and where their reality is. They can come and go as the actor pleases in terms of the soliloquy. The actor has the power to conjure, by a wave of the hand.
>
> Their [the audience's] function changes a great deal. So, it's difficult to call them friends because in the next soliloquy you might be railing against them. People who—people for whom, *for* whom I was unfolding a great secret [he says this with great emphasis]. But not WITH whom, FOR whom. Only *occasionally* I would hope that they would feel that it was WITH as well as FOR.
>
> All of the soliloquies very much included the fact that the audience were there looking at me. None of them were in the abstract. It was like—when I spoke to *myself*, I spoke to the *audience*. They were my ears. I addressed myself to them in the way that one would address oneself to oneself in an argument. I never asked them what I should do.
>
> I never made any demands on them, but I always let them share the questions that I was asking myself. I think it's very difficult—an audience can't respond. They can't help the play other than by listening. So rather than "what shall I do" [he says this leaning forward in an aggressive and pronounced way], it's more like "what shall I do" [he says this quietly but still to an audience]. It's a case of not begging for an answer but telling them that I was in a very difficult position and only I could find a way out. I often let them off the hook in the soliloquy by indicating, "You can't help me out, you know—this is up to me and I'll have to take care of it."

Kingsley believed in a delicately defined restraint that never actually pulled the audience inside the play's world:

I tried not to pick out individual members of the audience with my eyes because I think that's very difficult for them since they were very close. Some nights, you'd occasionally *flick* back to the same person.

Even though we were wonderfully near to them and they could smell us and our sweat and hear our breathing and sometimes see real blood if we bashed ourselves a bit in the fight, we would never touch them or stop and address something to an individual member of the audience. That's an assault. But the closer you can get to the breaking of that wall, the better. But the wall must *be* there. You can shave and shave and shave it away until it is the finest piece of glass between you and the audience—as indeed it was at one point where I actually left the theatre and then came back—I had shaved it down to a minimum, but it was still there. They were very secure throughout the evening in that the membrane was there. Our mode of doing the first scene signaled that nobody would shine a torch in their face and ask them for their driving license!!

They are part of a group consciousness that you address yourself to, that you share your dilemma with, but you don't include them in your dilemma. They're not part of it—it's not *their* fault. Yet you share it with them.

An actor's movement through a play is often described as a "journey," and Kingsley used the word "map" to describe both his emotional and his verbal progress. The soliloquies were map tacks that kept the actor on course. He felt the same way about the verse:

I don't have a philosophy about verse-speaking except in that I use it like a map. Like having to drive, perhaps, a very fast car. [The verse is] a map of what corners you can take at what speed, where you have to brake, where you have to change gears. It's a real technical working map which unlocks how to use the energy, the stress. Line endings. Hovering, hitting at line endings, or whispering. It works. It seems to give the speech its right rhythmic structure and help to contain and exploit huge amounts of energy that are released in these soliloquies. The verse is a way of utilizing your energy and therefore helping the audience to listen.

In discussing his advancement through the play, Kingsley used a triple metaphor, which helped him to make connections with the play's substructures and to link them to the emotions he performed. These are psychological narratives that aid in telling an actor which chords to play. The first, of course, is Shakespeare's story. What is actually happening is the controlling point in an actor's logic, not what he *feels* but what is going on in the plot. It might be called the master metaphor. A second, for Kingsley, was the acting company itself and its own metaworld—the theatre and the players within it, its in-jokes, its lore, its inborn magic, and its network of relationships. This particular cast and their awareness of themselves as practitioners of the art became a unit with unusual glue. That is one reason that the director and events which surrounded her were so influential, even took on layers of meaning as the run of the play progressed. Of course, much of that was reinforced in the language and imagery in *Hamlet*. The final metaphor was that of the family. Critics remarked on how domestically oriented (as opposed to emphasizing the politics of Denmark) was this production. Polonius and his children had a close and loving association. Hamlet and his mother shared a familial tenderness which poured empathy into the closet scene. The actor saw himself as a young man going through growth stages as he acted the play. The cast itself bonded like unto a family after the death of someone who seemed to be kin, director Buzz Goodbody.

Kingsley described I.i as important in creating an atmosphere of chill and questioning. It is peculiar to this first scene of the play that, as it closes, we have little concrete information about the facts of the play. Its function seems to be to tease and to lay false leads. Only when Hamlet himself comes out for the first time to talk with us in I.ii do we get detailed expositional material about events in Denmark:

At the opening of the play, before my first entrance, there was an argon street lamp—these are clever devices because they take quite a long time to warm up—you start with a pinkish, grayish pulsing light that looks somewhat like dawn—but it also looks rather institutional, like the outside light of a vast prison building—that was allowed to bleed light into the first scene. The chaps had torches [modern battery-powered hand flashlights] to look for the Ghost, and the audience's eyes simply followed the beams which picked out the faces of the guards on the battlements. The Ghost appeared behind the audience, so everyone turned around and thought, "Christ, it's there after all!" to a space that was blank before. There were incredibly simple devices like that used, ones that tricked the audience and undermined their original notion of what was true, what was happening. That was the format of the first scene.

Equally as interesting was what was going on in Kingsley's mind as he made preparation for his first entrance:

I used to stand behind these doors [at the back of the auditorium], waiting for the red light to go green, which meant I had to go onstage. My breathing was fairly regular, but my heartbeat was probably twice its normal rate—usually is when I stand in the wings. I was shaking and covered in perspiration and thinking, "I can't do this bloody play. I can't do this—I can't. Why was I cast in this role?" (You see what I'm getting at, don't you?) "Why am I standing here? What the hell am I doing here? I wish I was in the pub down the road." And so my first soliloquy to the audience is, "I wish I wasn't here. I am not a hero. He's as much like my father as I am like Hercules." In other words, I'm simply not a hero, I'm not Hercules. My first major soliloquy is absolutely reflective—my feelings at the opening of the play, my terror in facing that audience, at becoming the great, the major, the most famous of Shakespeare's protagonists, stuck out there with the audience saying, "Right. Come on. Deliver." It took me until the end of the run to realize the *extraordinary* coinciding of my own feelings as an actor with Hamlet's. *Why me* is the umbrella for the first soliloquy. And that is how it came out, night after night. It was highly personalized, and I was tempted to say to the audience, "I do not wish to do this play, ladies and gentlemen. I feel ill-equipped, I cannot do it." And then all this, of course, lends itself into the structure of the betrayal of the mother, the stepfather, the uncle, the real father . . . and so on.

In contrast to I.i, act I, scene ii began with a very long session of applause, so that the entrance of the king and queen seemed very public and crowded. Claudius delivered his opening lines to the court and then walked down into the center aisle of the theatre audience,[33] which transformed them into the gathered courtiers and provided a role for them within the play. His action also set up for Kingsley's directness to them shortly after. Within this scene, Kingsley presented a Hamlet who was "visibly fighting for control as he sits cross-legged and there is the sudden shock of the [king's] hands" that touch him from behind.[34] His "A little more than kin and less than kind" was not a whispered aside to the audience but a loud and tremulous comment directly to the king.[35] In fact, when Hamlet told the queen, "I shall in all my best obey you, madam," there was a sigh of relief from both king and queen, as if they had expected considerable opposition from the prince. As the group exited, they moved down the center aisle, through the theatre audience. Then there was that great theatrical hush:

> First you are standing onstage with other people and *they're* talking and then what does Shakespeare do, leave you on your own within the first five minutes of your entrance! Well, thanks a bundle, Shakespeare, thank *you*. I am defenseless, they've all gone and it's up to me now. If this play's to progress, it's up to me. At the beginning of it, I did not move, I was frozen, facing forward. I contacted them immediately. "O" is the first sound or noise of that soliloquy, as if in "ouh!"

Kingsley gave the first soliloquy from a position at the center of the front stage, as far downstage as he could stand. The vocal delivery of "O that this too too sullied flesh would melt"[36] was beautifully clear and well pronounced. The actor grew louder and more anguished on "O God, God, / How weary, stale, flat, and unprofitable / Seem to me all the uses of this world!" He literally shouted the section at "A little month, or ere those shoes were old / With which she followed my poor father's body, / Like Niobe, all tears" and "no more like my father / Than I to Hercules" was deeply ironic and cynical. Listening to this passage, one heard a man whose emotional clock was mercurial, very ardent and acute. The tension of unpredictability was transferred to the audience, and they remained more still than they had been since the production began.[37] Will he laugh—will he cry? They clearly didn't know what to expect.

Kingsley talked about the importance of this soliloquy, how much depended on its going well:

The first one is the hardest one because it has to lift you off—it is the engine of the others. These massive soliloquies are like rockets that thrust this play into orbit and then that one is jettisoned and then you go into another orbit and then another is jettisoned and you have to go a bit higher. They can take colossal amounts of energy.

In the second soliloquy, Kingsley took his energy from the Ghost itself, which "materialized halfway along the [prompt] side platform, was thence followed by his pursuers to the back of the auditorium, and from there led Hamlet up the central gangway to the 'more removed place,' which was the stage itself. . . . the Ghost delivered his narrative straight out to the audience. . . . At the cry 'O horrible! most horrible!' the Ghost placed his hands on the sides of Hamlet's head, and Hamlet threw up his arms in agony. The effect was powerful and it could be prolonged for, as the Ghost withdrew by the central gangway and his 'Remember me' receded, the audience remained fixed by Hamlet's frozen figure onstage."[38] This scene was noticeably absent of sound effects other than gasps by the actors. The scene was played very melodramatically, with the Ghost hissing, "Beast," and virtually shouting, "Murder!" Both actors set up for Kingsley to continue in a passion after the creature withdrew on three prolonged "adieus."

Kingsley decided to give the soliloquy "to Dad, very much to Dad. Except for that one line 'smile, and smile, and be a villain,' that line was suddenly to the audience." Rather than the traditional nervous breakdown, Kingsley saw this as a galvanizing of energy into a fury. He fell onto his knees, "dedicating myself, like a samurai warrior. I didn't collapse. I saw it as more formal than that," but he stood, four lines later on "sinews . . . bear me stiffly up." His first syllable of "O all you host of heaven" was a prolonged vowel sound on several notes with the shouting continued throughout the first whole line. He sped through "trivial fond records," using no props but pushing the thoughts into "the table of my memory," hands pushing into head. Again, references to "pernicious woman" and "smiling, damned villain" were curses given in a voice that could cut steel. The final vow at the end, "I have sworn 't," was howled triumphantly.[39]

Critic Benedict Nightingale declared that for him this scene was the beginning of the actor's showing all the various facets of the role, developing the other keys in the concerto. "Our first impression is of a starched, repressed, uptight youth . . . but there's plenty waiting to burst from beneath."[40]

The second soliloquy is only rarely performed to the audience in modern stage history. Even when an actor (and an audience) describes the soliloquies as generally being done toward the audience, this second solo speech is the one that requires the qualified answer. Perhaps a soliloquy which approaches the function of a classic tirade simply does not hold the same appeal for a modern audience that is likely to be embarrassed and not enthralled by an outpour of emotion.

Before the third soliloquy ("O, what a rogue and peasant slave am I!") Kingsley said he received a great boost of energy from the entrance of the players, as if they had jolted the play into another gear:

> I was very excited by the players' entrance into the play and how their presence is celebrated. They came in the back doors, as if they'd come in a van like the Cotswold Players or Theatregoround. They had things in a suitcase and it was lovely—to have an opportunity in the middle of the play to share with an audience the glory of acting and how exciting it is that these people work and learn lines and rehearse and learn technique. It also shows Hamlet's adoration of theatre and actors. He would have been an actor if he hadn't been a prince.

Kingsley overplayed the Pyrrhus speech to bait Polonius, who, of course, thought it very accomplished. Then the Player King, Bob Peck, completed the speech in a beautifully naturalistic and convincing way, crying at the end because he was so overwhelmed by the poetry of it. This choice helped to motivate Kingsley's profound anger at himself in the forthcoming soliloquy. Kingsley's "Look you mock him not" (about Polonius) as the actors left "was a warning that he is a cunning old bugger and he will get the better of you even though you might be mocking him." The topic of the theatre had now been introduced, and in this soliloquy Hamlet began to personalize the metaphor and wring his own commentary from it. He said, "This speech got angrier and angrier, and the anger turned in, against myself, physically. I was almost hitting myself with my fists. It was a very unwhingeing Hamlet."

The promptbook indicated that Kingsley drew the paper panels closed after he had shown Rosencrantz and Guildenstern off upstage left. This action gave more weight to the opening phrase, "Now I am alone," and said to the audience, "at last we can talk." He then walked to the center of the front stage, at the very top of the central gangway. He let the stops out from the very first lines, which were literally screamed. He spoke quickly the description of the player and came to a full falsetto on the very point of this self-lacerating speech: "And can say *nothing*." He began to walk and pace on the next section, a new build at "no, not for a king," where he was going at full tilt, top of the emotional chart. Yet the fury was directed toward himself and not toward the audience, who were nevertheless directly addressed. He showed a great deal of confidence in the relationship he had established to lose his temper at this pitch in front of them. He took the section through to the peak at "Oh Vengeance!" which was literally howled. Then there was a short pause before the huge change of tone at "Why, what an ass am I!" and a fresh build led up to "a very drab, / A scullion.[41] Fie upon't, foh!" at which point he ran out of the theatre! The audience was utterly silent for a long moment. He returned finally to devise his plot, his solution, which was intense but reasoned. Finally, he delivered the closing "conscience of the King" couplet in a determined and challenging way. Clearly, a gauntlet had been thrown down for Claudius.

Kingsley recounted it thus:

In "rogue and peasant slave," another layer of the magic of this play spins off and reveals another play: because this is a play about the potency of a play. This is a piece of art about how art can provoke a change in somebody. So, it's wonderful to be a part of a great theatrical event that celebrates the potency and the power of the theatre and of the confrontations it can release. At "I have heard / That guilty creatures sitting at a play" Hamlet's whole muddy disposition turned into a white-hot needle. I got very still and said these lines like a machine gunner. [Here, he stutters rather incoherently and then goes on.] It almost left me exhausted in a separate part of my brain—because if you pretend to go mad, then you think you *are* going mad. It's a very dangerous game to play—suddenly this huge insidious intelligence smashes through a layer of grief and anger and finds this great thought, this theory, this *idea* about using a play! It is found *by an actor* standing in the middle of a play *in front of an audience*—so again that double coincidence. It's all about *acting*—see, I can do this, I can do that, what do you want me to do, I can do it. The actor for a moment feels that he's the victim of the play, and then suddenly he realizes, "Wait a minute. As actors, we are *here* and we can do extraordinary things." So he then goes into over-drive and he's a commander again. The actor gets his sovereignty back and the character gets his sovereignty back at the same time.

Kingsley's decision to walk out of the theatre in the middle of this famous speech was one that two critics faulted. Although he lauded the performance, J. W. Lambert simply did not understand the activity ("an apparently purposeless dash down through the hall and back").[42] Richard David objected because he felt it violated the audience's aesthetic distance from the performer.[43] Kingsley explains it this way:

That's right. I ran all the way out. I said to the director, "Why don't I leave the play here? Why don't I just say [with my actions]—the play's finished—I can't do it—Fie upon it, foh." That was very much like saying "fuck it." It even *sounded* like "fuck it." FOH! As if to declare, "Good-bye, ladies and gentlemen. I can't do it, you don't think I can do it, I don't think I can do it, you probably don't think I'm a very good Hamlet anyway. So fuck it." Very angry.

Wonderful devices, these. To remind audiences of where they are and what they're doing there and what they are participating in. Very exciting. How simple it was for me to exit, as if to say, "I could leave the theatre. There's a car park out there. Once you're out the rear doors in this tiny foyer, you are literally out of the building. If I'd run off into the wings, the audience wouldn't have thought, "Oh, he's left the play." But if suddenly you went out the back door and got into your car, they realize, "Shit—we're left on our own!" Once I'd gone through the doors—the same ones they came in through, remember—they knew there's the ladies' loo, the gents' loo, and the car park. "That's where he's gone. Mr. Kingsley and Hamlet, too, are both gone!"

Once outside there, I used to feel exhilarated because I'd think,

"This is *my* play. I could walk around the car park for ten minutes if I wished. But I won't. I'll go crashing straight back in there." It was like pulling back on a piece of elastic and then catapulting myself into the play. Which I did. And essentially said, "The play can continue now. On *my* terms. Because I know about theatre and I know why we're all sitting here and I'll tell you all about it."

This third soliloquy, then, operated as a major turning point, a kind of peripeteia for the actor.

I had made this terrific resolution, but I hadn't got it all worked out. However, I knew that I had committed myself to the rest of the play. The play had to go on: the play's the thing. The only way to solve the problem is to do this play and also to do this play within this play. If the evening doesn't continue, neither I as an actor nor Hamlet as protagonist will ever resolve themselves.

That is like committing myself to the most dangerous part of the journey, where the stakes get vertical and the temperature drops another ten degrees and the air gets thinner. I have to climb the rest of the mountain and not turn back.

Reactions to Hamlet's next speech, "To be, or not to be," reflected that Kingsley's indecision was very, very real: "We really wonder what conclusions he (and we) will finally reach."[44]

Behind the sliding white doors again, I felt another wave of terror and exhaustion. There was deep questioning of the play, the whole event, the audience out there, knowing you have the most famous soliloquy in the world to do, two more difficult scenes, a sword fight—the toughest bits of the play are about to come and the speculating about them is over. You are going to continue with *a* play (the players' play) and *the* play (the one you're in). The strongest sensation before I went on was—is it worth continuing—are we doing anything by carrying on with this play? Is it worth it? Is it justifiable, this agony, drenched in sweat and shaky, all the emotions we were exploiting and playing with, in the best sense of the word? But if it went *wrong*, in the worst sense of the word—and particularly, I must say, after the death of our director, sitting back there I used to hit terrible despair and helplessness and questioned everything. I could have chosen to opt out, I could have chosen suicide. But I did not. I chose to cross over into adulthood, to go on like a man and an adult, to complete the journey.

I'd somehow had the courage to say to the audience [through the soliloquy], "I am terrified, and the fact that I am stuck up here as the hero does not separate me from you; in fact, it doth make cowards of us all." *All* was an encompassing embrace of the audience, like a passionate revelation—we're all scared and I'm no exception. And it was *such* a wave of relief to say that. You know when your good friends say to you, "Don't worry—lots of people feel like that—you're not the only one," you feel like crying with relief! And it's a very maturing process. It doesn't make you feel like a baby but as if you've joined the adult world and paid the price. Which is everything that that soliloquy is all about and that the play is all about: joining the adult world, having to make adult decisions.

Once he'd gone through this mental journey, Kingsley was ready to go onstage. He brought a chair in from the wings, banged it down, sat astride it. There is a loud bump on the sound recording as he does this: "I can't wait, can't mess about to tell you this. I've been working it all out in the wings and couldn't wait to get on to tell you what I've been thinking. I walked on while the other scene was walking off, I was in such a hurry. This is it—the crossover moment is about to come." He began the speech strong and sternly: "To be, // or not to be, // that is the question." He changed pitch at line breaks instead of pausing, and this helped to emphasize words. He seemed to punch the *actions* one can take in the speech. He worked perfectly with the sense of the speech; everything within it was obviously a very real consideration for Hamlet. The diction was beautiful, the energy powerful, and the understanding surpasseth all.

At this point, Kingsley brought in the other part of his thinking, the rest of his operant metaphor:

You see, this is what happened to Buzz. She got us all through "To be, or not to be" and said, "I'm not joining you on the other side." Knowing a bit about suicide, knowing a bit about that terrifying leap from childhood to adulthood, and knowing that she had a very difficult childhood, I understood that she found letting go of that and moving into adulthood very painful. She was very articulate about it, very eloquent. The process for her was mesmerizing—she dreaded, dreaded, dreaded it. It terrified her. She held it at bay as long as she possibly could. And then that soliloquy said, "Well, Buzz, you go with the rest of them into adulthood or you don't." That's what the voice said to her. And she must have answered, "Well, I can't do it. I just can't do it."

The New Statesman called Kingsley in this rendering "a dedicated mental explorer and spiritual discoverer."[45] One can understand how difficult it would be for him to answer the question "What did you *mean* when you spoke this speech?" For the actor, meaning is on many levels—social, personal, critical, contextual, psychic, and metaphysical.

Furthermore, the way he gave the speech affected the way he played the nunnery scene that followed. Although one critic found him "plainly beside himself with passion"[46] in the third soliloquy, another felt he was "at his maddest after 'To be, or not to be.'"[47] At first he greeted Ophelia (who entered up the central aisle) with tenderness, and then they sat down together on the steps and talked. As she had walked into the room, he felt that she was just the person he wanted to see after his stride into the adult world. After that point, however, the scene was emotionally and physically violent, with both characters weeping hysterically before it was finished.

> He says at first, "Thank god, because you're a friend, a lover." I still think the play could have gone off in a totally different direction if she'd said, "I'm still wearing what you gave me." But instead, *at that moment* she says, "Here you are," and hands back the jewelry. It is completely devastating; when he has arrived at his own virility the woman in his life says, "I don't want this stuff anymore." For such faux reasons, simply because someone else has told her to say those things, terrible. So that unlocked, understandably, a huge amount of venom and anger. And so, you see in the nunnery scene the cries of a very damaged man. I'm not saying that the way he treats her is justified [Kingsley even threw the trinkets at Ophelia] but that he is very ill.

In the next scene, during his advice to the players, Kingsley developed the theatrical metaphor even more. Here the outer image (the play's dialogue), as well as his inner image, is about the actor's experience:

I used to sit down with the actors on a beer crate. My experience in working with Peter Brook in *Midsummer Night's Dream* was still very fresh. He was the most intelligent man in the theatre at that time, probably still is, and I love the way he talks to actors. He uses language beautifully and he takes the actors with him. He never patronizes. He accepts that your speed of thought and your capacity to grasp an idea is at least as fast as his, so you run to keep up and you're privileged and flattered that he's running without slowing down for you, and you sit there and listen. So I decided to do that great moment of stillness like a Peter Brook note session. I gently intervened myself into the group and said, "Look, I think we should talk about how we're going to do the play." Not comic, not condescending, not apologetic, but more like, "Look, we're all committed artists here—" So the audience felt they were watching a rehearsal: "But we didn't come for *that*—we came to see a play. And yet it is a play as well!" So the Chinese boxes of *Hamlet* come out of themselves one more time, and you get the audience seeing a rehearsal and a play, just like Buzz had given us, and like Brook had given us, and Trevor Nunn and Peter Hall, and so the baton gets handed down in moments like that, no swaggering and swashbuckling, waving your sword around and sweating and screeching, but in moments of great concentration and responsibility and integrity.

The fifth soliloquy ("'Tis now the very witching time of night") was the only one to suffer cuts. The first six lines of twelve were performed. An examination of the promptbook gives the impression that the soliloquy was used as a transitional speech. Just preceding "witching time" was the business where Hamlet goaded Polonius into assuring him that the clouds are backed like a camel, a weasel, etc. The bit was played with lots of ironic comedy as Kingsley duped Polonius. Rosencrantz, Guildenstern, and Polonius left, but there wasn't the usual hush that precedes a soliloquy. In fact, it was Kingsley's intention to shock the audience:

That one followed lots and lots of laughs from the audience. You keep on reminding the audience that they are in the theatre and they are here to be stimulated and entertained, and then you float that black-magic, terrifying Halloween thing on this sea of laughter.

Great device on the part of the author which gives the actor the power to suddenly and sharply change the mood.

The soliloquy was said quickly and shouted. It started low and built to "quake to look on." The meaning was quite clear: Hamlet's intentions were renewed. Immediately after his last phrase, "Soft, now to my mother," the players came in and cleared away the gear that had been set up for the previous production of the play within the play. As the First Player, Bob Peck, picked up the prop sword, something important happened that helped to make clear the sixth soliloquy. This piece of business was the point of the transition:

> I ask Peck for the sword. I hold out my hand, and he gives me the prop. It's a real sword, the one I kill Polonius with. As I am the royal patron, the prince, and he is there at my behest, he has no choice but to give me that sword, but he gave it to me in a very special way—as if to say, "Manhood, here you are, here you are." Giving a sword is also part of the great acting tradition. The sword that Edmund Kean used in *Richard III* was given to Larry Olivier. It was handed down through a whole line of great actors, including Irving and Gielgud. So, this gesture is a magic talisman for actors. I have just done that Hecate soliloquy and I am now moving around the palace with a sword in my hand and then I open the door and there is that man praying.

What followed, of course, was the "double soliloquy" scene. One of the first things that needed to be negotiated was where the king performed his speech ("O, my offense is rank"), which fell just before Hamlet's speech. Claudius entered with Rosencrantz and Guildenstern at the beginning of III.iii. As they were dismissed, he chose as his chief playing area the space to the right of a table which was angled at right center and also functioned as a visual separator between the two men once Hamlet entered. Claudius' soliloquy was given in a very calm and very reasoned voice. At one point, he sat on the table, but as he neared the end of his speech (at "Bow, stubborn knees," III.iii.70), he knelt and continued praying with bowed head, facing forward. Next, Hamlet cautiously slid open the white panel at right center and entered. He stood in the entryway to deliver his first three lines.[48] He whispered on "Now might I do it pat" and built to a quick cry at the end of the second sentence, "And so am I reveng'd." He then frightened himself and so flung his body against the wall and fell on the floor. He whimpered like a child, having realized that it would have been a mistake to kill his uncle: "He's finding very good reasons for not doing it now. Sound reasons, sound philosophically and rationally, but he's postponing. I could do it now, but why am I not doing it. I am staying the execution, that's all."

Once he'd actually decided to wait until a more opportune occasion, his plan was spoken very quickly and he regained a measure of control. The closing couplet, "My mother stays," was said in a very low voice, but the ending was clearly a threat, "This physic but prolongs thy sickly days." He exited, and Claudius rose and left, after uneasily closing the panel Hamlet had left open.

Kingsley thinks that the reason the audience was never confused about whether the two men saw or heard one another was that he never entered the king's performance space. The audience merely accepted the convention that they were in two different areas and were consequently invisible and inaudible to one another. He always stayed at the back of the stage, inside the entrance he'd created or very close to it.

After this soliloquy came the closet scene and, for this production, one of the most powerful reinforcements of the theme of family relationships. Although there was some violent emotion—for example, Kingsley slapped Gertrude at one point when she accused him of "ecstasy"—the interaction was one of extreme tenderness rather than fierce confrontation:

The tone of it was, I love you, you're my mum; how could you? It wasn't accusatory. There was almost a plea within it to go back to the beginnings of childhood and motherhood and start again. The attitude was, how have we got from me on your lap as a babe to this. Let's examine the steps together. She can't cope and becomes hysterical, but it's my only chance to get back to the essence of the relationship when it was good and to discover what went wrong. So it's passionate, but it's reasoned. Not a screamer. There were moments when I had to physically get her attention, but not to hurt her—more to get her to look at herself. A son doing that to a parent is extraordinary and has great emotional power for the audience. Not a parent helping a child but a child helping a parent to confront. So Hamlet is the therapist in that scene, not the executioner.

Leaving the room was like a little boy dragging Polonius away, teddy bear replaced. I suddenly saw what she could see—her son, her child, her baby, dragging a dead man out of the room. I looked up and she looked at me, grief-stricken. In that look was—this is what has happened, this is real, this is what it's come to. She was devastated. She just broke down. Night after night, floods and floods of tears. The audience cried, too. It was an extraordinary moment, that complete loss of innocence, the body of the man I've killed—and I'm still me, I'm still that little boy that you thought was all right, that you didn't listen to, that you betrayed, that you let go of. Now look. "Good night, Mother."

The final soliloquy ("How all occasions do inform against me," IV.iv.32–66) was set up for by depicting a very macho Fortinbras. He was played as particularly commanding, someone who had not merely reached manhood but had gone beyond being human into something forbidding and despotic. His lines were strengthened to project curtness and absolute authority: the Folio reading of "Fortinbras *claimes* conveyance of a promis'd march / Over his kingdom" was chosen over the First and Second Quarto reading of "Fortinbras *craves* . . . " (IV.iv.2–3).[49]

Kingsley declared that this glimpse of reality pushed him into manhood. It was the final step:

Seeing destiny marching in front of him, our collective history, our past, Hamlet makes the ultimate resolution. This is one of those moments when the outside world impinges upon him and he suddenly sees distances, perspectives on his own dilemma. We were all walking along some path leading out of the buildings and into open terrain. There was the wind, I pulled my coat around myself, I was exhilarated to be outdoors and away from the dreadful castle. Leaving the house is also the act of an adult. The child leaves home. As soon as he is out, he has other thoughts. He sees other men, armies, the great forces of history of which he is a part, and he says, well, I must join in.

The Hamlet that gave the speech was a man in charge. He asked the others to leave him:

> That request was made with great authority. They didn't question it.
> They left the stage. It was the emergence of the man you could
> see—the tone of the voice, the need, the dignity, the acceptance. This
> was a way to illustrate to the audience how far Hamlet had come—
> not a totalitarian, like Fortinbras, but a person. He came from the
> first soliloquy, where he said, "I cannot do it" to here—now he's
> controlling the play. Before, he'd been left alone on the stage and
> he'd panicked, he wanted to melt away, but now he asks others to
> leave the play because he wants a soliloquy. It is a very great journey
> from being terrified of being left alone to saying, I want to be left
> alone. Many would say that these are two different worlds, in fact,
> two different people. It was that transformed character that ad-
> dressed the audience, and that was probably the most *mature* solilo-
> quy and probably the most *direct* to the audience because it was now
> man-to-man, man-to-woman.
>
> Perhaps because it was our last talk together, I made the strongest
> possible use of the audience—really debating whether or not it
> would be one part wisdom, three parts coward. It got very engaged.
> It came very close to crossing the line. If it got too close, I could
> always defuse it. I mean, I would come very close to asking them a
> question, and then I could say it's all right if you don't know the
> answer because I don't know it myself. It's like when you're talking
> to a friend very earnestly, and you say, "I'm not asking you what to
> do, I'm just telling you *I* don't know what to do." Sometimes we ask
> our friends what to do and they cannot tell us. But I think the audi-
> ence wanted to cross the line too—they wanted to join in. The lines
> are built so that you can handle it. And then, of course, I decide for
> myself. It's a wonderful place to leave the theatre and go out into the
> night air. Hamlet leaves home.

In this speech Kingsley was robust, almost bellicose. He stood stage
left on the elevated platform and took a long pause after the others had
left. Then he spoke with careful deliberation: "How *all* occasions do
inform against me, / and spur // my // dull // revenge." He conceded that
he had delayed and so slowed down on the "craven scruple" passage.

Then he became loud and forceful again; his tone of voice was very cynical about Fortinbras, condemning the man's actions. After "How stand I then," he began to build to a resolution and final vow on the closing couplet, "O, from this time forth, / My thoughts be bloody, or be nothing worth!" The speech ended dramatically, followed by an explosion of cannon fire in the background.[50] At this point, the second interval fell.

In a very real sense, this production of *Hamlet* was a result of the most propitious combination of elements: a fresh and talented director, a dedicated and gifted actor, and a skilled supporting cast. The final result was balanced and artistically coherent. The director chose to emphasize familial and personal relationships, but not at the expense of concurrent themes such as the question of madness or the insidious court politics.

The performance mode of the soliloquies was partly determined by the shape of the theatre, by practical considerations. As Kingsley said, "That space had so many choices built into it." However, we must remember that at that time The Other Place was a large open room in which almost all of the productions were staged in a kind of "basketball court" seating arrangement, with the bulk of the audience on two sides and occasionally some seated in the end zones. The designer changed all this, by manipulating the configuration of the actor-audience relationship and placing the main playing area at one end of the rectangular shape but still retaining many of the effects of a theatre in the round with his ramps and runways. The theatre's capacity also figured in—at under two hundred seats, it remained a small and intimate house.

The performance mode of the soliloquies was partly defined by the director and grew from her political stance regarding Shakespeare productions, i.e., making them understandable to a mass audience. She shaped a performance that spoke directly to them: the soliloquies set within that concept were equally direct. Rather than imposing a certain technique on her actors, she used the rehearsal time to generate and explore various possibilities. Also, the cast saw themselves as a family and had a feeling of unity and solidarity that she helped to create.

The production was very much an outgrowth of the social history of the middle seventies, having absorbed and integrated local events into its theatrical function as a mirror of the times. In fact, one of the popular ideas of the middle seventies was a focus on improving human relationships and communication. One can see within the production, in the cast and in the influential lead actor, a propensity toward and interest in feelings and interpersonal relations, for exploring and defining them and finally dealing with them. It was also revealed in the quality of the ensemble acting of the group. Interaction was tight; people really listened to one another and took cues off the moment. Levels of intensity matched, sparked and ebbed, waxed and waned, despite a truly breakneck speed of delivering the verse. The result was high excitement on the stage. The interaction intensified when the group lost its director and felt a need to bond to one another for the common purpose of doing their best work each night. Clearly, this was a cry of players who gave to the tragedy its ultimate commitment as professionals.

However, what made it all work was the final factor in the formula: a lead actor who, through the very important device of the soliloquy, made the audience feel as if he was being very intimate with them. The result was a performance mode that captured the audience and thoroughly engaged them in the experience of the play.

We see in Ben Kingsley the prototype of the actor-manager Hamlet. He had a respect for the power of illusion in the theatre and knew how to use it to enlarge his character. He believed that it was not only within an actor's aptitude to manipulate the audience's reality, but that it was the duty of a skilled craftsman to define and channel performance energies so that they served the aesthetic objectives of the play. He brought to the role a delicious sense of danger via his own vitality; the humor and wry wit of Hamlet emerged along with a feeling of terror as he controlled the audience, snapping their laughter short directly after making them comfortable. Indeed, the entire production combined laughter and tears in close juxtaposition—even in the tensest moments of the duel scene, the audience tittered. Kingsley was skilled vocally and physically. He was not oblivious of technique; in fact, his mind was very often on how he used his eyes or his voice. One critic commented, "He took the lines and shook the meaning out of them."[51] He managed to make the famous speeches of the play seem like set pieces, staged just for that moment, as well as giving the feeling that "the soliloquies . . . always spring from the action itself,"[52] were always well integrated into the play's narrative. This delicate balance is indeed rare in a Hamlet.

The issue of control and manipulation was not a small one for Kingsley. He spoke with great accuracy about his relationship with the audience, yet insisted on that aesthetic distance which assures an audience that it will be safe. Even though a number of devices were used to draw the audience in, Kingsley never stepped out of the play to become a Brechtian narrator. He had at his fingertips the ability to involve them but he refrained from allowing them dialogue. Always, he safeguarded the spectators' integrity as well as his own. However, he was the man in charge. Always the wall was there—not the "fourth wall" of the proscenium arch, but the boundary that must be there so that the play never fuses with real life.

MAHER: So you would consider yourself having tentacles out there the whole time with an audience, listening, responding to small sounds—

KINGSLEY: Yes, yes.

MAHER: Do you get driven nuts when they are coughing?

KINGSLEY: No, no. I always think it's our fault.

5

DEREK JACOBI : *The Courtier, Soldier, Scholar*

For Derek Jacobi, acting goes beyond an occupation to that
rare sphere of vocation or calling: "If you've got a crush on the theatre
or a great desire, be wary. You have to need to be an actor. If it's just a
desire, a want, a love—that's not enough. You have to *need*."[1]

Jacobi's experience with *Hamlet* has encompassed the middle decades
of his life in the theatre. He first acted the role just before he entered
Cambridge as a student in a production in 1957 which was highly praised
at the Edinburgh festival.[2] Of this early experience Jacobi mostly remembers its zeal:

> I was lucky enough to do Hamlet at seventeen. Actually, it was a
> week before my eighteenth birthday. As a schoolboy, I think I tore a
> passion to tatters. What I lacked in experience and technique and
> skill and craft, I made up for in enthusiasm, passion, and just plain
> noise. I don't remember how I did the soliloquies. . . . I really think
> you have to be in your thirties or forties to do the role well. That
> young Hamlet had great energy and was very loud.[3]

Jacobi spent the next twenty years developing his acting career. He had
periodic associations with *Hamlet*, because his formative years were
spent in the leading classical repertory companies of England, the Birmingham Repertory and Olivier's Chichester Theatre, which became the
core group of the National Theatre's[4] first company. Jacobi debuted in
London by playing Laertes to Peter O'Toole's Old Vic *Hamlet* in 1963.
He also saw a great many Hamlets:

Derek Jacobi in Hamlet, *1977. Photograph by Chris Davies.*

I'd seen Olivier's film and onstage Paul Scofield, John Neville, Michael Redgrave, Alan Badel, Richard Burton, and David Warner. I've always been a great fan of Scofield's, but I think the one that made the most impact on me was the Olivier film. It was my era, it was from my age, it was film, and I was very young. *Henry V* and *Richard III* also made a great impact. I'd not consciously patterned anything after these other actors. . . . I was kind of far too young to appreciate any technique they were using or even to know if they were using any. And they were far too good to let it show. The glory of them was that they had this wonderful technique that never looked like technique, that always looked spontaneous. So in watching them, I wasn't aware of a particular thread or attitude to the part—or even a convention they were following.

In 1977, after the very successful television series of Robert Graves' *I, Claudius*, Jacobi began an association with *Hamlet* that was to saturate his life for the next three years. He opened in the role at the Old Vic with the Prospect Theatre Company on May 30, 1977. This production ran through August 1977, then it toured the Near East, going to Egypt, Amman, Teheran, Greece, Cyprus, and Athens. It was also seen in Dubrovnik, and at the Edinburgh festival, toured parts of England, and returned to London, so that it was still playing in 1978. A year later, the performance was revived at the Old Vic, and Elsinore was the first stop on a second world tour which included Sweden, Finland, Australia, Japan, and the People's Republic of China, where Jacobi was the first English-speaking actor ever to give *Hamlet*. He stated that these were separate productions "only in the sense that there was time in between the two. But it was really the same director, virtually the same set, not totally the same cast, but *all but.*"[5] He has performed the role 379 times, a total that rivals only John Gielgud's.

Jacobi's interpretation of the role received unanimous critical approval. London critics perceived that something noble had been restored to the stage. Tired of controversial productions and experimentation with basic character conception, they felt that Jacobi had found an essential core: "Recent performances of the play . . . have mangled or upstaged its protagonist. This time Hamlet is back in control. Derek Jacobi restores the figure of the Renaissance prince . . . equipped with all the courtesy, irony, and masterful variations of tempo and weight that traditionally belong to the part."[6] The return engagement was equally applauded: "This is a solid workmanlike evening at whose center Derek Jacobi shines with undiminished fervor."[7] "Not many revivals of *Hamlet* are any longer as straightforward, intelligent and balanced than this three-and-a-half hour version which comes back to London with Derek Jacobi better than ever in the title role."[8] And the *Times* guaranteed that the "production is still richly rewarding on second viewing."[9] To draw wholehearted approval from the major London critics is a feat indeed. Although characterization was commended, there were other parts of the text that remained inviolable in certain reviewers' minds. More of that later.

The decision to place the play in the traditional Elizabethan period had been partly a result of the practicalities of touring. The set was relatively unadorned, a "rather bare . . . empty arena . . . where emphasis goes onto actions and interactions of the actors"[10] and where the "natural element is its darkness, probed at strategic moments by lighting."[11] Jacobi explained:

It had to be a production for all seasons. It was not just mounted to the Old Vic but had to fit into large theatres, small theatres, square ones, round ones, indoor ones, outdoor ones, raised platforms on flat surfaces, raked and nonraked stages. So it had to be very *mobile*. A production that couldn't be too conceptual because it had to appeal to all cultures—a *representative* play, which is much more interesting in some ways than a director's concept.

Julian Glover, who played Claudius, added:

The rehearsal process was somewhat like the Royal Shakespeare Company's but a much shorter period. Ours was three and a half weeks. . . . Toby Robertson is a very eccentric director, someone who has brilliant ideas or terrible ideas. . . . The first entrance of the king and queen was quite remarkable—the music he organized for it stated that there was no fiddling around with anything except *power*. We made an entrance from the left and right wings accompanied by a hurtling drum roll, and we met at the center at the first blast from the brass and came downstage in rhythm, slow motion, and then we separated and were enthroned right and left. His staging of the play scene was brilliant: he made it work with the King and Queen upstage—this is a directorial problem in every production—but he managed this difficult situation and never lost focus. [The production] was costumed not richly, not opulently, but *decadent*. There was lots of dark blue and dark red velvet. This was obviously a household which was hanging on for dear life through military power. The production took a very militaristic line.[12]

Audiences on tour responded in unique ways, said Jacobi:

At Elsinore, one-quarter of the listeners were tourists and three-quarters were Danish; the Danes loved the remarks about Denmark. Considering that we were rained out the first night, their good humor was welcome. Fortunately, the queen of Denmark came back the following night to see the performance through.

Fellow player Glover recalled this added drama:

There is this strait [Katte Gat Strait] between Denmark and Sweden which has the busiest shipping traffic in the world. A great foghorn in a lighthouse guides the ships through the strait, and it so happens that Kronberg castle is on the point of that peninsula. Every twenty seconds or so, and especially in the dark when the fog was impenetrable, the foghorn blew. The director tried every single official channel that he could and finally went out to the lighthouse and knocked on the door, and the man came down and said, "No, I won't turn off my foghorn." Finally, after much persuasion, the director said, "Not even for two tickets to the play?" And the man said, "Right. I'll turn it off and then put it back on straightaway when the curtain comes down." The fog was very thick and had a certain resonance in the play, especially in the beginning scene, where it was very helpful.

Playing in China was a particular surprise, since the convention of audience behavior is much different. Audiences do not rivet their attention onto the stage to get involved with a performance. Julian Glover described the experience:

The Chinese had got a tape of our Old Vic production. The eight leading actors of China had been working on the text of the play for three weeks and did a simultaneous translation from the English to the Chinese via headphones for the audience as they watched from behind a glass booth at the back during the production. We'd made some minor text changes on tour, but they worked around them. I must say, sometimes they got laughs we didn't deserve. On the first night, there was this noise out front which was not only the noise of the simultaneous translation—it was people talking to one another in low voices. The actors were in *despair*. Derek came backstage and cried, "My God, we're dying out there—we're losing them completely!" And then the interpreters came round at the interval and said, "Ah, isn't it wonderful—they're loving it." We were astonished, so we asked why they were talking all the time. They answered, "They're living through it *with* you. 'Oh, isn't he an awful murderer and isn't she pretty—look out, here comes the Ghost!' They are so involved in it." Well, once we knew that, the second half of the play went like a hot knife through butter.

Jacobi added:

The Chinese had never seen *Hamlet* acted by a Western company, and the reactions, to put it mildly, were loud and enthusiastic—and when I say loud, I mean LOUD. Once I learned that they were actually enjoying the performance and discussing it virtually line by line as we played it, we relaxed. It was rather like having critics dictate their notices to secretaries as they watch opening night. And the Chinese also *ate* quite a lot during the performance. The whole thing was the nearest I've ever felt to playing before the audience at the Globe theatre in Shakespeare's time.[13]

The big laugh of the evening—the *big* laugh—was over the dead body of Polonius, "Thou find'st to be too busy is some danger." It was a major joke in China, and they found it hilarious. There must have been something in the translation which made it sound like a comment about the local bureaucracy. On the last night they asked permission to televise the production, and we braved all the Equity rules and said of course. Peking was empty that night, even the hotels, because everyone was watching *Hamlet* on television. It was a very great compliment and a memorable evening.

Many more people saw it when the production moved to Japan:

They weren't buzzing or talking, though, they were very quiet. Those that didn't speak English were hearing the text in Japanese through earphones. Must have been very odd for them—watching me but hearing somebody else. Still others who knew English didn't use the earphones, and those of us onstage could still hear the translation coming out of the speakers sitting on their laps. So you'd be acting in English and all around you ringing in the air was Shakespeare in Japanese. Job satisfaction was not always of the highest quality on tour.

Jacobi recalled that Egypt offered challenges too:

There was one night in the Sahara desert, in Giza near the Sphinx. The Egyptians did son et lumière [a light and sound show] over the monuments and we had to follow it. Since it didn't stop until almost ten o'clock at night, we were sometimes still doing *Hamlet* at two a.m. in the morning. Then there was the night the British ambassador was coming and he was late—he didn't come till half past eleven—so everyone was cutting to cue. It was "O all you hosts of heavens—my tables meet it is I set it down," end to end like that, there you go, thank you very much. We cut it down to about two hours, and it went so quickly that Rosencrantz and Guildenstern missed their first entrance because they were still changing! Then Claudius ended up breaking his leg on a hasty exit offstage. It was an evening of incident.

Considering some of the places I performed, outdoors, late at night, often very noisy and in record time, I mean, it had to be loud. And in those circumstances, some of the nuances of soliloquy performance just went out of the window. You couldn't afford to be at all pye[14] about what you were doing—you just had to say the words and get through it, like actors do, with very little idea of *how* you're going through it.

Upon returning to the United Kingdom, Jacobi was invited to do the plum of roles for the Time-Life BBC "Shakespeare Plays" series. He had, through the accolades gathered with his stage role of *Hamlet*, quickly become the actor of choice to videotape the play he calls "the Everest of acting." This television venture, which included all of the plays in Shakespeare's canon, has become the teaching tool of the twentieth century, since the series was unilaterally used by most American and British universities and secondary schools. To most students and to a great many schoolchildren, Derek Jacobi "is" Hamlet.[15] In between the demands of this enterprise, Jacobi also made an audio recording of *Hamlet* for Decca.[16] In the spring of 1988, Kenneth Branagh, founder of the Renaissance Theatre Company, asked Jacobi to direct him in a *Hamlet*[17] which toured the provinces and then went into the Phoenix Theatre in London. Branagh describes Jacobi's direction as "blocking the moves of the play with immense speed and then filling in details with a white lightning of perception. He is never in the stalls but always on stage, demonstrating and dispensing wisdom confidentially to the actors."[18]

The picture that develops of Hamlet's soliloquies must be set within the frame of Jacobi's extensive involvement with the role. His perceptions are the product of having said the lines to a world of audiences and having organized the play from behind the scenes as well. His insights are a running commentary about what the soliloquies meant to him, what ideas he felt were most important to project, and what internal meanings he intended to manifest externally. It would be impossible to speak of one production as if it were typical or to say that he performed them in an immutable way, unless we were referring to the BBC production, in which approximately eight days of videotaping were electronically preserved for history. What follows here is an accumulation of Jacobi's intuition, intellectual penetration, and sheer practical theatrical wisdom.

Since the 1977 production was intended for touring, an all-purpose philosophy had to be developed:

> What we were thinking at the time and how I was feeling at the time—and forming the lines at the time—was really irrespective of the space we would be playing on. Obviously, I'm very aware of the audience because that's who we're doing it for—to get lost in the part is rather defeating the object, because if you lose yourself totally and you lose your awareness of where you are and what you are and who you are and WHY you are—then it becomes kind of masturbatory and you won't need an audience. You are acting for other people, to engage their attentions and sympathies and emotions,

not your own. Otherwise, it's just amusing yourself and it's showing off.

Sizing up the actor's space is really a very practical matter, once
you've seen what it is—well, I've got to be there to make that exit,
I've got much less space to do the sword fight in, I don't need that
much voice—the physical things that stand out in whatever time you
have to do rehearsal, and it's often somewhat short when you are on
tour. From then on, the internal life of the character is as you've
chosen it to be in your rehearsals at your home base. . . . About the
soliloquies, I think they were both internal and external. I shared
them. But, you see, you can be *very* internal in the theatre and still
project.

In this regard, Jacobi remained eclectic and let the text determine where
the performance energies would be directed during each speech.

The first soliloquy ("O that this too too solid[19] flesh would melt,"
I.ii.129–59) had a natural transition built into it:

Yes, it's the first time you are left alone onstage with the audience.
Hamlet has got a long evening ahead, it's his first foot on the first
rung of a very high ladder. I tended *not* to come out of a mood I was
in in the earlier scene where I wasn't really with them or part of
them. I was cut off from where they were. Of course, I was talking
to my mother and a couple of lines to my uncle (Hamlet doesn't say
that much)—but I tended to do all that in a kind of removed way so
that when they left, there wasn't a gear change. They just happened
to leave me alone.

I think I welcomed the sudden silence and peace of being alone
onstage, of moving around without the other people being there.
Also, there was a lighting change—the lights went down, so it made
one feel more isolated. That always helps because your space is more
defined. So the audience were waiting for this soliloquy. All of them
know the play and that Hamlet talks to himself a lot. So they say to
themselves, "Ah, this is the part where he talks to himself." "Is it 'To
be, or not to be'?" one says and then the other says, "No, that comes
later." There is a *huge* silence that comes when an actor is left alone
onstage because the expectation is, what is he going to say? It's
lovely. But it's also terrifying.

In this beginning solo, Jacobi had a strong recognition of himself as part of a tradition of the acting of the play and also a sense of the pressure to succeed. Again, he returned to the text:

The soliloquy essentially repeats itself. It says what it's got to say many times—information-wise, there is nothing new in it. Hamlet's anger we get with his mother, married to his uncle too soon after his father's death, the untimely wedding, and that he's disgusted by it. He repeats and repeats himself—there is nothing in it that we do not know. Except, of course, for the *speed* of all these events—the time frame—it all happened in a month. So, it can be said very quickly.

For the actor, there are two opposing forces in it. There is the man who cannot hold it in any longer, and it comes bubbling, bubbling, bubbling out. The other force is—"I must hold my tongue—let me not think on't." So there is "I mustn't think these thoughts, I mustn't tell you" (and this happens in the scene with the Ghost as well). He holds his head and says, "I mustn't—please, please, *please stop*." The man is clutching them all down, trying to hold them in, but it comes bursting out—he cannot *not* speak because of the frustration and the horror of them. So that accounts for the structure of broken sentences and incomplete thoughts. Those little parentheticals bursting into the main thought—that's how you actually *think*—a major thought and then a small little digressive thought hits you and then you get back onto the mainstream thought. "Heaven and earth, / Must I remember?" is probably the first time in the whole soliloquy he stops to draw a breath. The whole speech has only one or two full stops in it. And then "Let me not think on it" is another stop. The lines pour out, pour out, and it all happens with the actual speed of thinking. It keeps on going and is pretty unrelenting.

You know, it could be a very *dull* soliloquy because it's so emotional—especially if the actor plays it as an endless litany of complaint, moaning, and indulgent wallowing. I think it should be the quickest of all. It has to go very fast because thinking is very fast. I didn't move that much, probably wandered a bit—I'm a bit of a wanderer onstage, one of my faults, I should be stiller. But in this speech, the action is mental.

There were changes of emotion—on the second "within a month" Jacobi was near to weeping. Although the actual rendering of the soliloquy was brisk, it held showers of nuances.

A reviewer described Jacobi's entry into the second soliloquy ("O all you host of heaven!" I.v.92–112): "After seeing the Ghost, he rolled in agony on the floor."[20] This physical gesture precluded any direct contact; the actor demonstrated great agony and suffering but did not share it with an audience:

> He is very out of control here. The *largeness* of the passion in this soliloquy is very important. The lines are scripted in physicalized terms much of the time. He says, "Hold . . . my sinews . . . bear me stiffly up." He's talking about his body not actually being able to work, saying, "Come on now, let's get me together. Brain, help me to get my body on my feet." And of course, the scope is heaven and earth—it encompasses everything.
>
> I always used my hands on "my tables"—otherwise you've got to get out this diary and a pencil and put it all down, and somehow that just doesn't work for me. The tables are not actual objects, they're in my head, the tables of my *memory*, so I used a hand gesture to the head as if to say, "I'll get it in there."

Jacobi felt that Hamlet was very close to the edge. For the most part, the character was "passionate, a few moments of madness, but not over the line. This soliloquy is the first sign of his frenzy."[21] Furthermore, Jacobi felt that Hamlet's "humour" (in the Jonsonian sense of temperament or disposition) grew in the role as he played it. This subtle shading resulted in his enlarging the character's "antic disposition," something that not all critics approved of: "Derek Jacobi, a well-graced actor . . . is a volatile, near-hysterical Prince determined to live up to the description that he waxes desperate with imagination and uses wild whirling words."[22] Jacobi explained that Hamlet underwent a true decline because he was a man of action, not a delayer: "In the grip of passion, he can do anything. Once the passion is gone, he becomes a thinker. And then things get tough."[23]

The second soliloquy was another in which the burden of the speech was to release emotion. Jacobi saw this juncture as one of the major shocks that disturbed Hamlet's equilibrium. He wanted to convey to the audience that the character had a hypersensitivity to events in Denmark, a reaction that few others in the court seemed to manifest. A moment alone gave him the opportunity for complete abandonment to his inner feelings. Again, the actor worked "solitariness" to his advantage.

Next came the virtuoso soliloquy for Jacobi, "O, what a rogue and peasant slave" (II.ii.550–605). To him, the text dictated a direct-address speech. However, he did not invite a verbal response from the audience:

Here, he is talking absolutely, directly, to the audience because he's asking them questions. He's not asking *himself* questions—"Is it monstrous what I've done? Am I a coward?"—no, he's asking the audience. It's total audience contact. Also, he's not expecting answers—they're rhetorical questions. They're addressed to the theatre audience, but I don't expect people to shout back at me.

In a way, it starts with [Hamlet] desperately upset—that somebody in a fiction, in a dream, could be so moved, so genuinely emotionally moved, and he himself doesn't seem to be able to do that in a "real" situation, so he ends up talking himself into another way of gaining his revenge. He tends to be saying to the audience in this speech, "Well, we have got this far. Are you with me so far? You know my problem—I know my problem—perhaps I know my problem *too well*. We've just been watching a man talking about something similar, except he [the First Player] was acting and he got the kinds of effects that come from acting. Am *I* acting? Am I *real*?" The speech is a kind of summing up what state we're in now—how far I've got. It's a kind of gathering-in of all the strands, of all the possibilities so far of what the Ghost is, what it could be or might be, and how he's going to deal with it, how he has so far unsuccessfully dealt with it. Then he gets this idea, about the play within the play and the guilty creatures sitting at it. This seems at least a way of finding out, in the course of events, if the Ghost is true. And he even jollies himself up about it, as if to say, "Right. Now I've got to do it. Okay, it's the *play. That's* what I'll do."

For Hamlet the whole concept [of revenge] is anachronistic. Since he is a student and a philosopher, his mind quite naturally begins to question. It is interesting that so soon after the second soliloquy, so soon after seeing the Ghost, he immediately begins to doubt the vision: "The spirit that I have seen / May be a dev'l, and the dev'l hath power / T'assume a pleasing shape . . . "

This speech is, by the way, the big number, the bravura one, the showstopper. It's such a wonderful actor-y thing with so many opportunities to do an emotion, stop it midair, and suddenly do another. It's a fascinating speech and I was always very, very physical in it, with lots of business and movement, very *acted out*. I always physicalized "Bloody, bawdy villain! / Remorseless, treacherous, lecherous, kindless villain!" I used one of the wooden swords that had been a prop of one of the players in their first entrance, a kind of theatre-within-theatre comment, borrowed fake properties.

Jacobi also let the stops out vocally. He let pauses run on dangerously, and he colored words like "mad" and "drown" with pyrotechnic energy. The "Oh" prior to "Oh Vengeance!" had a wonderful operatic build to it. The speech was "shaped" vocally to reach a peak which then allowed the actor to comment on his own elocutionary mastery with punctuated naturalness on "Why, what an ass am I!" He gave the closing couplets with speed and a whispered intimacy to the audience, as if to seal their conspiracy.

Jacobi had strong feelings that the interval should fall after the third soliloquy: "If it's placed there, it puts an enormous physical strain on the actor playing Hamlet, but it makes psychological sense, and a lot of the problems associated with the great middle section of the play disappear." For Jacobi, this placing of the interval enabled what he saw as the three phases of the play to come clearer:

> In the first section you see Claudius's guilt, about which [Hamlet] remains doubtful, even when he has evolved the plan for "The Mouse-trap." Then after the interval you have that extraordinary succession of scenes: the nunnery scene, the play scene, the sudden failure to kill Claudius as he is praying, and, immediately after, the closet scene, in which he kills without hesitation, followed by his exile to England. I think these scenes must follow one another like hammerblows. There must be no respite, either for the audience or for Hamlet. When they happen in that way, then the inconsistencies become accountable. It is no longer odd that Hamlet should be considering killing himself at one point, organizing the performance of

"The Mouse-trap" the next, failing to kill Claudius when he might "do it pat," and then killing Polonius in mistake for the king only minutes later. Those actions might seem inconsistent on the page, but in the theatre, when you see the succession of events and the pitch they lift Hamlet to, they become utterly convincing. The stress is acute, and people under stress behave wildly and inconsistently—the whole sequence has absolute emotional and dramatic truth.[24]

It was essential to Jacobi's interpretation that the second series of scenes begin with "To be, or not to be" and the nunnery scene, because it was at that moment when Hamlet felt utterly betrayed by Ophelia's lies and evasions that he came closest to madness. This narrative line convinced Jacobi to take a fresh approach to the famous fourth soliloquy, something that the BBC found too radical to use and that elicited a wide variety of comments from critics: "To be, or not to be" became a dramatic speech to Ophelia within a scene, part of an interaction between himself and her rather than a solo speech. The long sweep of events had to begin with the soliloquy, and the pace had to be tight and breakneck up to his departure for England. It was imperative that "To be" not retard this forward motion.

There were a number of textual clues that Jacobi felt reinforced his decision. One of the issues that Shakespeare leaves open is the quality and depth of Hamlet's relationship with Ophelia:

> I think you have to assume, or at least *we assumed*, that they were lovers, that it was a consummated affair. And that they're both still "in it" emotionally. Him, too, although other things have gotten in his way. The seeds of their relationship, the bottom line of their relationship, have taken place before this interview.

Corollary to this was the very real fact of Hamlet's isolation: "One of the problems of Hamlet is that he has these needs to tell, but he has no one to confide in. Horatio is one person, up to a point, but Ophelia overall." Thus Jacobi chose to feature Ophelia over the two possible confidants for the prince, a non-traditional choice but not an impossible one. These two basic interpretative decisions helped set up the remaining scenario. Jacobi's attention was also drawn to the fact that "To be, or not to be" had no dialogic stage direction to introduce it:

Because in all the other soliloquies, Hamlet (or Shakespeare) emptied the stage. There was a mass exit of some kind, as there was in the first soliloquy, "O that this too too solid flesh." Or Hamlet simply asked them to go—"Good-bye to you"—and then said, "Now I am alone" or "Leave me friends," as he did before the fifth soliloquy, or "Go a little before" prior to "How all occasions." Hamlet usually gave some kind of transition line so that the actor was left alone onstage. But there wasn't any of that before "To be"—he just went straight into it.

Jacobi's reasoning about the scene proceeded as follows:

Claudius says, "We have closely sent for Hamlet." Whether or not Claudius has signed the message or even if Hamlet doesn't know from whence it has come, he's obviously gotten a message to be in a certain place at a certain time. It is not a case of his wandering around the castle thinking of killing himself. Hamlet is on his way to a rendezvous—with whom, he does not know. He has obeyed a message to *be there.* When he arrives, he sees Ophelia. That is rather a surprise. Their most recent encounter, in the sewing closet where he took her by the arm and looked her up and down, had frightened her. He'd made a kind of mute appeal to her to which she did not respond. She'd just looked at him as if he was odd and strange, which indeed he was being, but she couldn't see *beyond* that. At that time, he'd just wanted to lock eyes with her and find out what her reaction to him was. And it was fright, it was fear, it was terror. From then on, he didn't see her for several weeks. Or if he had, she'd run away. When he'd glimpsed her down at the end of a corridor, she'd ducked back.

All of a sudden here she was, just standing still, reading a prayerbook. Now she doesn't normally do this, but the theatre audience knows that Polonius has said, "Walk you here. . . . Read on this book." Under ordinary circumstances, it is Ophelia's command to *not* walk you here and to *not* read on this book—she's hidden behind something or scurried away. However, here she is. Very odd. But what a marvelous opportunity to actually be able to voice his thoughts and to tell her what is troubling him—to tell her that he is complicated, that she's the only one that he could possibly tell these things to.

What he says makes him very vulnerable. He tells her that he worries about death, that what comes beyond death is so unknown. He confesses that he is a coward like every other man because his thoughts of suicide are not necesarily *new* thoughts. In fact, they have been there from the very beginning—"'gainst self-slaughter," even from the point of the first soliloquy. This has occurred before— "I'll kill myself"—but now he needs to *tell someone*—preferably the person he loves most—not so much to confess, but to release pent-up feelings so that he can go on. He needs a confidant, and of course he cannot talk about subjects like suicide with just anyone. He is, after all, a public figure too.

Jacobi played the scene very physically, as if he were speaking to someone he loved very much: "I sat at her feet for most of it. I touched her on the face when I said 'Nymph,' before all the realizations began." In fact, Jacobi felt that the matter was so personal and so intimate that he didn't really want an answer from Ophelia:

> Because, you see, he's saying it *to* her, but he's also saying it *at* her, *through* her, *around* her. He doesn't need her response. And I think that it's legitimate to say that she's *about* to *say* something and so the lines at the end, the "Soft you now, / The fair Ophelia"—just remember me in your prayers—is how he quiets her. In all the other places in the text when he says "soft," it means "hold on, hang about, wait a minute." This is the only time where he says "Soft *you*." Now the word "you" could be to himself. There are other places where the word "soft" is not coupled with the word "you"— but at this point in the play text, it is. And "the fair Ophelia" is just one of those little titles we all have for one another.

However, Ophelia had an assignment:

> Now she's got to keep him there. She's a decoy in this scene, and Dad and Claudius have set it up that way. She's in a fearful position and doesn't know what to do. So she says, "My lord, how have you been lately?" ("How does your honor for this many a day?") From the

actor's point of view, that is a major clue. He thinks—of *course* it's all wrong, the fact that she was standing here is all *wrong*. And so his reply, "Well, well, well," is totally ironic. He knows her father has set this up. He detects the falseness in her voice, and he knows that the whole situation is phony. And then he sees the curtains moving, little indications, and then it all dawns on him and contributes to the *horrendousness* of the nunnery scene that follows.

Of course, this rendition of the fourth soliloquy required a certain character conception for Ophelia. Suzanne Bertish played the role from May to September 1977, and Jane Wymark played it in the spring and summer of 1979. Although they were two differing Ophelias, both played a passionate love for Hamlet and both felt that being the recipients of the "To be" soliloquy helped them with character, especially in setting up for Ophelia's suicide later on. Jacobi stated:

> I think Ophelia's madness has to do with how people *use* her. She is literally an object, a thing, and everybody tells her what to do and how to live her life and how to behave and who to talk to and who not to talk to. She can't get out of the situation. She has to sit there and take it. There is that awesome metaphor in the Russian [Kozintsev's *Hamlet*] film—she wears an iron corset—wonderful in its accuracy. Ironically, Hamlet's soliloquy contains the seeds of her destiny—she goes mad and commits suicide. He *talks* about it, but it never happens to *him*. You can almost see her mind begin to fracture in her own soliloquy in this scene.

Fellow actor Julian Glover responded favorably:

> I thought the idea was quite miraculous—direct eye contact with Ophelia during the soliloquy, as if to say to her, "Do you know what I'm going through, sweetheart—this is what I am about." By the end of the scene, she was a wash. Because she loves this man and sees him in such despair and there is nothing she can do to help. It was wonderful, wonderful. We watched fascinated every night.

Messing about with the most famous passage in all of literature was something few critics were prepared to let pass without comment. Even if the respondent loved the production, he needed to blow a whistle of warning to potential audience members. The reactions were unusually varied. Geoff Brown in *Plays and Players* merely reported: "[Jacobi spoke] the soliloquy fingering Ophelia's mouth and ended up crouching down, an arm around the back of her chair."[25] B. A. Young in the *Financial Times* complained about giving the soliloquy to Ophelia, "toying with her the while," but added, "I thought the speaking in all the parts intelligent; there was hardly an emphasis I didn't agree with, save in extent."[26] Irving Wardle in the *London Times* was suspicious about the soliloquy, yet felt that Suzanne Bertish's "crack-up, presented in case history style, wholly drained of pathos, silences all objections" to the change in traditional delivery.[27] John Barber in the *Daily Telegraph* was flatly critical: "'To be' I cannot believe . . . to Ophelia as he tickled her nose and put an arm around her shoulder."[28] And when Jane Wymark took over the role, Michael Coveney in the *Financial Times* praised the unique treatment of the soliloquy as "beautifully elided into the performance."[29] Jacobi closed the subject with a sporting comment: "It was an approach. I will take it to *my grave* that it was not a gimmick and we never said, 'Well, how are we going to do "To be, or not to be" *a new way?*' It truly wasn't that. It was an attack. But for me, the situation and the emotion really bear that out."

The fifth soliloquy ("'Tis now the very witching time of night" III.ii.388–99) followed the play-within-the-play scene and two summonses (one from Rosencrantz, another from Polonius) to Gertrude's chamber. It was the first time after "The Mouse-trap" performance that Hamlet was alone with the theatre audience (no other character was within earshot), so it was the first time they heard his true reaction to the plot to catch the king. The first five lines composed the reaction, summed up in "Now could I . . . do such bitter business as the day / Would quake to look on." He had already assured Horatio, "I'll take the Ghost's word for a thousand pound"; consequently, the indecision of the fourth soliloquy had effectively been reversed.

The shift to the second topic of the speech, the waiting Gertrude, was signaled by the word "soft." Although he carried a dagger, Jacobi wanted to make clear that he had no intention of harming Gertrude: "I will speak daggers to her, but use none." The speech was held within, like a fervent stage whisper. Its purpose was to build and hold high tension in the audience, a verbal equivalent to the edgy and high-strung music one hears in mystery thrillers as the hero advances down a spooky corridor. The closing lines spelled out his paradox, his dual signals to the audience: "How in my words somever she be shent, / To give them seals never my soul consent!" That word "seals," said Jacobi, "is a clue to the dramatic purpose of many closing couplets in that they are like seals on an envelope: they close the thought for the moment, put it aside. That does not, however, preclude the speaker from taking these thoughts out and looking at them at a later time."

The sixth soliloquy ("Now might I do it pat," III.iii.73–96) followed Claudius' attempt to pray. Hamlet entered behind and above the king, whose character was interpreted as very Machiavellian. The soliloquy was played as a rhetorical argument. Hamlet posited the "givens" in the first line—"I could kill him now"—and the dagger he carried intensified the lines. His pitch stayed up, making a question of "And so am I reveng'd." There was a short realization passage on the succeeding couple of lines, when it occurred to him that he needed to consider that judgment. He concluded that he'd rather wait until his uncle was in the middle of some guilty act, and there was relish and glee as he decided that. The final lines were soft and mean, even hard, as he carefully pronounced, "My mother stays, / This physic but prolongs thy sickly days." In this passage, Jacobi considered himself to be rationalizing but not delaying the ultimate act.

The final soliloquy ("How all occasions do inform against me," IV.iv.32–66) was cut from the earlier 1977 production of *Hamlet*. The director, Toby Robertson, much to Jacobi's chagrin, decided that it should go:

> Toby saw no need for it and I wanted it. It was a fight between us and Toby won. I wanted it rather desperately because I saw it as a punctuation mark in Hamlet's journey. But because we were doing a production that was primarily a touring production, he was looking for cuts. You see, in the provinces, the buses stop at a certain time in the evening and the play had to be over so that people could catch them. However, when we came back to London and did it at the Old Vic I got it back because I argued to Toby, we don't have to worry about transportation in London and if we're five minutes long, it won't matter. . . . If one has to cut soliloquies, this one would

be a likely candidate. Once again, it repeats itself, and its basic sentiment is something Hamlet has pledged before.

Jacobi was loathe to cut the speech because it marked a transition in Hamlet:

After "My thoughts be bloody, or be nothing worth," Hamlet no longer needs to think, to analyze, to question, to ask, to ruminate. He goes away with bloody thoughts and he puts them into practice, which is one of the indications to me that he was close to madness. At the beginning of the scene, there was an accident in killing Polonius—at the end of the scene, he is talking about premeditated murder, removing "my two schoolfellows. . . . O, 'tis most sweet / When in one line two crafts directly meet" with sardonic humor. I quite enjoyed saying those lines.

Jacobi felt that Hamlet had found the killer instinct in himself:

That is the moment, I think, when you see Hamlet begin to harden. By the time he returns from England he will have killed two more people—Rosencrantz and Guildenstern—and will indirectly have caused Ophelia's death. When he sees Fortinbras and his army, another son avenging his father, waging a war for a patch of land, then I think he finally reaches a resolution beyond questioning or doubt. . . . Earlier there was something hysterical in his tone, as if he were deliberately whipping himself up. Now when he says it, I think he means it. Certainly he does what he says. When [he] returns from England, you see a man transformed. He is fatalistic now, as if the events before had drained him in some way. Some great suppurating wound had been cleansed and now he is filled with cold resolution. "A man's life . . . is no more than to say 'One.'" He can kill now without hesitation and without compunction, and he seems to be prepared to bow before events. He will no longer try to influence them.[30]

As if to emphasize this sense of resolution, Jacobi delivered this last of his soliloquies directly to the audience in a very deliberate manner. He needed to have very strong breath support, because the sentences are long and unbroken with few parenthetical interruptions and no broken thoughts. In fact, one sentence is ten lines long. On the final couplet he was exceptionally quiet and determined.

When asked where he would place an eighth soliloquy had Shakespeare provided Hamlet with one, Jacobi replied:

> I always feel "fall of a sparrow" is like a soliloquy, even though it is spoken to Horatio. It doesn't actually need anybody there—there's simply a sympathetic being there, absorbing what he has to say, and that could be a theatre audience as well. It's very like "To be, or not to be" in that he is speaking his inner thoughts.
>
> You see, the man who comes back from England is a man who is now just biding his time. The answer to his problem upon his return is "If it be now, 'tis not to come; if it be not to come, it will be now: if it be not now, yet it will come—the readiness is all." The "To be" question has been answered—que sera, sera—whatever it is will happen. He's in a kind of state of grace. There's no talk, no worrying about it, no thinking it through, no letting it get to you, no upset. The calmness of the man who comes back is extraordinary, because somewhere he's acquired the knowledge that absolutely things resolve themselves. A state of acceptance. Let be, let be—that same word "be" that is found in other soliloquies. The fight will determine itself—let revenge come to me.

Jacobi's method of dealing with the soliloquies was to begin with the play's context as a whole and then to approach each one individually as it occurred in sequence. He was not in any way influenced by the architecture of the theatre he would be working in, because his touring production had to adapt to all sizes and shapes of theatres, some unknown at the beginning of the endeavor. Moreover, his director had no set plan or directorial concept that these soliloquies need fit into; neither Robertson nor Jacobi had preplanned how the soliloquies were to be done. In the late seventies, there was no predominating vogue or fad in enacting soliloquies. Jacobi's strictly textual penetration into each solo speech was partly pragmatic, partly common sense, and partly intuition, qualities this actor holds in quantity. As it turned out, his analysis of the play guided him toward playing the third ("O, what a rogue and peasant slave am I!"), the sixth ("Now might I do it pat"), and the last of the soliloquies ("How all occasions do inform against me") directly to the audience. Another three were still projected, as Jacobi maintains, but quite clearly addressed to Hamlet himself and not to the audience, a definite mixture of modes of performance. "To be, or not to be" was a distinctive spice in this heady mixture of styles in that the passage was not performed as a soliloquy at all.

This chapter has encapsulated the experience of a veteran actor acting the most famous of stage roles under the best and the most adverse of stage conditions at the pinnacle of his career. A conversation with Derek Jacobi confirms how much can be learned from a superbly skilled craftsman—about acting, about acting Hamlet, and about acting Shakespeare. He has experienced all facets of the art, and his work is a combination of pragmatics and aesthetics, the pendulum never swinging too far one way or the other, the balance never tipping too much toward showmanship nor toward esoterica. Julian Glover said of him:

> I'd rather work with Derek. First of all, he is a great problem solver. If there is a difficulty with the text, he works it out quickly and with dexterity. But it's all firmly rooted, firmly rooted in the mind. I find him more electric to work with . . . his eyes are flashier. He is an actor who revels in the craft.
>
> He is also a very generous actor. He gives totally on both an intellectual and physical level. He hurls himself into it. But, you know, this is not by accident. He is a great conserver of energy. We'd go out to dinner as a group, and he'd keep up the energy until he'd had his meal and a glass of wine and then, plop. He's suddenly gone. Then he'd sleep late and rest in the afternoon. That evening in the show, he was like a typhoon. The fight was excellent—I used to watch it night after night.

Jacobi commented on this quality:

> I think that's important . . . that word "energy." Because energy is visual and it's tangible. . . . it's the great communicator, really. And the audience can plug into that energy, becoming *anything*. It's not that the actor has got to sweat all night. It's a mental energy; it's thinking at the speed of light; it's a physical fastness, a physical awareness and instant adaptability, a vocal adaptability and an emotional turning on a sixpence, if necessary, without appearing to be

tricksy. . . . People say to me . . . one moment you are streaming with tears and it's highly emotional and you went upstage and you turned around and came down and you played the other scene. How'd you do that? [The answer is that] you do it with energy. You do it by flicking that switch, that emotional switch. You just exchange one truth for another truth, but you do it quickly. It doesn't need to take time. You don't need to agonize over it, because that's what acting is about. If acting is art, then it's about a technique that can create art. So, to say that "technique" is a dirty word is wrong. It's not a dirty word. It's an essential word in an actor's bag of tricks.[31]

However, in Jacobi's mind, the performance ought not to slide into "demonstrating"—the actor's job is to deliver the text and its meaning:

For them [the audience], in my terms I succeeded because what they talked about was the play and the man and the subject. They didn't talk about my technique, or my talents. . . . Let's take an actor's talent proverbially. Let's say, All right, you're an actor. You can act. You don't spend the evening convincing me of that. You use that to take me on a journey, to take me to places, to make me think thoughts and feel feelings that will surprise me or that I haven't thought or felt for a time.[32]

Jacobi appeared to have the simultaneous vision of a director and an actor. His relationship with Toby Robertson was exemplary:

I've worked with Toby Robertson a lot—we were friends and working partners in my student days at Cambridge. There was a great deal of mutual trust, which there needs to be. Toby can be inflexible and dig his heels in when he wants to. But then so can I, but I think in a subtle way. I am one of those actors who needs, oh indeed, needs a director. But rather than argue or confront on a textual issue, I'll say yes, yes, that's not going too far. I won't say, "I don't want to." I'll usually go ahead and do what I think is correct and then say to the director, "Is that what you mean?" And he'll say, "Yes, it's coming." *Or* he'll say, "No, you didn't do what I told you." And then I'll say, "Oh, but I thought—all right, I see, right, okay—."

You play games. Of course you play games like that. And directors play games, too. If you feel that what he's got to say wouldn't really work for *you*, then by all means try it first, but then forget about it if you both feel it's false. I'll often see an actor do something which is absolutely from left field, and the director will pick up on what you've done and then tell you to do it, so that the suggestion seems to come from the director—and then he'll reject it so that you can save face from having done something wild or irrelevant. It's all based on trust, though, even those games are based on trust. I just don't like the confrontational type of director . . . who terrorizes a performance out of you so that you end up really *only* acting to please him—to stop him chatting at you or to make him be nice to you. Toby wasn't like that . . . for example, when I originally suggested that "To be, or not to be" be done as a speech to Ophelia, he said yes, let's try it. And then after we'd worked it through, he let me have it. What I'm saying might imply that I go my own sweet way and do what I want to anyway—that's not true. I need a director to know more about it than I do. An eye I can trust and somebody whose judgment about what is going on is greater than mine.

It's ideal if the director knows the meanings in the text better than I do—so that if I just say, "What does this phrase mean?" the director will know. It's ideal if their knowledge and culture and intellectual grasp is greater than mine. Someone like a John Barton or a Terry Hands is good. Terry's wonderful in that he has an intellectual breadth which is a marvelous rock to have in the maelstrom of rehearsal. He doesn't rewrite the text as much as John—Terry actually has much broader strokes than that and trusts actors a great deal. Barton goes ferreting about in the punctuation, and Terry's a bit freer than that. For me, that's better.

I very much enjoyed my first experience at directing Ken Branagh in *Hamlet*. As an actor, you've got your own problems and you're very concerned with finding your own way through your part. As a director, you've got all sorts of people with problems coming up to you and saying, "Well, this doesn't work and what can I do with that—what does this mean?" You've got to make decisions because you're in charge—of sets and lighting and costumes and what you want and what you need. You problem-solve all the time—about when and how long and which days to rehearse, the coffee breaks, the logistics. And then there is the *people* dimension. Ken and I came to a modus vivendi. I tried to really let him have his head and be very *minimal* in my direction of him in the soliloquies especially—because I think they are highly personal. When Ken came to me and said, "Well, I'm having trouble with this section and what shall I do here? Can you help me with this?" then I would. I did *not* want to say, "Look, what you do with this soliloquy is—" or "This is *how*—." I wanted him to find out for himself, so I helped him only when he couldn't answer a particular question. Ken deals very instinctively with Hamlet's problems in his own way. Any director who works with a Hamlet has to give him his own freedom to deal naturally with his own impulses, how he reacts in given situations. Within that framework, a director is free to guide and to manipulate and to help steer a course.

Hamlet really is the personality of the actor who's playing him. Of all the great roles, it is *the* personality role. That's why there is no such thing as a "definitive Hamlet"—which is essentially a critic's convenient tag. The role is infinitely accommodating.

Jacobi also had very strong notions about the body and the voice:

In Shakespearean acting, the body language is terribly important, as well as the face. Attention does wander from your face to your feet and legs and to other parts of the body. And they've all got to be part of a whole. In Chekov, for example, the feet often tell a different story from the head. When you apply that to Shakespeare, you have to remember that all parts of you are seen and you can express contradictory things with this knowledge.

I don't count out the iambic pentameter when I am preparing to perform. There is that school that does that, and the actor knows the exact end of each line. I think I have the healthiest respect for versifying and scholastic punctuation. However, if you want to make a full stop, to make it mean a particular thing, and the punctuation mark is not there and it needs one to make vocal sense, then by all means do it. Especially if it makes the text alive and much clearer. Face it, we don't know exactly how it was punctuated and scholars disagree even about where the commas came. The genius of the writing is that it has a poetic bloom—the rhythm is there and even the worst verse-speakers in the world can never wholly mangle the line because the actual choice of word is in-built into the line in such an extraordinary way. The thoughts are so beautiful and so poetic, so if you've got to muck about with the punctuation to get it expressed correctly, do so. Scholars will be aghast, of course.

The important thing is to go for the *sense* of the line, to make it accessible for the audience so that they can understand the *meaning*. If you in any way give the impression that what you are saying is not your native language, not the way you naturally express your thoughts, you are in trouble. Excessive versifying can be a barrier to actually speaking your thoughts, in fact, because there is the danger that you will get into a vocal pattern and the audience will stop listening. They will have to work so hard to perceive the meaning that they cannot understand what you are saying. And you must make the language sound absolutely real and believable.

Then there is that school that sticks slavishly to rules. For example, if a thought ends mid-line, then you should omit the stop and go right on without taking a break. I do not subscribe to that at all. It can violate the sense of the line and also railroad two thoughts together that ought not to be. Also, establishing rules like that prevents any newness of interpretation, any imaginative leap on the actor's part. To make the thoughts new-minted, to speak the words so that they come out fresh and truthful, it sometimes means approaching punctuation and iambic pentameter slightly different from how it is regulated. You should approach Shakespeare the way you approach any other play. The trouble is that a lot of very, very good actors in the presence of Shakespeare seem to have all their instinctive techniques and skills desert them. They put on a voice, a walk, and it all starts to "go classical." All the things one would normally do in a flesh-and-blood modern play—all that reality, all that imagination, all that talent, all that theory, all that "re-creation of the text"—seem to vanish. Directors and voice teachers encourage this, I think. In a modern play, the voice is informed with tonality. You can hear the comment on the lines in the voice—you can hear someone say, "I love you," knowing that they hate the person they've said it to. The correct message gets communicated in the *way* that it is said. So if you versify out the line, ta-da ta-da ta-da ta-da ta-da, if you *assume* an artificial voice, then you cannot communicate with those words—and it's there to be done.

All those aitch-ays [ha's] and aitch-oh's [ho's] and oh-aitches—such as in "O, what a rogue and peasant slave am I!"—in Shakespeare are very useful to an actor. They can be a scream or a cry as well as an "O." They are there for sound and can be very effective. Use them for vocal underlining.

Now all this is *not* to say that you *don't plan* and don't rehearse. Of course you do. But within that planning, the essential quality you are working for is that it must look onstage as if that is the first time you've spoken that line. And even within a well-rehearsed sequence, you can occasionally change something, absolutely, change the way of saying a line midperformance or change a bit of business. But it does require maximum confidence in what you're doing to make changes—and you must be extra careful when you go off on another track that you don't crash the gears and derail the train, that you don't complicate the lives of other cast members. But, quite frankly, I *would* have a soliloquy so planned that I would know ahead of time which lines are more direct with the audience and which are less—although I usually think in terms of beats and smaller chunks when I perform lines. So, you see, preparation and spontaneity go hand in hand.

Shakespeare was making his plays for actors. That interval break, after "How all occasions," for example, is profound evidence that Shakespeare was an actor. Hamlet couldn't go on without it. At that point, he is in a right good sweat. Most Hamlets go off and shower and change their costumes. . . . You just rest and have a breather so you can get into that last calm state to end the play.

Upon being introduced to the young Hamlet he directed (Ken Branagh), Jacobi commented, "'Ah, my parts,' and then remembered John Gielgud saying the same thing to him some years before."[33] Indeed, there are many parallels in the careers of Jacobi and Gielgud: both had seen a number of Hamlets before they acted it professionally; both had performed Hamlet as a young actor; both had extensive experience in touring the role of Hamlet; both directed a younger Hamlet later on in their careers; both have been noted for the skill of their voices in handling Shakespearean verse; both are extremely practical men who are accustomed to paying attention to the details of performance. There are often parallels in the lives of distinguished actors. However, it is typical of Jacobi to tender the compliment to fellow players of Hamlet: "The other ghosts of Shakespearean actors—Sir John, Sir Michael, Sir Laurence—are up on the battlements with the Ghost of my father."[34]

Anton Lesser in Hamlet, *1982. Photograph by Sophie Baker.*

6

ANTON LESSER : *A Noble Mind*

British actor Anton Lesser has performed extensively on the London stage, with approximately half of his stage credits in classical roles from Shakespeare to Chekov. For the Royal Shakespeare Company he has played Richard III, Romeo, and Troilus. He has numerous credits in British television, and over the last few years he has worked with award-winning American playwright Richard Nelson, playing the lead roles in three British premieres: *Principia Scriptoriae, Some Americans Abroad,* and *Two Shakespearean Actors.*

In 1982, at the age of thirty, Lesser played Hamlet under the direction of Jonathan Miller, with whom he had worked earlier in his career, playing both Troilus and Edgar in the Time-Life BBC "Shakespeare Plays" series. This was Miller's third *Hamlet* in twelve years. An old hand at Shakespeare, Miller was famous (or infamous) for bold strokes of imagination and iconoclastic interpretations, often using classical painters as sources of inspiration for his production designs. He occasionally directed for the large Shakespearean companies in England but preferred to be unfettered in style and unrestricted by institutions.[1]

Lesser's *Hamlet* was originally staged at the Donmar Warehouse in Covent Garden and opened on August 17, 1982. It then transferred to the much larger Piccadilly Theatre on September 22, where it continued to play for ten more weeks. The austere set, consisting of simple, spare furniture (such as a plywood throne and a bench) was on a three-foot raised platform of gray boards backed by a black-curtained wall. The actors wore costumes of varying shades of gray (Hamlet's was the darkest) with buttons, tight bodices, and farthingales, somewhat reminiscent of the clothing in seventeenth-century Dutch paintings. This was clearly a neutral country of some kind and a smaller, more domestic notion of Denmark. Other Miller touches included a medically graphic mad scene by Ophelia, whose clinical insanity offended some critics and drew horrified responses from others. Benedict Nightingale described Miller's style: "In his undeniably skilled hands, the Shakespeare production became spare-parts surgery. Plays come off the table the same but different. A new heart here, an extra arm or leg there, a brain transplant over there—anything seemed possible in Dr. Miller's operating theatre."[2]

The character conception of Hamlet was in tune with other modern productions. Lesser's was a youthful Hamlet, sullen, sly, fond of adolescent jokes, and prone to tears, who managed to mature as the shocks of experience washed over him. Obviously, Miller had envisioned an anti-romantic interpretation: "I have always been interested in the idea of Hamlet as a rather unattractive character . . . volatile, dirty-minded and immature."[3] Most critics recognized in Lesser, stubble-chinned and small of stature, abundant intelligence and a charismatic energy: "an actor who holds the spotlight of our attention simply by being on the stage,"[4] "he has the great actor's ability to give familiar words a freshness and make us hear them as if for the first time . . . his stage presence is undeniable and often transfixing."[5]

However, there were a couple of heavy-handed negative reviews which focused on Hamlet's callow unprinceliness. Moreover, he had clearly squared off with his new stepfather. A reviewer from the *Daily Mail* commented: "This is the first Hamlet I've seen which asks why Claudius cannot bring himself to kill Hamlet, instead of the other way round. It is a good question, but would any director other than Jonathan Miller have thought of it?"[6] Lesser explains how the idea came about:

This was a young Hamlet, yes. There were scenes when I was actually sobbing. He was very funny at times that are not textually required, a lightness that was useful. I didn't consciously think, "I'm going to play him quite young." I just tried to let the text come through me as I was then, at age thirty. I can't remember Jonathan being uncompromising about concepts—saying, for example, "I really feel in this scene, this is what's happening and therefore we should go in that direction." But he often said, "What about this . . . let's try so-and-so"—which is a much more enjoyable way of working. He would then arrive at an idea. He always began with an openness and then said, "This is how it's going to be." I wouldn't have accepted doing it under any other circumstances.

Lesser discussed the experience of working with a renowned director, talking about both the rehearsal and the production process. As with any Hamlet team of actor and director, the two needed time to forge a working relationship:

The first time I worked with Jonathan Miller (as Troilus, on TV) was probably one of the biggest crisis points in my career. It wasn't his fault, but it certainly didn't help that his ideas were so fluent, so prolific, so constant that I withdrew and sort of disappeared in that rehearsal process. I felt that I was superfluous—what was there for me to do? It was all being suggested for me—"you do that, now go there and do that—and I think what Troilus does here is this." I sort of felt, "I don't know how to act it anymore." Yet I saw other people's performances blossoming all around me. Not Jonathan's fault—but it was that I hadn't really understood how to make the best of our alliance. Luckily, by the time we went into the studio to video-record—I think through sheer terror and panic—I managed to find a performance that was spontaneous and actually did things I'd never done in rehearsal. By the second time I worked with Jonathan, I was a bit more forewarned and forearmed and enjoyed the process because I could receive this torrent of imagination and yet say, "Yes, but I want to let it filter through me, and I will find what you want. Let it come organically." I gave myself more space and I had more confidence. Despite that earlier experience, I discovered that he'd actually *liked* what I'd done. By the time we got to *Hamlet*, it was a more equally balanced situation. I could say, "Well, I might take that option, but then again, I might take this one."

When Troilus was completed in the BBC-TV's "Shakespeare Plays" series, he came to me and said, "It's all arranged, then. Hamlet." Surprised, I said, "Oh!" Thereafter I don't think we spoke a word about it or about his ideas until the first day of rehearsal. I had played Hamlet once at grammar school in Birmingham when I was sixteen, so I had a familiarity with the text. When I came to do it professionally, the first thing Jonathan said was "memorize the text before we start rehearsal"—which is a very interesting thing to do because usually one's character develops *during* the rehearsal period, and therefore the intonations and inflections start to become *yours* because of the way you're rehearsing it. Different directors do different things and sometimes it's quite nice to be "thrown" in that way. It can give you a new avenue for creativity.

Lesser felt that Miller's different way of working pushed him further much faster:

> You really had to be open to anything that happened, anything that might come out of your mouth. The safety net was gone. You simply knew the words—they were there in your head—you knew the way the speeches were constructed and the thought that went through them. How you expressed that thought was a complete adventure. Essentially, it made you listen to yourself and cue that process of self-critique that leads to exactly how you want to speak the lines.
>
> With book in hand, half of you is trying to communicate—the other half is puzzling over half lines and bits of text. Without the script in hand, you are really focused on the other person and making those words effectively change the person you're talking to. The *director* is doing the analyzing and the academic speculating—saying to himself, "Well, did that make sense—did it fit in with my overall view of the piece?" Released from those corporate decisions, you have a greater range of interaction possibilities sooner.

One of the cautions of this method of working is that an actor must be careful not to sneak by phrases or sentence constructions without unscrambling them to find out what they really say. He might be in danger of memorizing lines for which he has not yet assigned specific meanings:

> For the price of learning it quickly, you can get into nasty habits. One has to go into rehearsal without preconceptions about what the text should sound like. I prefer that, because there is no way I can be similar to another actor. People say, "Don't you mind the fact that you've got all those sounds in your head from the great performances of the past—such as Olivier's Hamlet"—and I say, "No, I

don't mind that, because there is no way I can be similar to Olivier. I am totally unique as each individual actor is totally unique."

I am discovering I can let go of the residue from other performances because I want to find what sort of Hamlet comes through myself, through this little frame and this little voice. Maybe then I can touch somebody in my generation and my particular social milieu. Instead of "building a character," my own process is that a character *unfolds*. In a Shakespearean role, I have a vision of my character that isn't totally whole, not all the details are there. How do I release that persona and confirm my vision along with all the decisions that we make in rehearsal?

Lesser had formulated a personal method of character creation that was consonant with his interest in meditation, which he also teaches:

The more I make myself into a neutral state, the more I'm in touch with what is unique about me. The more I put myself in touch with the rational part of my mind—the more I make a mental list about what words I want to inflect in "To be, or not to be" and how I *don't* want to sound—the more I get my mind tied up in knots. My particular route through a part is to become totally nothing, a neutral state in the beginning of the rehearsal. I don't stand in the wings thinking, "Now what's Hamlet had for breakfast and where's he just come from?"

Lesser did not have "models" that he emulated or imitated in creating his stage characters. However, he had watched a number of other actors perform Hamlet:

I had seen Michael Pennington's at Stratford in 1981. I saw the film of Olivier's Hamlet. I thought Jonathan Pryce's Hamlet was extraordinary! I saw Derek Jacobi's and Nicol Williamson's on TV. Edward Fox's *Hamlet* was playing at the same time as mine at the Young Vic. I think we were as different as chalk and cheese.

I would have to say that the most impressive one for me was Olivier's. It is perfectly natural to say to oneself, "Um, I don't think I would do it that way" or, conversely, "Well, I want to remember how X did it." Those choices and decisions happen very intuitively with me, and my monitoring process is largely unconscious.

Regarding the stage device of the soliloquy, Lesser felt that Shakespeare had forged an extremely useful theatrical tool:

The soliloquies do a great many things—Shakespeare kills forty-nine birds with one stone. He gives plot very economically. He lets the actor explore the unsaid, the subconscious of the character. He gets a lot of the play's emotional journey contracted into a short space of time. Instead of playing out a scene in which four or five characters in a long interaction scene would reveal the state of Hamlet's mind, Shakespeare simply has him say, "To be, or not to be—I live or I die. What's death, anyway?"

The language of the soliloquy operated as a discovery process for Lesser, helping him to define his character. Correspondences in his own life aided him in determining how Hamlet expressed his inner thoughts:

I am more articulate when someone is listening: when you are telling *someone else* how you're feeling, you're telling yourself how you're feeling. I do some teaching, and I find that whenever I teach, I'm telling people what *I* need to hear. The best ideas come out because you've got to put your thoughts into some kind of form. As you hear yourself, you think, oh, yes, that's exactly what I feel. The soliloquies are learning processes for the actor. By teaching them, the character is able to learn about himself. That gets tricky in acting. That's why the blank-page process is so important for me, especially at the beginning of the role.

Even though the production originated in a small theatre with a slightly elevated (three feet) thrust stage, this Hamlet chose not to address the audience directly. His performance mode was internalized, yet he knew the importance of making himself available to the audience. Indeed, he used the audience in talking to himself; however, he did not pitch the performance energies at the listeners in an effort to connect:

The convention we used was one of the soliloquy being a form of expression where the audience eavesdrops onto a man talking to himself in order to understand himself. One may look up and, as it were, occasionally address the audience. But one is addressing the audience not as impartial, objective bystanders listening to what's going on in one's head. Rather, the audience is one's alter ego, another bit of oneself to appeal to, as if to say, "Am I mad—what's happening here?" Consequently, the actor doesn't actually focus on persons in the audience or look at them and treat them as recipients of the speech. One of the keys is what the actor does with his eyes. I try not to see faces. It's more of a glazed look that goes in front of the eyes. However, I *look* in that direction so that they get the benefit of the sound being projected forward. I don't want to pop them out of the play. They should never feel affronted or intimidated by an actor talking to them, because he's not communicating with them as people. They don't lean back in their chairs because there are actors shouting at them—rather, they lean forward because you are letting them into your head, so they want to listen and to see more.

At the moment, that's how I think I would operate with any soliloquy. If I were in an audience, I wouldn't want the actor to break the spell by treating us as a group in the middle of Shaftesbury Avenue in a theatre. I would want the performer to weave a spell. There may be moments (if it works well) where I forget totally and feel an extraordinary magic, forget myself and imagine that I'm a fly on the wall in the palace at Elsinore.

After the initial four-week run of the play, the production transferred to a much larger theatre. Naturally, some adjustments had to be made in the performance:

The danger is that you will lose more than you gain by transferring into a big auditorium. The Piccadilly wasn't a vast theatre like Drury Lane, but it was a change of performance space and it implied a different style of heightened acting. After all, we had moved from a theatre with two hundred seats to one with a thousand seats, and we had moved from having audience on three sides to a proscenium arch theatre. We had to reblock the production slightly so that all the action was focused more out front instead of in the round. Automatically, the actors *bring up* the performance to match the space. A change like this is never as big a shock as you anticipate. At first, you panic because you think the production rests on intimate communication and that you've evolved a wonderful way of doing the text that seems natural and is accessible to modern ears, and now you'll have to yell it to the back of the gallery! Eventually, you adjust and, after a day or two, you begin looking at the gains you've made. Of course, we felt as if we'd lost a little, too.

However, it is a great benefit to transfer a Shakespearean production because Shakespeare seems to accommodate an intimacy and truthfulness in communication as well as a strange sort of lifted and projected style as well. The combination of these two is very exciting. There was something special about the closeness that evolved in the smaller theatre first that came along with us to the new house. We only took three days to re-jig [re-block] it, and the director took us through the transfer.

The decisions I had already made about the convention of the soliloquy—that I wanted to draw them in rather than to "tell" them—made the transition purely technical. I had to be louder, the blocking had to be changed (if I'd made a quarter turn, now it had to be a half). The circle of concentration became wider—I could literally focus on the Exit sign up in the circle for my outside perimeters.

An interesting phenomenon occurred for Lesser. The larger the theatre was, the more private (or inward) his soliloquies became:

It is extraordinary, isn't it? It's having to be internal in a bigger space. You have a man thinking alone in a bathroom versus a man thinking alone in a cathedral. You must bring the performance up vocally so that the people in the back rows will have a *similar* experience to those in the front.

Lesser decided that the first soliloquy was chiefly about Hamlet's internal revulsion. Even the aside was spoken to himself. The speech focused attention onto his judgment of Gertrude and emphasized the growing conflict between Hamlet and Claudius. The soliloquy exemplified the classical "psychomachia," or "war within."

I did not look at the audience and say, "Ha! A little more than kin and less than kind!" That would have destroyed the effect. Jonathan allowed me to mutter the aside as if it were a sarcastic remark to the self which is not meant for anyone to hear, yet is heard by the king. So Claudius said, "Hmmm?" as if to say, "You were going to say something?" and I responded with one of those "I didn't say anything" shrugs, which said, "I wouldn't dream of speaking when *you* were speaking."

In the transition from the court scene to the soliloquy in I.ii, I sat and thought, "If these people don't shut up or leave the room in a minute, I am going to explode." When they finally left the stage, I thought, "Oh, Christ. What a relief. I cannot describe to you what I am feeling because I cannot believe my mother and this man, in a short period of time . . ." The soliloquy was a tension released—like a coiled spring—after the people had gone. It created its own energy. I remember sitting for a time in the chair that Claudius had just vacated. I got up and moved around, picking up some of the documents that the king had left on the table. There was no lighting change for the speech.

At the point of the first soliloquy, I hadn't decided yet that Claudius had committed murder—it was more disgust and Gertrude having left my father for this licentious, slobbering beast. It takes Hamlet nine lines to get to the word "married." The lines are filled with self-interruptions that do not allow him to say it.

The second soliloquy was performed as a major realization, Hamlet seeing for the first time that assumptions he'd made in life were false and unreliable. Instead, villains prevailed in the life of the court:

In the second soliloquy, which follows the Ghost's exit, he goes from tears in the nervous breakdown to anger with himself for breaking down when he should be making some cosmic statement about the condition that he's in. Then he gets himself together in order to work up to that statement: "This is what I'll do—I'll wipe away all trivial fond records." Then the lights came on, and the landscape [of the court] lit up, reminding him of the pernicious woman and the smiling villain. He thought, "I'd better now look at every person on this planet as potentially a liar, a cheat, a thief." His whole view of humanity expired and he became a complete, bitter cynic. "My tables, my tables" kicked off this whole internalized series of thoughts— "all my education and upbringing have been wrong—Denmark is a synonym for hell from now on." The last bit, "So, uncle, there you are," was unemotional: "Okay, I have given vent to what I feel, I have established my new philosophy about this hell I'm living in.

Now what am I going to do about it?" But he *doesn't* do anything about it! He simply tells himself that he will *remember.*

Jonathan worked with me on that speech. In early rehearsals, I was trying to play the end of the speech at the beginning, and you cannot do that. There is a journey through most of these soliloquies. Just because they've got exclamation marks early on doesn't mean you can expend a lot of emotion at the beginning of the speech.

There was something else we added here. The Ghost and the Player King were "doubled" roles. When the Player King came on later on, there was a shock for just a moment, because he looked so much like my father. Jonathan added that.

The third soliloquy was given as a youth attempting to cast himself into the role of a posturing and overtheatrical avenger. However, Hamlet found that he could not force true emotion, so he gave up with an embarrassed shrug:

That one was more direct to the audience than any other. Hamlet was a bit caught up in being the Player King and in saying the soliloquy lines as the Player King would. [Here Lesser does an imitation and draws out "kinnnne-less-a villun" in an elocutionary way.] In the first part of the speech, Hamlet was like an *idea* of grief and tragedy, "making points" and ponging in the old declamatory style. Then, there was the sharp break at "Why, what an ass am I!" He started, appalled at the level to which he'd sunk. There he was, raving around the stage and *still had done nothing* about his father's murder. So, it went from amazement to the thought that "I am lower than the low" because I have cause for *real* feeling and I haven't done a *thing* about it, a feeling of futility about his own inaction which carried throughout all the soliloquies, even to the last.

That business about "Who calls me villain, breaks my pate across" harks back to playacting also. No one had pressured Hamlet, and he'd not convinced or moved one other person by revealing the true story of corruption in Denmark. If anyone had actually challenged me, I would have to "*take it*"—I would have to admit that I had not played my part very well. In this speech, the actor and the man Hamlet merged.

"O, what a rogue and peasant slave" was my favorite of the soliloquies because there was a lot of color in it, great possibilities and potentialities for acting.

"To be, or not to be" was yet another series of discoveries, the first of which was major and focused on the opening lines:

Jonathan and I felt that the point where the audience eavesdropped into Hamlet's mind was at the conclusion and not the beginning of a journey. In other words, when the audience saw him begin "To be," it was catching him after he'd been up all night thinking about his dilemma. He'd arrived at—not the answer—but after going round and round, he'd come to the fundamental *problem*. I remember when I came on to do this, I tried to give the feeling that I had been pacing around somewhere, thinking "I know what it is—it's the fact that I'm a coward. That's what it is. No, it's not, no. What it is is that I have a sexual problem—I need to get laid. Then I could understand—no, no, it's nothing to do with that. It is—that I hate women. No, no, no, I don't though." So when he came onstage and said, "To be, or not to be, *that* is the question! *That* is what I've been trying to find all night!" you can see that Jonathan and I definitely wanted to avoid the feeling of a set piece in speaking this speech.

In terms of the relative focus, this soliloquy started off very internalized, not looking at them at all. "To die, to sleep"—as if to say to himself, "What's dying about? Sleep, isn't it—no more than that." On that part, I lifted my head a up little more to include the audience, as if to question or to sound them out about this. "Everybody knows that—about sleep, when we end the heartache and the suffering and it's a nice anesthetic, isn't it? To die, to sleep. Uh, oh. To sleep, perchance to *dream*. Oh, no, there's the rub." "*There's* the respect"—I had great difficulty making sense of that line. At first I thought that respect caused calamities—which is an interesting idea—too much adherence to convention causes calamities and your life is ruined by formalities. But then I came up with "it's the dreams, the dreams, *there's* the respect that makes calamity of so long life."

What it all came back to was cowardice—because it's so simple to end life, so what stops us is—"I'm frightened." The whole natural logic of a very idealistic youth whipping himself for what he hasn't yet done in life—and also for his fears about death.

The final soliloquy was difficult for Lesser because it had more of a single message and was less histrionic than the others:

> Of all the soliloquies, I remember that "How all occasions" was the hardest, not because it's difficult but because the colors are less defined in it. The changes are less easy to negotiate. It's a bit boring because he's said an awful lot of it before. I always felt, as an actor, that the audience were saying, "Don't tell us once more that you're a strange sort of person for not doing anything, just *do something*!" This soliloquy was, for me, a lot of words with nothing behind them.

Because the soliloquies were so internal, the temptation would have been to depict a teenaged Hamlet who had gone off the deep end; however, Lesser eschewed the idea of a volatile and insane prince:

> I didn't take that stance because I think it is too easy an option. Hamlet is much more interesting if he has to deal with his problems within the framework of being an ordinary, normal, well-balanced person. Yes, his world has crashed, but it doesn't send him mad. I remember Jonathan talking about his view of madness. He felt that people don't just abruptly go mad. Ophelia was orchestrated to show that she had certain tendencies—right from the top she seemed an unstable lady, but she did not just suddenly go potty.

This production featured internalized soliloquies even though it was first performed on a three-quarter thrust stage, the kind of stage historically associated with direct-address soliloquies.[7] It then transferred to a larger, proscenium arch theatre, where, Lesser stated, the soliloquies became even more inward. The playing space, then, had little bearing on the performance mode selected. Interestingly, neither actor nor director found it necessary to explore Hamlet's madness, something well within the production's interpretative scope and easily reinforced by a Hamlet holding dialogue with himself. Both actor and director drew from a known convention and certainly Lesser, when he saw actors like Michael Pennington and Nicol Williamson perform direct-address soliloquies, knew that other options were available.

The lead actor was wary of being too easily led by a man most artists would label a "strong" (i.e., authoritarian) director and one known for implementing distinct visions or concepts within his Shakespeare productions. Lesser felt he had learned from his first experience of being directed by Miller and was determined to present an interpretation that flowed truthfully from within, not to have an idea externally imposed upon him. The production was, in the best sense, a collaboration. Miller envisioned in Lesser a very young Hamlet, one who could believably curl up in Gertrude's arms like a baby in the closet scene—and Lesser delivered that. His Hamlet was iconoclastic, also somewhat puerile and occasionally obstreperous. However, he did not become a rebel and bolt out of the play seeking solace and support from the audience. Instead, the focus was on adolescent emotional states and Romeo-like fluctuations of temperament, including periodic bouts of self-hatred. The soliloquies were designed to elucidate these character traits and not to create a rebel without a cause. A Claudius who was clearly overreaching the bounds of king and leader provided the youthful stepson a worthy opponent. This interpretation served the play and also preserved both Lesser's working processes and Miller's point of view.

David Rintoul teaches Hamlet *on an ACTER tour in 1986, when he also played the role. Photograph courtesy of ACTER, Santa Barbara, California.*

7

DAVID RINTOUL : *Th' Observ'd of All Observers*

British actor David Rintoul has numerous stage and television credits in London, including work at the Royal Shakespeare Company, the National Theatre, the Old Vic, and the BBC. He is a mainstay of the Association for Creative Theatre, Education, and Research (ACTER),[1] a U.S.-based international organization which tours American and British colleges and universities with master classes and productions of Shakespeare prepared by professional actors. Consequently, Rintoul has built part of his reputation as a classical actor within a select group of educational institutions across America.

ACTER is one of the most important pedagogical links ever forged between the study of Shakespeare and the study of performance. Because ACTER productions are often the first professional performances of Shakespeare that college students in the United States attend, the group is a strong influence in creating future audiences for Shakespeare in the United States. The organization is headed by Homer Swander at the University of California at Santa Barbara. ACTER was Swander's brainchild after summers of going to Shakespearean productions and discussing them with actors at the Dirty Duck in Stratford-upon-Avon, a theatrical hub near the Royal Shakespeare Theatre. Swander realized that performers provided a rich source of knowledge on Shakespeare's plays, so he assembled groups of actors (usually five at a time) to tour college campuses for eight weeks during the fall and spring semesters, staying on each campus for about a week. The group offers scene-study classes focused on Shakespeare's plays in performance, and they also give public presentations of them. Most actors who tour are British, and all have played leading roles with one of the major classical companies, the Royal Shakespeare Company or the Royal National Theatre. By the end of the eighties, after two decades of operation, more than one hundred actors and more than one hundred educational institutions had participated in this very successful venture. In addition, ACTER has spawned television projects, research conferences, numerous books and articles, summer tours, and vital liaisons with other professional theatre groups within the United States. ACTER is especially well known among academics in Shakespeare studies and has had the immediate and salutary effect of drawing closer together the research and teaching on Shakespeare at all instructional levels throughout the English-speaking world.

The ACTER plays that are performed on each campus are unique in that five actors perform an entire Shakespearean play by dividing up the roles and by utilizing a very streamlined production style. They also direct themselves. David Rintoul played Hamlet in a five-actor version of the play that toured American colleges and universities for eight weeks in the spring of 1986. It was offered, along with master classes, at the University of New Hampshire, Memphis State University, Goucher College, the University of Southern Maine, Lawrence University, La Salle College, Rice University, and Brandeis University, reaching a geographically varied selection of American audiences.

Although Rintoul had played numerous roles with ACTER, this was the first time he'd performed the lead in a full-length version of *Hamlet*. He was interviewed about this experience on January 18, 1988, in London. Rintoul opened with the comment that his prince was not traditional: "I played him as an angry, aggressive, keyed-up Hamlet—he certainly wasn't romantic or contemplative." Another aspect of the production was that it had to be portable. Since this, like all ACTER productions, was specifically prepared to travel to different locations and a variety of performance spaces, adaptability and flexibility were important to the enterprise. Rintoul explained:

First of all, the play was suggested by Patrick Stewart, one of the founders of ACTER, whom you may recognize from "Star Trek" on American television. He rang me up and said he thought this would be a good year to do *Hamlet*. And I said yes. Having got the play, we then cast it, which is a slightly different way of selecting plays—ordinarily, the five actors do it as a group after they sign on for that season's tour. However, it does happen that the first two or three people to commit themselves (in this case, Vivien Heilbron and myself) definitely become the nucleus. Then these select the other members of the group. So, you see, the process is organic right from the outset.

From then on, the five of us made all the directorial decisions. Also, there was doubling and tripling and quadrupling of roles. For example, I played four roles—Hamlet, Bernardo, Fortinbras, and Voltemand. Vivien Heilbron played Gertrude, Ophelia, the Player Queen, and also the odd soldier and messenger. John Burgess played Polonius, Gravedigger, Osric, and Norwegian captain. Philip Voss played Claudius, Ghost, Player King, and Michael Thomas played Laertes, Horatio, Rosencrantz, and even Guildenstern!

The play had to be ready to adapt to *any* performance space we encountered. In anticipation of that, we prepared it to be played in a twenty-foot square, marked out with tape, with a specific arrangement of chairs around the perimeter of the playing area. Any actor who was not "in the scene" at any given moment sat in one of the chairs. We also had two props tables around the edge, because we did decide to use a few selected stage properties in what is essentially not a very "proppy" play. We used a scarf, a prayerbook for Ophelia, letters—that sort of small hand prop. The props all fitted into one very small suitcase. The chairs occasionally came onstage into the performance space and helped to create a scene. For example, the grave was made of four chairs back to back, with Burgess standing in the midst of them digging a grave. So that when Laertes jumped into the grave, he jumped into the space between the chairs.

Furthermore, we tried to continue a stylistic unity with costumes that were all neutrally colored. I was in black, Philip had black trousers and a gray shirt, Vivien wore a white blouse and black skirt, Michael wore gray shirt and trousers, and John wore a gray jacket (up until the time that Polonius was killed). The costumes were all modern clothing of very simple styles. We also decided to go with no light changes at all and just use general lighting.

Those who have participated in ACTER projects verify that audiences accept all of the changes in personae as well as changes in locale. They adapt well and even enjoy the conundrum of identifying new characters as the actors assume their "doubled" roles. Of course, Shakespeare's "spoken decor" helps the audience in locating the various scenes in the play. In addition to these casting solutions, the play texts are somewhat edited for tour presentations:

> We made a decision to cut one hour out of what is usually a four-and-a-quarter-hour play because we knew about how long this five-actor version could hold the attention of college-level audiences. I did a completely instinctive and unscholarly actor's cut on a beach in Greece during a holiday before rehearsals began. I chose from the Arden, the Cambridge, the Penguin, and the Signet [editions], using a mixture of the four. When it came down to the crunch on textual decisions, I went with the Cambridge edition most often. I then marked out five scripts with the cuts I'd made. Soon after, all of the actors met as a group and talked about my suggested cuts, which were mostly done to get the ball rolling. These were negotiated among us, and some remained and some didn't. The interesting thing was, not having referred to Folio and Quarto[2] at all, we then went and *looked* at them. And a lot of the differences between the First Folio and the Second Quarto—the areas of discrepancy between the two scripts—were, in fact, often the areas that I had just instinctively cut.

Cuts were made "by committee" rather than by a director or dramaturg. Historically, this experience could lend credence to the theory that certain alterations were regularly made by Elizabethan actors to make the text more portable, perhaps to take it on extended tours.

A second group decision then had to be made about the dilemma of where to place the intermissions:

> We found a textual challenge in placing the interval—which is of fiendish difficulty in *Hamlet*. We tried one interval, we tried two intervals, we tried one long and one short, and we never got one which absolutely satisfied us. My first instinct was to have a single interval after "the play's the thing / Wherein I'll catch the conscience

of the King" (directly following the third soliloquy, "O, what a rogue and peasant slave am I!"). It's such a massive soliloquy, so tormented and passionate, so to place the interval after it would leave the audience wanting more. The downside was that "To be, or not to be" then fell very near the opening of the second half. It struck me as weird that Shakespeare had written those two great soliloquies so closely together! We then eliminated that interval, and I grew to love playing the cooler, more rational "To be" so soon after the emotional "O, what a rogue." We eventually narrowed our options to one interval only, (1) after the closet scene (my Hamlet's emotional high point and a ball-breaker of a scene to play), its disadvantage being that it breaks the flow of action as he goes off to England, or (2) after "How all occasions," a very natural completion but a hellishly long first half and tricky for Ophelia to kick off the second half with the mad scene. What did they do at the Globe!

Since there was no final directorial arbiter, one of the five actors (if free) could sit out front and look at what other actors were doing. However, Rintoul explained that that was rarely a possibility:

That was the hardest four weeks' rehearsal in my life—eight hours a day with five actors with pretty strong personalities. Of course, it had to be a fairly high-octane group to take on a play like *Hamlet*. Although we got along very well on the road and stayed together as a group, we argued quite heavily in rehearsals. But I was exhausted throughout rehearsals—I remember being just dead. You see, we'd all worked with really awful directors where we sat there and thought, "How much longer am I going to have to take all this worthless bullshit!" so that when you got the chance to make directorial contributions yourself, there was the danger that you would become the worst director that you'd ever worked with.

Rintoul stated that few of the adaptations the group had made for going on tour influenced the way he ultimately decided to perform the soliloquies. The soliloquies were determined to be Hamlet's territory, and the cast left him to make decisions about them:

I decided *not* to use a convention but to treat each one individually. In a funny sort of way, I felt nearer to Hamlet's true self speaking the soliloquies than in any other point in the play because the closest relationships in the play were all so complicated (except for Hamlet's with Horatio—that relationship was fairly straightforward). You felt that Hamlet was always doing something with the people onstage—protecting himself, being aware of being manipulated by them and even manipulating them, doing to people or being done to. The soliloquies were Hamlet talking to himself, and the experience of playing them was a release from all this other crap. He was less mad in the soliloquies somehow—he was less disturbed. Even though he lacerated himself in "Rogue and peasant slave," he was truer to his real feelings. In the solo speeches, he's not compromised, he's letting go, whereas the other relationships are jeopardized, flawed, difficult, twisted relationships. His relationship with the audience wasn't—it was absolutely straight. The audience was Hamlet's best friend in the same way that Horatio was; however, he didn't really talk with Horatio until after his return from England.

Rintoul felt a great deal of independence about sorting through the performance options and then making his selections. A well-educated and enormously articulate actor, always current on research and performance topics, he made a considered judgment:

How each soliloquy is performed, I feel, is a decision each actor has to make for himself. I remember at RADA, where I studied [the Royal Academy of Dramatic Art, London], we got a very, very eclectic kind of training, which was enormously helpful because you could take the best from each person. You got violent arguments between two members of the faculty who came from completely different camps—I mean a pure, obsessive Stanislavskyist versus a director trained at the Comédie Francaise. I remember an argument between two members of staff, one saying the soliloquy must always be a direct-address speech to the audience, eye contact with individual members of the audience, and another saying the soliloquy is not like that at all, you are bringing the audience into your imagination in an *un*focused way, so you are focused only on your own thoughts and you don't make eye contact with the audience. I hold neither position nor subscribe to either theory. I think the wonderful thing about playing *any* soliloquy—and Hamlet's in particular—is that you have the *choice*. You can vary it according to your instincts.

Besides, the soliloquies are all very different animals from each other. My instinct led me to do different things with each one. For example, the first soliloquy, "O that this too too solid flesh" (I chose to use "solid"), I never felt like giving directly to the audience. Most of that soliloquy was unfocused but trying to bring the audience into my head. At the other extreme, the final soliloquy, "How all occasions"—the whole of that was very, very much directed to the audience, with definite eye contact. "To be, or not to be" was more unfocused, and by that I hope you know I mean very *internalized*. It's the difference between "come here"—focusing inwardly and drawing the audience to you—and "listen to this"—direct address. So that "To be" was "come here" until "Thus conscience does make cowards of us all," which was direct-address. "O, what a rogue and peasant slave" was internalized at the beginning when I was lacerating myself. And then I had direct contact on "Why, what an ass am I!"—at that point, it became externalized. I made definite decisions about which lines were inward and which were directed outward. I am generalizing about how I *intended* to do them, of course, because so much of any performance is how I feel it in the moment.

Because we were on tour, I was not depending on the size or shape of the theatre to tell me how to do them—and I'm fairly sure I was consistent about how I did them. We did perform in wildly different houses—from Brandeis (over a thousand seats) to a lecture theatre of two hundred seats in Maine to the Guildhall studio [next to the Barbican Centre] for thirty or forty spectators.

In direct-address performance of the soliloquy, there is usually enough bounce off the lights so that you can pick out faces in the first ten rows. You definitely take them all in with a look and often move your head in order to pick out different people in the audience. Naturally, it would make one audience member nervous to be singled out and given the benefit of the whole speech, i.e., an entire soliloquy. I would also look out into the balcony and take in that audience—I suppose any actor would have an instinct for spreading it around the house.

Rintoul explained conscious technique in delivering solo speeches. He occasionally made accommodations in response to larger and smaller theatres, to different shapes and sizes of playing areas, and to varying acoustical challenges:

Adjusting to different performance spaces has to do with voice and technique. With experience, you know what it takes to play a particular house. You can misjudge, of course. A wonderful teacher at RADA called Maria Fedro (a Polish dancer originally) talked about "ze hook under ze bra strap." Imagine a hook under the front of your bra strap, from the base of the sternum, that helps you to accommodate to the size of the theatre. The bigger the house that you're playing—there's a slight millimeter of lift under the bra strap. And even if you are playing a collapsed character, don't completely collapse at the sternum. This is a wonderful image for actors, and it's a very small adjustment that I'm talking about. An actor of experience will walk around the stage and assess it, which is partly practical and partly mystical. Because of its extraordinarily wide stage opening, an actor can never really keep still in the Olivier [Theatre],[3] because you're not going to be able to take in the whole house [with your eyes]. Watch Michael Bryant, who is a master at that theatre. He is always slightly on the move, gently rotating his head like a radar disk.

Next, Rintoul discussed each of the seven soliloquies, describing how he performed them and what he intended to project as *meaning*. He also recounted how he made the transition into each. He saw the first soliloquy as related to the asides which preceded it:

During the court scene at I.ii prior to the first soliloquy, I experimented a bit with "A little more than kin, and less than kind." Sometimes I played it as an *aside*—"listen, audience, let me tell you something"—but more often I used it as dialogue and looked Claudius right in the eye to make a pun at his expense. I varied it a bit, but I quite liked it public, to him. (Of course in this production, you had to imagine members of the court present.) The other *aside*, "Not so, my lord, I am too much i' th' sun," I used as a very public put-down, so that the audience got the impression of Hamlet being a bad boy in front of everyone.

Also in this scene, Philip's [Claudius] instinct was always to come close to me, even occasionally to put his arm around me. I hated that, loathed it. Partly due to Claudius' physical proximity, but partly because my actor's instincts were screaming, "No, no—don't come near me. Keep this scene public." I was very strong on that and found it almost impossible to get the soliloquy started because I was so bound up with residual anger. He had played a very hearty Claudius who laughed off Hamlet's replies as if they were satisfactory to him. On his exit, he got a big laugh from the audience as he spoke about the king's rouse and about drinking in Denmark. So, at first I had a hard time cranking up on "O that this too too solid flesh." After a while, I really learned to work with it. I'd sit there and wait until the laughter completely died, let the pause happen a bit, and then I spoke—all of it to myself.

I performed the first soliloquy downstage left (within the square) because that's where I was after drawing back from Claudius and the court. I moved more to the center as the speech proceeded. There are some important audience issues in this scene. Claudius has been as charming as possible and conducted some very tricky business for the state—so that at this point audience allegiances between king and stepson were very mixed (especially to the uninformed audience). The first soliloquy was Hamlet establishing himself as the hero of the play, giving his own side of the matter, expressing disgust at Claudius, venting his anguished disappointment at his mother. A soliloquy is the direct theatrical equivalent to a cinema close-up— "let's see what this guy thinks"—which is why actors like them both so much. Notice, by the way, how *very few* of the lines in any of Hamlet's soliloquies are end-stopped: thoughts sweep on to the next line, reinforcing his emotional and intellectual quickness.

Before the first soliloquy and after a delayed entrance orchestrated by Shakespeare, Hamlet withheld commentary or emotion, so that the speech came out in a burst of pent-up fury. Nonetheless, the second soliloquy was even more emotional:

"O all you host of heaven!" was not done directly to the audience. I did it from center stage, kneeling—closing with "Adieu, adieu! remember me," and collapsing onto the stage. I loved saying "this distracted globe"—the triple resonance to his head, the Globe Theatre, and to the world. I stood up on "My tables—meet it is I set it down," and pulled out a small black notebook I had in my pocket.

The function of this soliloquy was very simple—it was to show the audience his reaction to his father's murder. This one provided a fuller release than the first one. And, I believe, cut Hamlet in two, and down the middle of him you will see that he believes that the Ghost was telling the truth from the start. The first thing he said to the others after its appearance was "It is an honest ghost, that let me tell you." Of course, there was a shade of doubt expressed, and that was in the first line, on "shall I couple hell?" Actors and scholars debate about whether Hamlet *genuinely* suspects the Ghost is a devil or whether he uses that doubt as a justification of his inaction. I chose the latter.

Here, he was not adjusting to the hurried funeral and the o'er-hasty marriage but to *murder* and to his mother's possible complicity in it. If the first soliloquy is like taking the lid off the pressure cooker, then the second one is attempting to put it back on—but it just won't go. He really lost it in this speech. And during the scene, his were wild and whirling words and he was all over the shop. His idea about the "antic disposition" came toward the end of the scene. His reasoning was that if he played mad, it would give him some control over circumstances and also a release from the immediate obligation of revenge.

Look at the line to the two lads right after the Ghost's appearance, "There's ne'er a villain dwelling in all Denmark / But he's an arrant knave." It's an incomplete line: "But he's an arrant knave" has only six beats, as opposed to the customary ten or eleven, which indicates the playwright is inviting you to pause either before or after the incomplete line. Lay a pause between "Denmark" and "But" and it suggests that Hamlet was going to say something else but changed his mind. In other words, he was about to reveal his knowledge of the murder to Horatio and Marcellus but decided against it. That, like the strange appearance in Ophelia's sewing closet, was a decision *not* to communicate. Hamlet had a number of attempts to communicate that got censored or somehow failed.

Rintoul sensed distinct tonal differences between the third and fourth soliloquies. He was very direct on the third soliloquy because of the abrupt stylistic change after "Oh Vengeance!" and also because he felt that the pattern of questions was most effective audience-addressed:

The third soliloquy, "O, what a rogue and peasant slave," I spoke from off-center right, ending up "Oh! Vengeance!" falling on my knees, downstage, not too far right. This was the one soliloquy I always dreaded because, for me, it was the most difficult to memorize and the most difficult to do. I always took a deep breath and thought, "Here we go!" It was partly because the speech was driven by such emotion, but it was also long and complex. "Am I a coward?"—most of that outburst I delivered straight to the audience. There is always a danger in direct address because if you catch somebody's eye, the person sitting there looks at you as if "Am I supposed to say something back to you?" I never got an audience member who talked back to me. However, I can imagine it happening!

I used the word "scullion" for "stallion."[4] And then came "About my brains!" as he had an *idea*—to confront Claudius with his guilt in the form of a play. However, the idea *wasn't* new. We'd already seen him in a prior scene ask a player to insert "a speech of some dozen lines, or sixteen lines" into *The Murder of Gonzago* play. In the soliloquy, I think you *have* to play "I'll have these players . . ." as if the idea had just that moment come to him. It seems like a cheat—perhaps it is Shakespeare making doubly sure the theatre audience was informed about Hamlet's tampering with the *Gonzago* play.

Rintoul performed "To be, or not to be" entering upstage left, from the same physical position as the first soliloquy. He noted that all the more reflective soliloquies were done from there. The decision was not conscious, however. The scene before and after the fourth soliloquy was one which was discussed frequently in master classes (in the various colleges) because Shakespeare had left a number of decisions up to the players:

Hamlet's emotion and his rationality take him very, very quickly in "To be" to "'tis a consummation / Devoutly to be wish'd. To die, to sleep—" which is his inclination was toward suicide—"I can't take what life has landed me with." He then proceeded to rationalize himself out of suicide—"undiscovered countries, yes, that's it, that's why I don't kill myself!" I would actually take myself away from the space [move to an entirely different place] in which I'd played and give the closing lines "Thus conscience does make cowards of us all" as if I'd just talked myself out of killing myself, as if distancing myself from the facility of rationalization and despising the quickness and agility of mind that I had just displayed.

Look at the end of "To be, or not to be," going into the nunnery scene. Did Hamlet know that he was being overheard by Claudius and Polonius, and if so, when and how did he realize it? As Hamlet you must decide at what point in the scene this has happened. Of all the scenes in the play, this one was perhaps richest with performance options. It was a scene we often worked with in master classes because it offered so many possibilities. The ending lines go like this:

And enterprises of great pitch and moment	85
With this regard their currents turn awry	86
And lose the name of action.—Soft you now!	87
The fair Ophelia! Nymph, in thy orisons	88
Be all my sins rememb'red.	89

Say Hamlet chooses to see Claudius and Polonius sneaking into position behind the arras at this point. You have the choice of saying, "Soft you now!" either to Ophelia, as I did, or to the audience as I saw her coming onstage. Now, if you choose to see them sneaking, there isn't enough *acting time* to do all you've got to do without breaking up the verse in the most extraordinary way. You have to play it "and lose the name of action"—*pause, stop, think*—which takes a long time. And then you've got a line directed to her: "Nymph, in thy orisons," et cetera. What I'm arguing is that line 87 is an enjambed line and that the verse structure is too tight for you to enact seeing Polonius and Claudius at *that* point. The verse is saying to you: "Don't try to do stage business on that line." At least, that's my theory.

As the scene progresses, there are several other opportunities to see them. I chose not to look at people rustling around behind arrases but to see Claudius and Polonius in Ophelia's eyes. Hamlet must know that there was something weird going on because suddenly Ophelia's been loosed to him after being forbidden his presence. There are a couple of verse breaks early on in the nunnery scene—line 95 after Hamlet says, "I never gave you aught" is an incomplete line. There is a pause after that phrase, look for it, and if it's psychologically right, take it. It could be either Hamlet's pause or Ophelia's, because Hamlet could pause after "No, not I," which precedes it on line 94. If it's Ophelia's, she would pause after Hamlet utters, "I never gave you aught" and before she answers, "My honor'd lord, you know right well you did." This second choice is the one we played. It made psychological sense to us. She had the letter in her hand, so the pause was valid for her to take.

These are the kinds of knotty problems we discuss in the master classes. Students get very involved in the arguments about performance choices.

The fifth soliloquy, "'Tis now the very witching time of night," was connected with the previous play-within-the-play scene:

"Witching time" especially relates because Hamlet now knew of Claudius' guilt and so he delivered this Macbeth-type windup to himself. However, he did not conclude "now to my stepfather to put an end to him," but rather "Soft, now to my mother."

For the sixth soliloquy, "Now might I do it pat," I came on from upstage right because it had to look as if I was traveling to my mother's closet and then saw the king. On "now I'll do't," I was fairly well center stage. I had a sword for this one and pointed it toward Claudius on "This physic (meaning this praying that you are at) but prolongs thy sickly days." A prop in my hand genuinely changed the quality of the rationalization. It was also needed because of the dialogue in the closing beat of the soliloquy, "Up, sword." I left that scene with the sword sheathed in the holder on my trouser belt. Many Hamlets go directly into the closet scene with sword in hand, which works to frighten Gertrude into speaking her lines. I did not do that, however; I drew it afresh once in her chamber.

Rintoul viewed the last soliloquy as a kind of summation and farewell to the interaction he'd had with the audience. For him, it was an occasion for a speech about man in general and then a thoughtful and determined public statement:

> For the final soliloquy, "How all occasions," I was absolutely bang stage center. That is such an extraordinarily ironic speech in that Hamlet has absolutely made up his mind, "To hell with all this, I'm going to do it," and then gets on a boat to England! One of my favorite illustrations of irony and ambiguity is the line "Led by a delicate and tender prince, / Whose spirit with divine ambition puff'd." The choice of those three words "divine," yes, "ambition," yes—Fortinbras the absolute model for what Hamlet should be, but then look at the verb "puff'd"—so what *are* we to make of Fortinbras, this great male model? I played the line "The imminent death of twenty thousand men" very cynically, as if to say, "The world is very screwed up—what am I doing here anyway?" There are lots of options on those lines: you could play them very quietly, as if this were a farewell to his former self. The soliloquies end after this one because Hamlet finally knows where he's at. "How all occasions" was my favorite because it was the last and it was the simplest and I did it the best. It's the speech in the most sustained major key, if you like. What is a man—someone who sees his line of action and goes for it like Fortinbras, or someone who constantly asks questions?

Rintoul rejected the use of a convention, i.e., that an inward soliloquizer signaled one kind of Hamlet and a direct-address soliloquizer another kind. Instead, he subscribed to a method of working from textual moment to textual moment as a way of deciding on the performance mode of each. He did not pre-plan a character conception—e.g., a near-insane inner-directed Hamlet—and then play all the soliloquies to fit that image. Instead, the characterization and modes of delivery evolved in rehearsal, an autonomous and self-reliant choice:

> I make decisions about a soliloquy as I encounter them. Giving a soliloquy in an "inward" way will necessarily give the impression of detachment and introspection whereas direct address is energizing to both actor and audience in that it gives the impression of public debate. Unless you subscribe to a theory about exclusively using one or the other method, text plus actor's instinct will determine which

you prefer to use. For example, "O heart, lose not thy nature!" (III.ii.393) seems to be a fairly obvious candidate for inward delivery, whereas "What is a man, / If his chief good and market of his time / Be but to sleep and feed?" (IV.iv.33−35) wants to be put directly to the audience.

Rintoul had also listened to many theories about speaking Shakespearean verse. From a great deal of discussion with actors, directors, professors, and students, he felt that a few simple guidelines kept recurring and were thus useful and serviceable:

> Here is the theory that I do believe (but, of course, all rules can be bent). One, Shakespeare should be played on the line at a good lick, a good pace: if you can get away without taking a pause when playing Shakespeare, great; if you can pick up the cues sharpish, not pause, and respect the line of the verse, great. Two, respect the last word in every verse line. Even if the line is not end-stopped, the last word has a special place in the meaning and in the poetry. In that same example I just used, "What is a man . . ." it's perfectly possible to run that on and speak it as prose. Try that. But the second time, pick out "man" and "time" and not only does it *become* poetry but the *question* somehow takes on its proper weight. Three, if you've got an incomplete line, have a look and see if that is not Shakespeare's way of saying "take a pause here." It's mostly a matter of remembering that there are options in playing lines in Shakespeare.

This last statement places David Rintoul in the vanguard of twentieth-century performance criticism. He is firmly rooted in the idea of rehearsal as an exploratory process. Of course, at a certain point, an actor has to choose what he intends to make his lines *mean*. However, his final choices must be defensible from a performance point of view: the meanings must have an aesthetic coherence as well as a logical meaning; the meanings must relate to the Hamlet characteristics he has chosen to feature in his acting of the role, as well as to the whole production style; and finally, the choices must "work" in a theatrical sense.

This principle of opening up performance options is counter to academic methods of writing criticism on the subject of, say, what Hamlet means in "To be, or not to be." Academics give a reading, then defend it in scholarly argument. Actors test several meanings and then apply a number of practical and aesthetic criteria before choosing. Generally, they find it limited and counterproductive to omit the practice of suggesting and exploring a wide number of choices. That exploration is a vital part of preparing to perform, an imperative in studying Shakespearean texts:

> Shakespeare's ambiguity is often deliberate, part of his art. For example, when I preferred "*solid* flesh" to "*sullied* flesh," there is very little difference in English and American pronunciations, so some part of the spectator's brain will have to ask which it heard. What I'm saying is that you get both meanings anyway. The poet is always asking you to reassess the characters and their actions. William Shakespeare: "Hamlet should be a revenger? I'll show you revengers. Here's Laertes, shouting his head off and manipulated by a clever politician like Claudius. Here's Fortinbras (fort-en-bras, strong-arm), "a delicate and tender prince"? Is Hamlet like these two revengers? Of *course* Shakespeare's ambiguous. He's a game player, playing with our minds. Which allows scholars such a rich divergence of opinion and actors such a multitude of choices!

One of the most valuable aspects of the ACTER tours is the constant evaluation juxtaposed with the interplay of text and performance. ACTER groups have been enormously important in widening the boundaries of interpretative discussions. Allowing actors an arena in which to articulate and defend has reestablished them as artists with reason and capability, rather than as people who perform for personal display or to sell tickets. Actors respect the text, an inheritance earned from their own performance history; however, they also view it as a tool for enactment.

Finally, Rintoul makes a strong case for the actor's independence from a director. He eschewed the selection of a "safe" mode of performing the soliloquies which would accommodate his tour—i.e., delivering all of the soliloquies internally would relieve him of having to negotiate each playing space afresh, as he encountered it. Here was an actor who literally declined conventions, who had both methods laid out in training: he was schooled and knew the options. He refused to be boxed in by fashion or tradition and chose to consider each speech individually. Unscathed by a number of encounters with professors, students, and critics, Rintoul emerged stimulated and enriched—and certainly ready to talk and argue again. Furthermore, his sense of humor remained intact:

Speaking of scholars, did I ever tell you that I almost cut John Dover Wilson's head off in *Henry IV, Part I*? I was portraying the Douglas in an English department version of the play, and I have to say that in this production the fights were rather underrehearsed. Wilson was at Edinburgh University when I was there, and he was very old by then. He was treated, of course, with enormous respect. We were in Pollock Hall, an old wooden lecture hall, a semicircular space with banked seating. He sat in the middle of the front row. He'd done an edition of the play and was making quiet comments to himself about the play all the way through the performance. At one point, I got wildly out of position and drew my sword back. I was far too near the front row of the audience, and 'tis said that everyone seated there ducked as the sword passed over their heads. Professor Wilson wisely bowed as well. However, the idea of actually decapitating the great John Dover Wilson—I have this horrifying image of a wizened old head lying on the stage, still muttering about our performance, attached only to the body by the means of his deaf-aid cord!

Randall Duk Kim in Hamlet, *1987. Photograph by Zane B. Williams.*

8

RANDALL DUK KIM : *Sir, a Whole History*

Randall Duk Kim is a Hawaiian American who has played Hamlet in the woodlands of Wisconsin. The American Players Theatre in Spring Green, Wisconsin, which Kim helped to establish in 1979, is typical of the regional Shakespearean festivals that have sprung up in the United States since the thirties. Cofounders of this summer theatre festival are Charles Bright, who manages, Anne Occhiogrosso, who acts and directs, and Kim himself, who was artistic director as well as its lead player. These three determined people spent years searching for the perfect site for their classical theatre. Finally they found it in a bowl-shaped outdoor arena planted firmly on seventy-one acres of timbered farmland near Frank Lloyd Wright's home Taliesin in Wisconsin, thirty miles west of Madison. The site even had a farmhouse and a converted barn in which they could set up shop. The American Players Theatre has drawn audiences from around the midwestern United States, as well as interested Shakespeareans from both coasts. A cadre of faithful volunteers, along with grant funding and the unflagging industry of its casts and crews, have helped to keep a mid-June through mid-October season afloat.

Kim's path to Wisconsin was certainly not direct:

The first time I played Hamlet was for the Honolulu Theatre for the Youth in 1977! I'm the odd one in my family, the only one to become an actor. My relatives were somewhat appalled in the beginning. They were concerned that I couldn't earn my living at acting. Given my race, they were worried that I wouldn't fit into the structure of theatre in the United States. But I was determined and I loved Shakespeare's plays, which have guided me for many years.

I've not had much formal acting instruction. What I know of acting has been learned through experience on the stage. I started when I was a senior in high school and our community theatre happened to be doing *Macbeth*. We'd just studied the play in class, and I was intensely curious to see how they would mount it. I screwed my courage to the sticking place and went to auditions. I was really frightened; nevertheless, I got cast as Malcolm. Next, I acted in a number of plays at the University of Hawaii. I then went to New York to begin work as a professional actor. I vowed that during the summers, I would leave New York to work with a Shakespeare festival. The Champlain Shakespeare Festival in Vermont hired me for three seasons. I had a shot at major roles like Titus Andronicus and Richard III. My chief interest throughout my career has been performing in classical plays, especially Shakespeare.[1]

Kim has played in more than a hundred productions since his debut in 1961, working at the American Conservatory Theatre (Richard III), the New York Shakespeare Festival (Pericles), Direct Theatre (Richard II), Guthrie Theatre (Hamlet), American Place Theatre, Yale Repertory Theatre, Baltimore Centre Stage, the Indiana Repertory Company, the Arizona Theatre Company, and many others. Based in Spring Green since 1979, Kim lengthened his flourishing list of classical characters with Petruchio, Falstaff, Shylock, Hamlet, Malvolio, Puck, Prospero, Tamburlaine, and Oedipus. One of the significant moments of his career was playing the role of King Lear under the direction of Morris Carnovsky and Phoebe Brand at the American Players Theatre in 1987.[2] Kim has literally forged a classical actor's career out of the regional companies and festivals in the United States.

Kim saw his earlier involvements with the role of Hamlet as preparatory for the definitive version he and Anne Occhiogrosso created for Spring Green audiences:

In my earliest attempt I found myself playing a very angry young man with a bitter sense of humor, a mean-minded cynic with tunnel vision. Slowly, I found my way around to a character who is a much more generous and three-dimensional spirit, whose death leaves a void in the world.

His appearance in the role at the Guthrie Theatre in 1978 was an important step in helping him define the later Hamlet:

It was an opportunity to become more familiar with the play. It was not the most important Hamlet that I did (despite the praise for my performance) because production-wise there were just too many things lacking. Our director had never done Shakespeare and announced that unnerving fact at the first rehearsal. The play was very chopped up—cuts were made when the actors were not meeting the challenge of the lines. Important pieces went—including much of the plotting scene between Laertes and Claudius. The reason given was that the play was too long and the audience would not tolerate it.

The directorial choices were not solid. One that somewhat typifies the production was during the dumb show when the poisoner mimed taking dog poop off of his shoe and flung it into the king's ear. There was also a lot of Freudian stuff injected into the relationship with Gertrude. And finally, I was encouraged to manhandle Ophelia and Gertrude, a more violent playing of the scene in which both women became hysterical. I had to shake them physically and throw them about—I even slapped Gertrude in the closet scene. It so offended me that from that point on, I simply felt that the character of Hamlet would never do such a thing. It was abhorrent and wrong and certainly against the basic character conception that was evolving from me. There is enough violence in the play without adding to it extratextually. The Guthrie experience was one in which arguments about text could not be opened—questions we had about performance choices got lost in all the hysteria.

Reviewer David George seconded this opinion in *Shakespeare Quarterly*:

The most striking feature of the Guthrie's *Hamlet*—its first since Sir Tyrone Guthrie opened the theatre with it in 1963—was its lead player, Randall Duk Kim. He is a diminutive Hawaiian (of about five feet four inches) of Korean-Chinese descent, thirty-five years old, and he has a pure, sculpted diction, entirely American. Duk Kim is a deeply committed and reverent Shakespearean performer, a man who in the opinion of his previous *Hamlet* director, Wallace Chappell,[3] is "one of the best actors in the country doing Shakespeare, if not in the English-speaking world" (*Minneapolis Star*, 18 August 1978). . . . As there was something amiss with all the rest of the principals' performances, I shall devote most space to the superior acting of Duk Kim and the peculiar odds against which this was achieved.[4]

Kim felt that his Hamlet at the festival in Wisconsin was the culmination of a decade of thinking about the role and examining what ought to go into it, given his own histrionic potentialities and his intellectual responses to the script. There, he was aided and directed by his longtime colleague in the Spring Green venture, Anne Occhiogrosso. Occhiogrosso directed the production that ran in 1987 and 1988.

> Annie and I had been working on *Hamlet* for a long, long time. We worked together on it in Hawaii, and she elected to direct the production at APT. Annie has always been on a quest, asking questions that made us understand what was going on in the play at any given moment. She would raise difficult issues. She expected us to look at all the source materials. We *had* to work out difficult passages—we couldn't slough them off or gloss over them. Since it is essential in Shakespeare to know the words you are speaking, we had lexicons and OED's [Oxford English Dictionary] and variorums. We were *required* to do our homework. She wanted us to know something of the history and the times in order to feed our imaginations. In rehearsals, we tried each scene a number of different ways and attempted to solve the performance problems as best we could by mutual agreement. We rarely had standoffs. Agreements were more common because we all had the same objective.

Together, Kim and Occhiogrosso evolved a philosophy about playing Shakespeare that grew out of their joint theorizing and experience with his plays. Their views about performance were steeped in Shakespearean and Renaissance origins, revealing a humanistic sense of history and a deep respect for tradition:

> We immersed ourselves in history in order to find our root system. Shakespeare's plays came out of a group of people who were earning

their living at it. We investigated Shakespeare's theatre, the society and culture that influenced him, Elizabethan life, his own sense of history and what he learned from the *Chronicles*, from Plutarch, from Saxo-Grammaticus. The story of Amleth as told in Belleforest's translation of Saxo-Grammaticus gave us insights into such matters as Gertrude's importance, Hamlet's madness, and the nunnery scene.

Such a historical approach was distinctly against the trend in the seventies, an era still heavily influenced by the sixties' notion of "relevance" in Shakespearean performances and throughout which there was a proliferation of "concept" productions. Asked if he believed in this practice of stylizing a Shakespearean production, tying it to a period, to some controlling design idea, or to a modern ideology of the twentieth century, Kim replied:

I find "relevance" limiting as a guiding principle. It is an approach that too often imposes upon the play something that distorts it. What I want to do is to learn from these plays. I confess right at the top that I don't know them and I want to see truly the inherent greatness of them, why they remain mysterious and fascinating. I don't want to lose any thread in the tapestry of the play. I won't simplify it nor cramp it by imposing a single concept on it. I want the play to reveal its complexity, richness, depth, all of its dimensions. I want to grapple with it in its own terms and its own fullness.

In fact, I find "concept" productions difficult to appreciate. When I get involved in them as an actor, I feel as if I am not learning anything about the play, especially if the play is cut to fit the concept, which it usually is. I learn a great deal about the concept though—a waste of time if I have cut out pieces of text and then imposed material on the play that may be relevant to us but totally irrelevant to Shakespeare. That method seems so narcissistic to me. What is passed on to the audience is not what the playwright has written nor how he has shaped his work of art but rather what the director's opinion is, his judgment of what is relevant for our time and what he thinks the audience can understand. I have heard of a production where King Lear steps out of a Cadillac—why? How does that serve the play? Why do we have to see these plays *in our own image*? How can we possibly affirm our common humanity with those who came before if we insist on viewing them with a limited vision? In trying to understand the life of another culture, another time, must not the effort be in trying to see that life on its own terms?

I want to find out what people thought, felt, the philosophic framework of the playwright's time. Great plays are *already* relevant, and you don't have to bash the audience over the head with something novel. I treat the script like a score, attempting to play it as the composer wanted it played. I want to see *Julius Caesar* done in Roman times, to see that terrible event unfold. I don't need to see a man get shot down by machine guns to make that leap about assassination. That's part of the delight of the theatre when it transports us to other places and times. Staying within the period that Shakespeare wrote into the plays unlocked worlds where my imagination could revel and live.

So, you see, relevance has far more to do with being able to recognize the human condition of, say, tenth-century Denmark. *Of course* we can identify with Hamlet—as a soldier, scholar, lover, son, prince, man, human being. What he undergoes tells us that there is nothing petty about unrequited love, suffering, murder, damnation. These universals need no updating.

When asked how he would respond to the probable charge that his convictions about history would surely result in the mounting of "museum pieces," Kim replied,

I love museums! Museums are not merely places where dead things are collected. They tell us something exciting about life as it has been lived. The past is not something we can put away and forget. Our ancestors were more than barbarians or savages. We have a great deal to learn from them. Here is a generation that has never seen a Shakespeare play as a story from a period long ago and far away. In the theatre we have a chance to do storytelling at its most basic, a handing down of history and myth. I prefer not to manipulate the audience into thinking my thoughts about the piece; I want them to think for themselves. I see myself as a transmitter. Let those who want to innovate do so, but I like looking into the past. That's very Confucian, by the way. To treat the past with some reverence for how others lived their lives.

In the theatre, there must be a clear moral sense that has been informed with humankind's history. We must be willing to grapple with truth and beauty and what those ideas mean. Otherwise, the theatre is just a commodity. You cannot place a dollar value on plays that deal with life-and-death issues. If theatre doesn't recognize and publicly examine larger issues, then I am afraid for our young ones. If their heroes are Superman and Batman and Ninja Turtles, how are they going to deal wisely with good and evil and human suffering? I'd much rather they watched a human being of Hamlet's caliber encounter the afflictions of life. A Superman or a Batman will bash someone, wipe him out, kick ass, and not suffer the consequences of what that means—a comic-book problem-solving. On the stage, characters like Prometheus, Oedipus, Antigone, Faust are either being neglected or, if given any attention, being twisted to fit some narcissistic view that seeks only to confirm who we are now while disengaging us from our ancestors. It's a very selfish cultural mind-set—me-me-me and what-I-want-now prevents us from delving into the past and advancing wisely into the future. We will sever our historical roots—and we will imperil ourselves and our society.

The Spring Green philosophy thus encouraged a study of the past, including, of course, the theatrical tradition. Kim's models of Hamlet came from the annals of theatre history:

I think that Edwin Booth was the finest Hamlet this country has produced—very advanced for his time. We dug around in the research, seeing what others—Henry Irving, Johnston Forbes-Robertson, E. H. Sothern, even Julia Marlowe[5]—had brought to the role. We looked at scholars to see what they had to say about the play—Roland Frye's *The Renaissance Hamlet* was very good, and Eleanor Prosser's *Hamlet and Revenge* helped us; also Bernard Grebanier's *The Heart of Hamlet*. Joseph Campbell's voice was important. The whole process consisted of asking questions and then looking at a broad range of answers. We felt that knowing what others had done before us *expanded* our choices. From something so small as a bit of business used in *Hamlet*—the deciding factor being "does it reveal or obscure a moment?"—we found our options.

Defining the past as central and indispensable to the theatre company's outlook determined a number of the basic operational premises of the organization. Hamlet's famous remark about "Words, words, words" became paramount. A certain way of exploring the text was essential to their process:

> The text of the play is *the whole of our ground*. Actors have to read and know the whole play, not just the scenes they are in: otherwise, you will only be playing your role and never know how it fits in with the others. Actors have to mine the dialogue in order to provide themselves with a map of performance. There is no relief from getting in there to find out what Shakespeare wrote *and* what goes on that is unspoken. There are big hunks of ambiguity—under the tip of the dialogue iceberg there is a whole bottom section and you've got to explore all of it to posit your performance choices.

Second, locating the most "authentic" version of the text was essential. Fitting into that quite logically was the policy of playing a Shakespearean text in its entirety and generally eschewing undue pruning of the script. Kim and Occhiogrosso chose the First Folio as the authoritative version of *Hamlet*:

> We sat down one night and read the Good [Second] Quarto and felt it was a difficult performance text. We wanted a complete text but one in which the line of action was clear. I feel that Shakespeare was present when cuts were made for the version that showed up in the Folio. It took Shakespeare's players time to get that play out. Over the years, they streamlined it to a more playable and active performance text. In our final version, we used the Folio text in its entirety with some additions from the Second Quarto. For example, we used "hoist on their own petar," just to elaborate that moment where Hamlet was betrayed by friends—to show he's already having to make kingly decisions. He learned that innocent people could be pawns.
>
> Once you've decided to do a "for real" version of Shakespeare, drawing on these original sources gives you strong guidelines for your work. We went to the First Folio also out of pure sentimental love for the actors who loved Shakespeare so much that they bound

his plays together. How close they must have been—sharing both success and failure! When you chose to do theatre back then, you chose a very difficult life.

The dictum regarding cuts in the text of the play was very specific. Also, the original texts were used as aids in speaking the lines:

Here at Spring Green, we don't cut. We say to ourselves—well, okay—we may not have succeeded in that specific moment, but we're not going to edit the script. Everyone will suffer through it, in rehearsal especially, until we understand how each line fits into the play. The playwright has stitched the play in a particular way—we will not deepen our understanding of the play if we snip away at the subject we are studying. Cutting is practiced in theatres all the time—either because the play is too long or because the actors cannot manage the lines. Those are the wrong reasons to cut. If the play is too long, start earlier in the evening and make an event of it—or don't do that play! In fact, I cannot *find* any good reasons to cut Shakespeare: it's like rearranging the arm position of Michelangelo's *David* or touching up Beethoven's Ninth Symphony.

In our *Hamlet*, we took courage from the Forbes-Robertson version, which Shaw commented about in a review, how wonderful it was to see it uncut. The running time, if one *indulges* oneself, can reach four and a half hours, but if you do not belabor it and "speak trippingly," you can play it uncut in three and a half hours (which ours was). As Hamlet, once you *commit*, your only obligation is to be strongly hooked into the action so that it pulls you along. Just plunge into it and be taken.

We looked very carefully at the Folio punctuation and also the capitalization of certain words, memorizing from facsimiles of the First Folio rather than from typed scripts. These seemingly picky details are part of the clues, part of the score. I suspect that punctuation back then was more closely allied with speech than it was with grammar as such. Punctuation marks are there to tell the actor when to breathe, how long a "full thought" is. Punctuation also tells you when a thought leaps ahead, when the new thought comes in. For example, in the Folio, because those lines in "What a piece of work is a man?" and "How noble in reason?" have questions marks following each phrase, I played them by leaving the ends up in the air to express doubt, as if asking, "Are men really like this?"

Furthermore, we don't follow the pentameter so closely that we pause at the end of each line, because following the punctuation often requires that you go beyond the end of a line to deliver a full thought. The pentameter is always there, it is your heartbeat, naturally built in without belaboring it—unless, of course, a particular point is to be made or special emphasis given. The pentameter operates on a subtler level than punctuation: you don't read *for* the meter, you read for the sense of the line. The object is to pull the audience into the event, not to call their attention to the poet's techniques. You want to give the illusion that the characters are creating the dialogue in the heat of the moment, not reciting something memorized.

We have just a few weeks of rehearsal, and we don't expect the best on opening night—it will be in whatever rough shape it is. As the run goes on and the play stays in our repertory, we continue to work on it, getting rid of bad ideas, incorporating new insights.

Kim's ideas about the character of his Hamlet were shaped as a result of much direct experience with the role and a good deal of research and contemplation:

Hamlet was a highly sensitive and keenly intelligent human being. He was also very aware of his own limitations—we hear that very powerfully in the soliloquies. His vision was moral and humane, his conscience ever engaged and demanding. He was essentially an active man, even in contemplation. He was passionate and knew the drawbacks—that touching moment when he expressed his love for Horatio and praised him as one who was *not* passion's slave. Passion was a very important element in my performance because it accounted for the many impulsive things Hamlet said and did.

From the beginning of the play to its very end, Hamlet struggled to govern the hellish feelings which threatened to overwhelm him. After the play within the play, this struggle was most intense. When Hamlet had the chance to kill the praying Claudius, he restrained his passion for vengeance in favor of a deeper damnation of his foe in the "Now might I do it pat" soliloquy. Had he killed Claudius then, he would have doomed him and averted the terrible deaths to follow. Immediately following this scene, Hamlet entered his mother's room, where he blindly and savagely killed an eavesdropper behind the arras—not Claudius but Polonius—the wrong man! He recognized in himself a furious capacity to destroy and his repentance was profound.

I felt a strong sense of nobility and virtue about the man. He had enormous moral courage as well. What his father's ghost demanded had cosmic implications and forced him to the brink of damnation. He had to avenge his father and to punish the *secret* murder of a king. His fulfillment of the ghostly command was more than private vendetta—the entire state was threatened. Through the play-within-the-play device, Hamlet made the murder public by openly accusing Claudius of poisoning old Hamlet. Whether or not the court (and Gertrude as well) perceived the accusation was an important directorial decision for us.

So there was this Hamlet who took stabs in the dark, trying to fix things, constantly and wildly searching for clear evidence of his uncle's guilt and for the moment to take action. In conflict with this was his keen awareness of the philosophic and spiritual implications of his actions. He entered at the duel scene having passed through crushing agonies of conscience. His father's command was now in the hands of Providence and Hamlet must wait. We must all learn this universal lesson—to wait for the event to unfold itself instead of jumping to inappropriate action. He began the last scene of the play thinking, "I simply have to be present and prepared to act. I shall wait for the moment to find me rather than my finding the moment. The readiness is all."

Hamlet died a king at the end of the play. His last thoughts were for his country and his people. When he dies, the audience must feel as if an extraordinary spirit has departed the world and left a void.

The production design itself was a combination of medieval fantasy and tenth-century Denmark created by Budd Hill, a designer of extensive experience and a partner in American Players Theatre since its first season. Kim's costume was an austere black velvet tunic with a wrought silver belt. The thrust stage of the simply constructed outdoor theatre represented a neutral playing space where Shakespeare's spoken decor was allowed to do its work. Simple architectural features, such as archways and levels, could be added to provide a balcony and a diversity of entrances and exits which created changes of locale. An interesting feature of the *Hamlet* set design was three large tapestrylike paintings (*Cain and Abel* for the lobby of the castle at Elsinore, *The Last Judgement* for the great hall, and *The Annunciation* for Gertrude's chamber) created by Wisconsin iconographer David Giffey, who paints murals for American and European churches. They were intended to look as if they might have hung in the castle at Elsinore and to underscore the play's spiritual concerns.

Kim's philosophy about the delivery of soliloquies remained flexible, since there is no direct evidence about how Shakespeare's players actually performed them: "I don't think of the soliloquies as *needing to be done* in one specific way or the other. There are no set rules about performance, only options." He chose, however, to perform most of them direct-address to the audience:

I think it was the thrust stage. I've often wondered how the physical plant [the arrangement of the performance space] affected the play that was being written for it. In rehearsal, we often ran onto what seem to be misplaced stage directions in the text that might indicate how far upstage or downstage characters were from one another. Whenever I do a Shakespearean play, I ask myself what Shakespeare's actors might have done at the Globe. My experience with working on a thrust stage has led me to believe that Shakespeare would have taken full advantage of the special actor-audience spatial relationship that operates in such a theatre by permitting characters to talk to the public naturally and directly—especially since many of the plays took place in daylight, as many of ours did at Spring Green.

On a thrust stage, I felt strongly encouraged to directly speak the soliloquies, to share my thoughts and feelings with the audience. They were almost on three sides of me [on slightly raised bleachers] and I felt an "all-togetherness" as they encircled me. I could see individuals, both at the sides and out front, even at night, and I "worked the house" because I wanted everyone to feel included—to feel like a crucial participant in the event unfolding before them.

It was a practical solution that gave an almost shocking imme-diacy and a highly charged vitality to the performance. Partly, this directness came from attitude toward the audience: I treated them as equals, even something more intimate, as friends. They were my confidants, as if I were talking to my own soul but it happened to be located in the bodies out front. They had seen things *beyond* what the characters onstage had seen.

Proscenium arch stages are entirely different—there is a dark-ness—the audience is part of a big black hole out there as you try to look at them from the stage. You are removed, detached, cut off. The audience observes on one side of the room and you are part of a happening occurring at the other. The picture frame acts as a separation.

I have often wondered how the performing of Shakespeare's plays on proscenium stages has affected the way we handle the soliloquies.

Kim felt that his directness with the audience reinforced his conception of the character of Hamlet:

It pulled the audience closer to him. It showed that he had the ca-pacity to display his feelings. He could speak to them as human beings who understood his dilemmas. He shared his struggle in de-fining his role as a revenger. They shared his painful wrestling with deep emotions.

You see, I don't think Hamlet goes mad, and I don't think the audience thinks he goes mad. If anything, he's *too* sane. The direct-address soliloquy has a way of confirming his sanity. After the Ghost scene, Hamlet said that he would put an antic disposition on, which I conveyed with an unkempt and negligent appearance. I didn't play for madness but walked a tightrope with a witty and scathing hon-esty. Look at Titus Andronicus—I suspect he went over the edge. His vengeance was horrible and insane, a case of the madman play-ing mad—a warrior's mentality with the capability for violence built in. Hamlet's mind focused on kingship and leadership. All the people we love and trust in the play—Ophelia, Horatio, the soldiers, the players—perceived Hamlet as someone to admire. The play isn't just the story of a man who could not make up his mind—look what he had to make up his mind *about*!

Kim discussed each of the soliloquies in turn, pointing out important interpretative aspects of his performance of them:

The first soliloquy was my favorite, played with a long and sustained sadness. It expressed Hamlet's moral outrage and the sorrow that came from discovering that the world was not what it seemed to be. It was the beginning of maturity, a shedding of a naïveté about life.

Very much in touch with his feelings, he could speak his first soliloquy simply, directly, to express his shock about the recent marriage. It was a moral offense, happening too quickly after the funeral. This was the lowest emotional ebb he could reach—overwhelming disillusionment and despair. It was the very first mention of suicide: "Or that the Everlasting had not fix'd / His canon 'gainst self-slaughter!"

Since it was the first time we see Hamlet alone, I liked to offer a somewhat comfortable visual stereotype of Hamlet the melancholic—to fulfill a few standard expectations of his look in costume and makeup. It helped put the audience at ease. As the story progressed, they traveled the real adventure with Hamlet revealed as more than stereotype. The peeling away of layers created surprise and fascination. Hamlet was not by nature a melancholic—circumstances brought him to that state.

In the first soliloquy, I also began to set up for direct address by finding phrases in the speech that could be spoken to the audience—a gradual initiation. It was not totally direct address but an outward sharing of an inward working-out of feelings. The concluding lines were less direct.

The second soliloquy was the taking of a vow to right the wrong of a secret crime committed by a kinsman who was also the current king of Denmark. Hamlet was wildly emotional about the Ghost's revelation. Imagine his response to his father—condemned to walk the night, had to return each day to eternal fires. All of a sudden a spirit, hell, heaven, fate, and divinity had intruded into the events of Hamlet's life. A hierarchy of supernatural powers existed, and this murder could unhinge the great chain of being, could disturb nature if it remained unpunished. Later, it drew Ophelia, Polonius, Gertrude, and Laertes into the whirlpool of tragedy. Here I stripped away the grief to show the passionate man within—it was an explosive soliloquy addressed primarily to his father and in a state of extreme physical agitation.

The third soliloquy, "O, what a rogue and peasant slave am I!" followed the arrival of the players at Elsinore, who provided the seeds of Hamlet's "solution":

Hamlet delighted in the actors—they were a relief, old friends, people he loved and trusted. In the soliloquy, he compared himself to actors: "Here is a player who could weep on cue, and here am I, aflame with real passion, and what have I done? Nothing! I have been unable to find a way to make sure about the murder and am still unprepared to avenge it." I left "Oh Vengeance!" in the text [the Second Quarto omits it] because I felt that the line punctuated the fact that he hadn't yet acted. He'd been in doubt about whether or not the Ghost was sent from hell to tempt him again to passion. He was too moral to commit unjustifiable violence—he needed sure evidence. The play within the play, which he began to devise in his last lines to the players, would provide him with proof, a reaction from Claudius, hopefully a public confession. (I've always been curious about where the "dozen or sixteen" lines he inserted *actually are*—scholars have battled to identify them.) If Claudius could be tricked into revealing his guilt publicly, Hamlet's revenge would be justified in both God's eyes and man's.

The famous "To be, or not to be" followed very shortly after the third soliloquy, another comment on Hamlet's wavering:

Polonius and Claudius, in a few short lines after the third soliloquy, had set up a trap to spy on Hamlet. He was summoned by Polonius to the lobby. The room appeared to be empty. He pondered his options should his plan to trap Claudius succeed. I took "To be, or not to be" as "To act or not to act." Was it nobler to bear evil without acting or to fight it to the death? When I arrived in the speech at the notion of death and the fear of what lay beyond it, I tried to convey Hamlet's conviction that choices in this life have eternal ramifications and this thought could drive you into paralyzing inaction. For Hamlet, the afterlife was a reality and what went on there was the imponderable. In the soliloquy, Hamlet had a moment of calm with the audience, sharing his thoughts and preparing for his entrapment of Claudius.

The moment ended with the appearance of Ophelia, not Polonius as Hamlet expected. To enhance the suspicion of the moment, we took a suggestion from the Saxo-Grammaticus story of Amleth, in which the Ophelia counterpart was painted whorishly to seduce him. We modified the idea and gussied Ophelia up a bit to make her more alluring. (There are textual references for this choice—Hamlet saying, "I have heard of your paintings, well enough.") As they talked, Hamlet realized that Ophelia had set him up and they were being spied on. The actress Julia Marlowe provided us with the idea that Ophelia was caught off guard by "Are you honest?" and began to weep from shame on "Where is your father?" Hamlet admonished Ophelia to go to a nunnery to save herself from the evil in the world.

The fifth soliloquy was born out of the play-within-the-play scene. Hamlet felt as if Claudius' reactions had provided him solid evidence about his guilt, and "'Tis now the very witching time of night" was spoken just before Hamlet went to Gertrude's chamber:

> Claudius reacted to the play in high agitation, rising from his seat and calling for lights, covering his guilt with outraged pyrotechnics: "Stop the play! No more of it!" For Hamlet, this response was sufficient proof, and he jubilantly told Horatio, "I'll take the Ghost's word for a thousand pound." He was ready, even impatient, to execute revenge as the scene ended.
>
> Rosencrantz, Guildenstern, and Polonius told him that Gertrude had ordered his presence in her chamber. After they left, he expressed his awareness of the bloody passions within: "O heart, lose not thy nature! let not ever / The soul of Nero enter this firm bosom, / Let me be cruel, not unnatural." He spoke his soliloquy struggling to calm himself. A compassionate nature ordinarily, these circumstances aroused destructive and ungovernable emotions.
>
> The Ghost had told him that his mother didn't know about Claudius. Hamlet needed to try to communicate with her—not to find

out how much she knew, but to let her know that she was married to a fratricide and a regicide.

The sixth soliloquy, "Now might I do it pat," was not direct-addressed to the audience. The speech had a number of performance problems built into it. Kim elaborated on these:

I always had difficulty with that speech. Whatever emotion he suppressed here would let blood in the closet scene. An enormous pressure was created when he decided not to kill the praying Claudius en route. It exploded in her chamber, in the impulsive and savage stabbing of Polonius.

I delivered "Now might I do it pat" to myself because the *object* of the speech [Claudius] was kneeling onstage. I did not think of it as a soliloquy—I thought of it as part of a scene with the unsuspecting Claudius. The convention we used was that Claudius didn't hear Hamlet but the audience did. During the speech, I had these thoughts: "I could do it now, but he's praying! I can remove this man from earth—but his praying soul might escape God's wrath! I will wait to kill him when he is committing sin. I want his soul to be eternally *damned*!" On "Up, sword," I didn't resheathe it but simply turned its point away from Claudius and unthinkingly carried it into my mother's chamber. There, I killed the eavesdropper Polonius. Hamlet had wanted to catch the king "drinking, swearing," okay, *spying*—he'd been set up a second time, very like the nunnery scene. I drew my energy for the murder of Polonius from the sixth soliloquy.

The closet scene was painful. Hamlet had to make Gertrude understand that her marriage was immoral. She may have loved Claudius passionately, but Hamlet had to open her eyes for the salvation of her soul. That difficult line "Not this that I bid you do" was spoken with a touch of sarcasm—"What should you do! Not this—continue living with this man, letting him touch and maul you and placing *me* in danger by telling him everything I've told you." Gertrude promised silence and did not inform Claudius in the next scene. Instead, she played on Hamlet's madness to protect her son: he could not be held responsible. She encouraged Claudius to send Hamlet away to give her son the breathing space he needed.

We mustn't forget that both Hamlet's father and Claudius had to marry Gertrude in order to get the throne. The old Amleth story clarified that she was important to order and leadership in Denmark. Gertrude is much more interesting if she is a woman who is a superb example of queenship. Her first real glimpse of the truth of her situation is in the play-within-the-play scene, brought home more fully in the closet scene, after [she was] forced to view Claudius in a different light.

The seventh and final soliloquy, "How all occasions do inform against me," was one of the Second Quarto additions Kim made to augment the Folio version used. He supplied his reasons for this textual change:

I did it to extend that moment of Fortinbras and to clarify how he tied into the action. In the more truncated Folio scene, Fortinbras and his captain pass across the stage and there is no follow-up [because there is no soliloquy]. I used it to link Fortinbras and Hamlet, both sons who were righting their dead fathers' wrongs. Shakespeare puts three sons in the play for us to compare. Laertes was willing to sacrifice morality and dare damnation, to slit Hamlet's throat in the church to avenge Polonius' death. Fortinbras would go to war for a straw, an eggshell. Hamlet had to take a different route, his own spiritual wrestling match. With his particular sense of morality, he suffered intense anguish before he could commit to revenge.

"How all occasions" came after the killing of Polonius, after Hamlet's arrest, and after the confrontation with Claudius in which both men knew what the others standing by did not know. Claudius felt he had the upper hand and had arranged that the king of England would get rid of this nephew who knew too much. Rosencrantz and Guildenstern escorted Hamlet out, carrying the secret orders for Hamlet's execution. He told them to stand aside and began his long reflective speech, comparing himself to Fortinbras, dwelling on Fortinbras' quick action and how he himself had not yet accomplished that.

I delivered the speech directly to the audience—telling them that

Fortinbras' action shamed my ineffectual activity and yet compelled me to take courage. I knew what I wanted to know, I had the justification I needed: "My thoughts be bloody, or be nothing worth!"

It's fascinating that after this speech Hamlet had no more opportunities to talk to the audience alone. He returned to being inside the play, totally engaged in his circumstances. I find that wonderful. The audience then watched their friend meet his end. What superb playwriting technique! It involves them deeply in the final moments of the play.

The soliloquies provided the end-stops for the two intermissions within the production: the first came after "O, what a rogue and peasant slave" (II.ii.550–605), and the second fell after "How all occasions" (IV.iv.32–66). Kim, as most Hamlets do, expressed doubt about where to place them, indeed, about having any at all. His choice provided a brief respite before the big duel scene, here carried out with the weapons mentioned in the text, rapier and dagger,[6] rather than the fencing foils often used in contemporary productions. Dean of theatrical combat choreographers Patrick Crean, a fencing expert with twenty *Hamlet*s in his credits (including the Olivier duel on film), choreographed this duel, as well as the one in the Guthrie Theatre production. Kim made specific decisions about the final fray:

> I've long thought that Gertrude can help Hamlet out in this final scene. After she drank from the cup and said that there was poison in it (her last line in the duel scene), she said it for both Claudius and Hamlet, "You were going to kill my son with this!"—which provided Hamlet the trigger to kill Claudius. There was something fishy about Claudius' wanting that fencing match so soon after he had watched the two young men fight over Ophelia's grave. Although Hamlet suspected that Claudius was about to make a move, he waited for events to cue his own action. Frequently, after having traversed the darkest parts of the play and having arrived at "the readiness is all," I felt relief and the opportunity to lighten up instead of thinking too precisely on the event. I wanted simply to be present and to enjoy the bout. Since there was no curtain on Spring Green's bare stage, the bodies were carried off to the sound of drum and

cannon, concluding the play just as Shakespeare did. I hoped that we had in some measure given our audiences a taste of the tragic experience—that we had moved them to pity and terror.

I often wish that instead of applause and the feeling of theatre as a commodity, we had a tradition of silence at the end of a tragedy, a moment to contemplate what we had seen as a community, to let the matter sink into our hearts.

Kim commented on the sheer arduousness of playing the role of Hamlet. He occasionally feared "running out of gas," wondering how long he would last on particularly hot days:

I had only one Hamlet suit—because we worked in repertory and I would never be required to do the play twice in a single day. (I couldn't have done it eight times a week!) My costume was thoroughly drenched in the hot summertime. My arms and legs would cramp up. My rib cage felt as if it had been beaten on, would hurt from drawing in enough breath to support the lines and the action for three and a half hours. At the end, there was one final mountain to climb—the duel. It's a killer role.[7]

Kim's final endeavor at Spring Green was clearly his most fulfilled effort, complete with all the study and analysis he felt the part required. He played the role for the last time in 1988.

Hamlet is not one of those plays you can do once and think you've done it. You have to live with it for a while. You have to nurse it along while you try different things with it at different times in your life. Both the first Hamlet I did in Honolulu and the second one at the Guthrie were superficial. I needed time to grow into the play—to nurture it, to become intimate with it.

Although Kim and his company of actors spent two seasons performing Hamlet, there remained a number of ambiguities and uncertainties in the performance. When asked how he solved those moments of irresolution, Kim articulated this guiding principle:

There were those occasions, certainly. What I would do then was speculate. As an actor looking at another actor—which Shakespeare was, remember—I would try to imagine how he and his fellow actors tackled the problem. From a base of practical experience, doing Shakespeare for over two decades, I believe I have a working foundation from which to decide.

This statement best summarizes the performance philosophy Kim developed. He believed, first and foremost, in finding and following the historical truths he felt were discoverable. He intended to stay as close as possible to Shakespeare's way of staging the plays. His loyalty and tenacity extended to the point of using primary source materials in rehearsal. That meant deciphering and analyzing Elizabethan punctuation and printing. The director involved the cast in an immersion process, requiring them to read and assimilate historical materials in order to find out what Shakespeare's actors did. The research and background materials opened up performance possibilities.

Although Kim and the actors also researched the stage business that actors throughout history used, the group was most interested in following Elizabethan playing styles. Kim wisely refrained from making a judgment about whether or not Burbage would have spoken the soliloquies direct-address; there simply isn't enough evidence to know. Consequently, Kim made decisions about his own performance options in his own space and delivered mostly externalized soliloquies.

Five of the seven soliloquies were direct-addressed. Kim cited the bowl-shaped playing space he worked in as a strong influence. Audience members were visible to him in the matinee performances especially, some of them quite close. The second soliloquy was internalized because of the strength of its emotional charge. The sixth was internalized because it, too, was pressurized agitation which Kim eventually used as motivation for killing Polonius.

Finally, Kim had a profound belief in the timelessness and universal values of Shakespeare's plays. He did not believe in imposing an updated concept (a controlling idea or an overriding production design) on the plays. Rather, he was adhering to what Shakespeare wrote, a powerful and simple historical strategy. He felt that the plays mirrored the important questions of human experience and that those could be discovered organically, as a cast explored the play. Nor would he see his own philosophy as imposing an "Elizabethan concept" on the play. For him, a return to historical settings and inherent humanistic ideas inside each play was the only direct path to "truth." This approach has the singular advantage of denying nothing in the text and crediting everything.

At the end of a performance I saw in August 1987, audience members came forward after the sunny Saturday matinee. They looked to be typical Wisconsin folk. "This was my first Shakespeare and you don't know how moving it was," she beamed. "We enjoyed it so much—took us out of the day," he added. Kim responded: "Well, you all deserved a medal for sitting there because today I drowned the stage with sweat!" They shook his hand, proud to have met a Hamlet.

I added, "It's a truly heroic adventure, this brave new world in Wisconsin."

"It's just plain madness," Kim laughed.

9

KEVIN KLINE : *In Action How Like an Angel*

"How do I manage it so that he doesn't split a lip, crack a tooth, or gag on a pearl?" said Kevin Kline, as he crouched over Claudius' body and forced the poisoned drink down the king's throat under the watchful eye of fight director B. H. Barry. Kline opened his second *Hamlet* by directing the production as well as acting its title role. This chapter is a look at the final stages of mounting the play, with the emphasis on performance as process, an endeavor which changed from day to day and continued to grow once the production had opened to the public. I was granted permission to observe and record during the final two weeks of rehearsal and the previews.

Kevin Kline is an American phenomenon. Equally at home with classical drama and films, he began his acting career at Indiana University, following a private-school education at the Benedictine St. Louis Priory. Then followed Juilliard and membership in a cry of players who became the Acting Company, touring for four years in a repertory troupe directed by John Houseman. Here began Kline's preparation in the classical repertory of Restoration drama, Moliere, Chekhov, Shaw, and Shakespeare. Next, he began to make a name for himself in that great American art form, the movies. Nonetheless, he continued his love affair with Shakespeare during and after the successes of acting a great variety of parts in films like *Cry Freedom*, *The Big Chill*, *Silverado*, *Sophie's Choice*, and his Oscar-winning kook in *A Fish Called Wanda*. Kline has now played Henry V, Richard III, Benedick in *Much Ado*, and Hamlet onstage for Joseph Papp's New York Shakespeare Festival. This range of artistry is

Kevin Kline in Hamlet, *1990. Photograph by Martha Swope.*

so versatile that *Newsday* declared, "Kevin Kline is a character actor trapped in a leading man's body."[1]

Kline's first *Hamlet* was in 1986 with director Liviu Ciulei, and he readily acknowledged his debt to that production:

> "Well, the first thing I will tell you is that . . . I could not have done this [1990] *Hamlet* without having done that production. And I'm not saying this one was a reaction to that one, although some of it is. Doing the groundwork first on Ciulei's production was extremely helpful. There was a great deal of fellow feeling about the play, and I owe him a tremendous amount for his guidance and his inspiration."[2]

Kline forged his own distinctive directing style in the 1990 production. His cast labeled him "an actor's director." He eschewed the usual direc-

tor's opening speech about his own concept of the play and began rehearsals with a few simple remarks. Actor MacIntyre Dixon, who played
the Gravedigger, described Kline's goal: "All he said was, I want it simple
and clear, I want the words to do the work." Kline expanded on this:

I wanted the play to be about *these* people in *this* situation—it's not
about thrones and crowns and pageantry. If we make the actors create the play, they'll have to use their voices and their bodies and the
words, the poetry, to tell the story. In that tiny space, there was not
room for much else. So, the production was simple, stripped down,
modern dress—clothes which say Student, King, Queen, Secretary
of State, Daughter, Soldier. As for the period, this is a story in which
kings squared off in single combat to decide the fate of the nation,
and yet by the end of the play, there is a courtly rapier-and-dagger
duel, so let's just not worry about anachronism because Shakespeare
didn't. Let's give the actors clothes that they're not going to pose and
"be Shakespearean" in—where they will have to talk to one another
and be *real*. I wanted to use the whole vocabulary of acting—of
naturalism and also of the most sweeping epic poetic drama. That
space can hold great raging tempestuous speeches and you can also
speak as I am speaking now and still have presence.

Kline's selection of a designer was essential to his straightforward idea
of playing the play. He chose Robin Wagner, who designed *A Chorus
Line* and *City of Angels*:

He was my first choice because I had loved the Art Deco set he had
done in my first big musical, *On the Twentieth Century*. I knew I
could have a dialogue with him . . . Robin wanted to begin with the
reading of the play in *that* theatre space. I sat down and did that,
playing all the parts, and we talked about each scene as I read it.
This hasn't been done much in this century—usually the designer
does a rendering, gives it to the assistants, they build it—meanwhile,
the designer has gone on to the next project. Robin was intimately
involved in the entire conception.

The playing space of the Public/Anspacher Theater had once been
the reading room of the Astor Place Library. Robin wanted to retain
and to continue the architecture of it. There were columns, half-

covered now, and a balustrade—we wanted to imagine the room before the seats had been put in. The irony was that I told him that the best set I'd ever seen for this play was for a ballet I'd seen years ago called *Hamlet Connotations*. It had a cyclorama as a horizon with a single high curtain that disappeared into the flies. The Ghost came unfurled out of it, and there was a wonderful pas de deux with Hamlet and his father. At the end, the arras dropped, and they carried off the body of Hamlet wrapped in it. Using the curtain in that way seemed to account for the ideas of hiding and spying so integral to the play. Then Robin said, "I know that set. I designed it."

We went through twenty models before we arrived at the simplicity of the set we chose. We decided not to use a cyclorama because I wanted an all-aural production, a floor without a carpet, a good acoustic bounce off the back wall—nothing soaking up the sound except the arras and the audience. The final set became a back wall painted like a horizon with a long, wine-colored velvet curtain hanging down the center of it. There were two smallish black pillars in front of that, holding up a "heavens" which happened to be made up of theatre lights. From the pillars forward, it was a thrust [stage]. From the pillars back to the rear wall, it was a proscenium, and when actors were behind them, they played proscenium style. We had to work to convince the actors that once they came in front of the pillars, they could turn their backs to the audience. It took a while to get to that point.

Kline's company was selected from the ranks of New York's most accomplished Shakespeareans—Diane Venora (Ophelia) had played the role of Hamlet before.[3] The younger members of the cast had wide experience in Shakespeare festivals throughout the United States. The assortment of voices was diverse—Guildenstern's deep and sonorous, the Player Queen's like a boy player's alto, Kline's tenor crispness. One actor confided during dress rehearsal: "In every other Shakespeare I've been in, the cast was hysterical at this stage. This one is so well organized and everyone knows Folio from Quarto!" That level of experience made it possible for the actors to make changes and assimilate them quickly. There was some doubling of roles—the clown and the Gravedigger were the same actor, so were the priest and the Ghost. Don Reilly, who played

Fortinbras, understudied Kline and stood in for him frequently while Kline adjusted the blocking. The cast was responsible for bringing on and taking off the few set pieces used.

Kline himself constantly watched details, warning players to beware of sharp edges on the scenery or to mind their costumes when candles were being used onstage. He did not deliver orders from the stalls but moved among the cast onstage, making jokes, delivering compliments, explaining an unusual word. He made sure that every actor had what he or she needed to perform each night—whether it was a specific property, a clearer understanding of a Shakespearean phrase, or a deeper explanation of the effects he wanted. As the cast neared opening night, he took particular care of sensitive egos. Kline described his directing style as a partnership:

> I had to live up to my own credo—that actors must assume the authorship of their own work. I made it clear at the outset that we are the ones who tell the story every night. It's not the director. I was careful to get actors who would take that responsibility. One who says, "Well, this is a job and I do what the director tells me" is not an actor I'm interested in. I want an actor who has a personal connection to the play and to his or her role. They would demand of me "Why?" And I would tell them "try it this way because then the scene becomes more about this than about that—do you agree? See what I mean?" So it was a *dialogue* with them. Of course, there were times when I simply wanted to say, "Just do it like I told you." I had to stop myself from that because I didn't want them betraying themselves as actors. If the bit of business or a way of saying a line is not ultimately *their decision*, then the acting won't be that good or that full. What's riveting when you watch a good actor—if it's an action that he or she has arrived at and has some ownership in it, then it has an air of instinctive commitment. It will come alive in a much richer way than if the actor is a puppet.

The philosophy meant that negotiation and discussion characterized rehearsals. Each actor had the opportunity to express a point of view. In a session that continued intermittently over three days, the group worried the phrase "Treason, treason!" (V.ii.323) as they analyzed the courtiers' reactions in the final scene. "Finish your thought," Kline said to one,

"Let's try it!" to close the discussion, and "You know what I'd love you to do?" to draw the actors to a decision—phrases uttered frequently in the course of rehearsals. Such exemplary corporate behavior created for Kline a company which gave more than its share, created a blend of solid prerehearsed activity as well as an improvisational climate. If Kline wanted to try something new in performance which would shift the timing, he was free to do so. Rosencrantz and Guildenstern especially had to be vigilant—they never knew when Kline, an extremely lithe and playful actor, would use the recorder as a fencing foil or break into a dance routine on one of their entrances. Rehearsal of the play was a continual act of discovery—of correspondences, parallels, serendipities, repetitions, déjà vus.

Nevertheless, Kline felt free to be authoritative. The cast was rehearsing a large group scene which he halted with "This is a MESS! Is there anyone who did NOT bump into someone else on that entrance?" One lone hand was raised. Even with his head in Ophelia's lap during the rehearsal of the play-within-the-play scene, Kline had difficulty not checking out courtiers' body positions in the scene. He monitored performances like a painter, moving this arm, asking for emphasis on a word, brushing up the Shakespeare—this in an era when directors often move to another assignment once the play has opened:

> As the run plays itself out, actors find out exactly what makes a character tick. Usually, they keep evolving in a role. But some people devolve and go back to comfortable habits or fall back on old tricks. So I had to check myself: Am I really pissed off because it's not going where I wanted them to go? Or is it that where they are going with it is still very true and I'm reacting because his or her role has grown and developed to something different from my original vision of it? Of course, casting plays an important part. You have to begin with people you know can do the job.

Kline had other partners in his vision. When he was *in* a scene as well as directing the scene, he depended on assistant director and dramaturg Barry Edelstein, who had trained at Oxford and had worked with theatre groups in London and the United States. Kline trusted Edelstein so much that he called him "not my third eye, no, *my second eye*." Kline, it must be pointed out, is a very visual director. The cast got used to his being fetishistic about debris left on the stage, such as Ophelia's crushed rose petals, which another actor removed after the nunnery scene each night. Edelstein said:

> Every actor was allowed a certain license. If you're going to be a liberal director, the contract you make with your cast must be "your instincts are as good as mine." The more experienced actors have good instincts—the younger ones, good as they are, would occasionally drive Kevin crazy in rehearsal by making inappropriate choices. When this happened, he checked them. No matter how good the production, if you play Bernardo sixty-five times, there is a limit to what you can discover in the character. Kevin would say, "I know how repetitive this is for you, but let's go back to the initial reason for doing the scene." Kevin understands that actors have fertile imaginations, and sometimes a director has to say, "Sorry." The thing a director can *never* say is, "Stop coming up with ideas." He would encourage them to keep on inventing and to get a sense of the world of the production. This way the actors could police themselves and know whether a choice was usable.[4]

Regarding textual matters and thorny questions of Elizabethan meaning, Kline relied on Edelstein's dramaturgical function. This was a Folio-oriented production, a choice made because the First Folio of *Hamlet* is shorter and considered by some textual scholars to be closer to the performance script that Shakespeare's company used. Edelstein added that the earlier rehearsals were more in line with the Folio version but that Quarto readings crept in—for the sake of clarity, for the audience, or to help bridge a difficult transition. The final text ran close to three and a half hours and comprised the material which Kline felt played best, with textual purity a major, but not the primary, concern.

Once the first night of the previews drew near, Edelstein put down his dramaturgical mantle and assumed the cape of assistant director. After that point, Kline empowered Edelstein to deliver director's notes to cast members. This was necessary because Kline had to make a total transformation into the character of Hamlet, who is, after all, not the director of the play but a character within it, one who has a specific temperament and very tangible relationships with supporting characters. Realizing that his role change was not without its inherent dangers, Kline was very straightforward about his giving over of directorial domain. He said to the cast,

> I won't be out there watching your work any more because I don't need to. I trust you. The whole rehearsal process has been very positive, and we each know that we're responsible for this play. I will be a bit more inaccessible because I've got problems to solve doing my own role. We're in good shape, though.

To Claudius, whose role was given heavy weight in the production, he gave a special caution:

> In the last two days of rehearsal, there was a subtle but distinctive shift. I gave Brian [Murray, who played Claudius] a note about the pace of the first scene, adding, "Of course, you and I are 'mighty opposites.' I am not sure how much of this is the director in me speaking and how much is Hamlet. Remember that I must have a residual dislike of you, which I am encouraging." Brian laughed and answered, "You're right. The scene has gotten too slow."

Kline declared that stage manager Maureen Gibson would be giving pre-curtain announcements: "I can't do it because I hope to be in character by then." Edelstein explained what happened most nights:

> I was in Kevin's dressing room with him from seven p.m. on. We would talk about details from the previous night, including observations about his performance, and then I would go out and give notes to other actors, leaving him alone to prepare. He would gargle, sing opera, sit quietly listening to classical music—things to warm up his voice and body and to make himself vulnerable and open to emotion.

Kline believes in bashing away at a scene until the text is unscrambled and made to work. Insisting that "you can't do the play for scholars," he does not spend much time in stopping to reason why he does a thing—he simply plunges in:

> When I was asked why I wanted to perform the role a second time and also why I decided to direct it, people said, "Oh, what a coura-

geous thing to do." I thought to myself that this would be either the most foolhardy exercise in self-destructiveness or a great learning and growing experience, but it's never felt like conscious courageousness. I knew the critics could kill me and laugh me off the stage and never take me seriously as a director, but I'd still have my acting career. So it's not risk, it's *caprice*. All I really risk is that NOTHING will happen when I'm out there—what every actor risks every night. Of course, I'm denying sleepless nights of utter fear, of all the things that I joke about. Most of the sleepless nights were about practicalities—like where is Ophelia's grave since we don't have any trap doors in the theatre.

There is a certain "readiness is all" quality about Kline's preparation, a seasoned familiarity with the play:

I have been accumulating experiences with *Hamlet* for twenty years. I usually had a Penguin edition somewhere on my person or within reach in which I would make notes during the years before I first acted it. I'd go watch anyone do it. I've seen about twenty Hamlets. I saw Richard Pasco in 1967, who came over with the Bristol Old Vic on tour. I flew to Moscow to see one. I saw Olivier's film. I've seen the Russian [directed by Kozintsev, 1964] and the Swedish [directed by Ragnar Lyth, 1984] films. I saw Michael Pennington's. I saw Derek Jacobi's Hamlet on TV, and I think he was best at showing the chain of betrayals that affect the character. When I did it in 1986, I was very careful not to *study* anyone's Hamlet because I did not want to be influenced. It had to be *my* Hamlet. Now, I've seen so many that I think I can say flat out that nothing I ever concocted in this production is purely original. I am sure that I have amalgamated into my unconscious twenty different Hamlets, which are now one great blur.

Kline's character conception was definite, sculptured, and clear. He gave a Hamlet far younger than his forty-two years, one critic placing it closer to the age of twenty-four.[5] His was an antic and quixotic prince, prone to tears and somewhat emotionally unstable. Because he chose to explore the potential madness of the character much more than in his

1986 characterization, he played on the fine line of jocularity and lunatic impulse. His mother and father saw him as a loose cannon. Tied in with the madness was a razorlike wit, sometimes whimsical, sometimes cynical, always enormously inventive. The darker side emphasized Hamlet's own sense of secrecy and mystery. Although he reacted with an idealism about humankind that had been thwarted by events in Elsinore, by real life impinging on a youthful and perfectionist vision, there remained about him an aloneness that he consciously protected. Kline explained:

> Even "What a piece of work is a man" is done to bewilder, to confound Rosencrantz and Guildenstern. Right after that, he informs them that he is "but mad north-north-west." That is one of the trickiest places in the play regarding whether or not he is truly mad. It worked best for me when he opened his heart to them—he knows quite well *wherefore* he has lost all his mirth, a man who had faith in mankind that has been shattered. He has the presence of mind to say that "there is nothing good or bad but *thinking* makes it so." There is something in him that would love to be able to tell what has happened, but a major part of the madness is the need to keep it secret. Look at the number of times he emphasizes the secrecy: It *is* "particular with me"—"I have that within which passes show," "But break my heart, for I must hold my tongue," "You would pluck out the heart of my mystery," and after the Ghost's appearance, "No, you will reveal it." He never exactly explains "what is between us, o'ermaster it as you may." Then there is the famous line, no coincidence that it is the last in a chain of secrets that he never tells: " . . . the rest is silence." I do not even tell Horatio who I am and what I am about—in many ways, I am a mystery to myself.

Kline made some interesting choices about the soliloquies and how to deliver them. The Public/Anspacher Theater and the set presented a playing area (at least in front of the pillars, which would be the logical place to do such important speeches) that roughly equated a thrust stage of approximately twenty-four feet by twenty-four feet. The house sat about three hundred audience members and was a very intimate space. One would therefore expect that the actor would use the most intimate of the ways of playing the soliloquies, a direct addressing of the audience. Kline's decision went precisely counter to that, and his reasoning considered both the shape of the space and certain qualities he wanted to emphasize in his Hamlet, especially the secretiveness. He explained:

When I played the first Hamlet, at the Public/Newman Theatre in 1986, I thought that all the soliloquies should be done to the audience. I insisted on it, and Liviu Ciulei was always against it. In that space, it seemed like they should be direct address because it was a long, proscenium house and I felt that I should reach out. I convinced him eventually and he finally gave in. I still feel they should be *that way* in *that theatre*.

Once you start doing audience-address, it forces a kind of clarity. You see, Liviu felt that Hamlet was *feigning* madness throughout. At one point, a scene was invented where he was running around the castle in white makeup with a candelabra, singing loudly and *pretending* mad. However, in the 1990 production, I felt that what I wanted to explore this time around was how Hamlet flirted with madness and even attained a kind of madness at times. One time in the 1990 production, I did do direct address and it got didactic and preachy, such as in "Thus conscience does make cowards of us *all*"—with "all" meaning "you-all," both the audience *and* myself. It took the onus off Hamlet, off me, and let me share it with them, diffusing the moment entirely, making it a general moment instead of "so particular with me." That's why it was wrong to do it that way in the present production. It can let you off the hook, can take you off the spot as Hamlet, and thus keep you away from madness.

Also, if I say into their eyes, "Is it not monstrous that this player here, / . . . Yet I, / A dull and muddy-mettled rascal, peak / Like John-a-dreams" [from the third soliloquy, "O, what a rogue and peasant slave"], then I am explaining it to them and I'm not going *through* it as I should be. If I am discreetly alone, I am free to express it, to *act* it as I should.

I am certainly not saying that one way of doing it is right and another way is wrong. I simply chose here to use the inner-directed soliloquy because it fed my need to explore the more emotional Hamlet. I'd explored his thoughts in the other Hamlet I did, and now I am much more interested in his feelings. In general, my earlier

Hamlet was always too professorial. At least in the [1990] soliloquies, I think the lecturing to the world ceased.

Kline thus made an interpretative choice. He gave a Hamlet who mani-
fested extreme inner turmoil and was struggling to handle the conflicting
emotions inside himself. The soliloquies became inner counsel, Hamlet's
dialogue with himself. He shared Claudius' misdeeds with Horatio, but
he never processed his turmoil with Horatio. That was saved for his moments alone.

What follows was recorded from the first preview night on April 10,
1990. It is important to state that because I observed during rehearsals
and previews, I was able to see the soliloquy speeches evolve. Quite naturally, the soliloquy was not performed in precisely the same way every
night. Once into a soliloquy, the actor does not have to stick to the prerehearsed rhythms and movements of a dialogue or to interact with another cast member, and so he can, to a certain extent, improvise. In this
production, the beginnings and the endings of each soliloquy remained
fairly constant because the lighting technician, the sound technician, the
stage manager, and other actors had to take cues from these, so as to
know ahead of time where Hamlet would be standing onstage. Physical
movement (the blocking) tended to remain the same for those reasons as
well. However, if Kline was affected by fatigue or injury (e.g., pulled
muscles or sprains from the duel) or was reacting to the audience's attention or inattention, the inflection and expression varied on those nights.
The words emphasized may have changed somewhat (although this was
rare), the size of builds may have varied, and the phrasing may not have
been spoken exactly as rehearsed. Of course, these changes could, to a
certain extent, affect *meaning*, even though meaning is somewhat stabi-
lized by the lexical definitions of the words (for example, "To be, or not
to be" would almost always be about Hamlet's contemplating death).
Most actors strive to keep the *intention* the same from night to night
because each speech has a function within the overall performance design, and the play will suffer if the design is drastically tampered with.
One thing that always remained stable in Kline's production was the performance mode of the soliloquy. He never suddenly shifted from an introspective soliloquy to a public address soliloquy, because that kind of shift

would have undermined other carefully predetermined aspects of character conception.

The emotional tone of the first soliloquy, "O that this too too solid[6] flesh would melt," was set up during the I.ii court scene, where Kline stood against the upstage left wall in a suit of mourning, grieving and occasionally wiping his eyes with a handkerchief. During the scene, he continued to weep as his "unmanly grief" was described by the king. The king, queen, and courtiers left the stage to a trumpet-and-drum fanfare accompanied by cannon fire. The general light darkened, and a "special" lit Hamlet as he leaned against the stage right pillar and then sat down on the pedestal, his back bent forward, his hands over his ears as if to close out the noise. On "resolve itself into a dew!" he took a long pause, to let the thought sink in. On "Or that the Everlasting had not fix'd / His canon 'gainst self-slaughter! O God, God," he looked to the heavens. On "'tis an unweeded garden," he looked toward the Danish flag. After "That it should come to this!" he played astonishment at his mother's actions, always punctuating the references to time, such as "But two months dead" and "A little month." On "winds of heaven / Visit her face," he brushed his cheek, and "Must I remember?" was angry. "O God, a BEAST" was fairly spat out, after which he sat down again. The remaining lines were played with increasing amazement at the choice of husband his mother had made. There was occasionally laughter from the audience on "no more like my father / Than I to Hercules." When he came to "post / With such dexterity to incestious sheets," the sibilant consonants were hissed out with rancor. He then stood to pronounce the final closing couplet.

Thus, the audience's initial introduction was to a prince not rebellious or flippant but enmeshed in deepest grief. He then moved from melancholy to stunned anger. Kline used demonstrative hand gestures and physical movement around and through the lighted area, but there was no "posing" or artificiality—this was a genuinely aching man. He said the words first and foremost to himself, in an effort to work through "a situation that is bad and it will *stay bad*." At one point he threw down a drinking cup—he later eliminated the prop because it had helped him find the emotion he needed and now he could perform that instead. Kline said this soliloquy was the most difficult because it had so much to do with the rest of the production, especially the relationship with Claudius and Gertrude. He felt that the weeping restrained him from admonishing his mother. The point he reached in this soliloquy was one from which the rest of the show had to be negotiated. When he presented a sensitive, wounded, confused soul—neither too weepy nor too brittle—then that was for him the correct springboard for the rest of the performance.

The second soliloquy, "O all you host of heaven!," held a surprise. The Ghost had just left the scene, and Kline fell to the floor, sprawled on his back, shouting the beginning lines near hysteria. On "hold, my heart, / And you, my sinows . . . bear me stiffly up," he writhed and clutched his heart, unable to rise as he begged his body to respond. He rolled to hands and knees and did a sweeping gesture to "WIPE away all trivial fond records," seven lines of verse which he spoke without pausing. He virtually screamed "O most pernicious woman!" Next, there was a change of beat as he began to stand on "O villain, villain, smiling, damned villain!" On "So, uncle, there you are," he sprinted to the downstage left exit and suddenly appeared to scale it. The final "rememberr-r mee-e-e" was shouted upwards from the top of the exit shields, his face well lit and seen by the surrounding audience as he fell backward from about five or six feet into the arms of Horatio, Marcellus, and Bernardo.

This was indeed a thrilling move, totally original in the performance of this soliloquy, and perhaps one of the things audiences came to see. It took some intense maneuvering and careful backstagemanship to bring it off. The spot from which Hamlet fell was the same spot at which the Ghost had made his initial appearance. Small stair risers, extremely difficult to see, were temporarily lodged in the exit, which was shielded by black masking flats; Kline scaled those. Bernardo had to be added to the scene to ensure safety in catching Hamlet, and three or four small lines were cut after the fall to allow him time to recover from the swoon.[7]

A comment from Russian Hamlet Innokenti Smokhtunovski (who played the prince in the Kozintsev film) that Hamlet would have been extremely surprised if his father had *not* returned and that he was indeed eager to see the Ghost, had rung true with Kline: "That movement begins with Horatio and Hamlet's quick interchange at 'My lord, I think I saw him yesternight' (I.ii.189), where a line of tension begins to tighten, and it carries all the way through to the fall." Kline explained that it integrated into his idea of a character who set himself heroic goals and then could not quite accomplish them, fell short of his aims. "If you find the right rhythmic values," Kline believed, "the scene will reveal its own direction." In any case, Hamlet did indeed wax desperate with imagination, and this stirring performance of the soliloquy integrated totally into the preceding scene with the Ghost.

The preparation for the third soliloquy, "O, what a rogue and peasant slave am I!," was almost as interesting as the speech itself and certainly full of cues and clues for the audience. At this point, Hamlet was somewhat disheveled and barefoot—the madness beginning to bloom on him. As the players entered for the first time, he was filled with delight at seeing them and welcomed them heartily as reinforcements: " . . . look where my abridgement comes." The players erected a small platform stage between the two pillars, on which one of them spread open a satchel of stage properties—a dagger, a white commedia mask, a mandolin, colored ribbons. Then Hamlet pleased them by remembering a large chunk of the Pyrrhus speech, as they clustered around him in a stage picture lit in golden Rembrandt tones. He delivered the lines, dagger in hand, and near the end, at "Old grandsire Priam seeks," he brandished it toward Polonius. The Player King delivered the remainder of the speech, choosing also to play with the sword in hand, which at II.ii.479, "seem'd i' th' air to stick," an icon which reappeared throughout the production. Thus was established a metatheatrical context for the upcoming jewel of the soliloquies—a context of a stage on a stage, an actor (the Player King) just having left off from playing as the beginning of Hamlet's next soliloquy states.

True to the soliloquy's purpose and placement, Kline gave it in a very theatrical manner. He began by circling the platform stage, making references to the speech that he'd just witnessed. He touched the bag of props, showed how "this player here" would "drown the stage with tears" by gesturing with hands to the playing space. Nearer "Yet I, / A dull and muddy-mettled rascal," he jumped up on the small stage. The short questions "Am I a coward? / Who calls me villain?" were addressed to the imaginary audience of courtiers that would *soon*, in the play-within-the-play scene, surround the platform stage, but never to the "real" audience in the Public/Anspacher Theater. (The lines "Who . . .

plucks off my beard," et cetera, were omitted because Kline did not wear a beard.) The acceptance of criticism, "'swounds, I should take it," was quiet and then moved to self-laceration on "THIS SLAVE'S OFFAL."

Almost as if in parody of the highly declamatory speech of the Player King, he began cursing Claudius, heavily metering out the words "Bloody, bawdy villain! / [no pause] Remorseless, treacherous, lecherous, KINDLESS VILLAIN!" On "Oh Vengeance!"[8] there was a huge gesture, arms upward. After keeping them frozen for just a moment, Kline spread his fingers, which mocked the gesture, looked at his hands and said nonchalantly, "Why, what an ass am I!" Thus Hamlet realized himself in a pause, like Pyrrhus, and called himself an ass. He took the next section lightly and quickly, leaving a brief pause after "Fie upon it, foh!" At this point, Kline said he used "About, my brains!" (he held his head) to cast backwards into his memory for some unfinished business hanging there—ah, yes, the plan beginning "I have heard / That guilty creatures sitting at a play" that he had initiated with the players—he wanted to talk about it more fully now. He visualized himself inside the plan, carrying it out and emphasizing "I'll TENT him to the QUICK." He began it softly and built it to an action eager and mean on "TO DAMN ME." Finally, he left the stage with a hand gesture that seemed to catch in its thrust fist the conscience of the king.

During rehearsals and up through the final performance, this speech was performed with much expression and a great deal of physical action. Initially, there had been a blackout at the end; however, it invited a sustained applause which nosed into the next scene (where Claudius and Polonius bestowed themselves behind the arras), so the blackout was cut in an effort to dampen the applause. Nonetheless, audiences continued to applaud about 25 percent of the time.

Very soon after the third soliloquy fell "To be, or not to be," for which Kline entered from down right, looking slightly more disarrayed than before. The thump-thump of his purposeful footsteps was obvious before he was actually seen. In high contrast to the previous soliloquy, this one was much less physically active and certainly less histrionic. Picking up on a staging pattern used in the earlier speech, Kline came onto the playing area and completely circled the smaller platform stage once without speaking. Occasionally, his hands would flutter down toward it, indicating that his mind was still on the players and playacting. He seemed to be working out something very difficult for himself that put strong intention behind the opening lines of the speech. He stopped at the center front of the platform stage (facing forward) and delivered quietly: "To be, or not to be, that is the question." He did not make eye contact with the audience—this was an inner dialogue. On the second "To die, to sleep—" he closed his eyes and wished for sleep. On "perchance to dream," they fluttered open fearfully, to conclude that "THERE'S the respect / That makes CALAMITY of so long life." The long catalog of whips and scorns that one has to bear was cynically and sharply spat out up to "bare bodkin." The second catalog of fardels was just as sharply enunciated up to "fly to others that we know not of." There was a pause, then, before the conclusion of the speech, "Thus conscience DOES make COWARDS of us all," as the proposed events lost the name of action. However, up through previews, Kline did not vocally conclude the speech but left it up in the air in order to "discover" Ophelia entering for the nunnery scene. By the end of the run, he sat down on "lose the name of action," near to sobbing, and finally lay down, dejected and weary. This second way, Ophelia discovered *him*, and the whole sequence seemed more complete.

Furthermore, there had been a change in the manner of lighting the scene somewhere about three weeks into the run. As Barry Edelstein explains it,

> The old school of "put out the spotlight and let the tenor sing the aria" was not an option. But during the run, we realized that we needed to mark it out [the soliloquy]—and subtleties in lighting are Jules Fisher's [the lighting designer] specialty. At first, we had general lighting over the stage throughout the entire sequence. We changed it—now the backdrop was lit with blue backlights, there was a "special" that came up from Kevin's left onto his face. So lights were much colder for "To be," and then afterwards modulated back into warmer lights. As to his lying down, this turned out to be one of the places at which he did that.[9] The sequence did, however, present some difficulties with "Soft you now, / The fair Ophelia."

Kline spoke the speech in a calm and quiet way with a few controlled gestures, most below waist level: "The risk is that it is too cool and unengaging and will be a man looking at the *idea* of death rather than really yearning for it." Overall, "To be" was much more contemplative than the preceding solo speech and more dependent on vocal color for variety than on movements of the body.

The nunnery scene also underwent a sea change from the opening previews to the closing nights. As it was originally conceived, Hamlet kept the focus inside the scene and did not acknowledge that he and Ophelia were being observed. He conceived the scene as if he were suspicious of something—not that he knew Polonius and Claudius were observing but that something was amiss:

> His treatment of her resulted from his feeling that she had a natural purity that was akin to his. What happened in rehearsal was that when he said, "I love you not," she was just crushed. She is like Hamlet in that regard. Both are perfectionists with an absolute set of values. Both have the highest aspirations for man and the highest standards for virtue. When that is shattered, when he faces the world's reality, that we are all flawed, *then* that purity is shattered and our old stock will relish of it. Ophelia is too pure to live in this world—it will kill her. He tells her to go to a nunnery and not to populate the world.

At a certain point in the performances, Diane Venora began to signal to Hamlet after "Are you honest?" that there were observers behind the arras. At first Kline resisted the idea. After he thought about it, he decided that Hamlet must suspect he'd been betrayed—especially after her weird doggerel about "givers prove unkind." Since the notion did not disturb the character conceptions they had established—Hamlet very drawn to Ophelia but ultimately having to wrench himself away from her, Hamlet always involved in the greater business at hand—it was permissible to play a reaction to her signal. Kline felt it stole focus a bit but did not contend with the line of action planned. The next major scene, the "advice to the players," was played for maximum metatheatrical subtext:

> "Speak the speech," I played for a certain amount of intimacy and playfulness, Hamlet not remotely conscious that he is any more than a prince directing an evening's entertainment. It was also done that way because I thought there might be those in the audience who

would remember my being the director. They were all there, sitting at my feet—you get a Pirandellian effect because the play's about acting and about someone not directly taking action. The scene contains all those themes we've read about—illusion and reality, acting and not acting, acting and seeming to be not acting.

It turned out that these scenes were among the critics' favorites and that the general audience did indeed remember and relish Kline's allusions.

The fifth soliloquy, "'Tis now the very witching time of night," was carefully connected to the preceding scene. Directly after the play-within-the-play scene, there was great confusion in the court. In the darkness that followed Claudius' exit, Hamlet experienced euphoria as the platform stage was struck. He grabbed Lucianus' prop knife, mockingly thrust it at Lucianus, twirled Ophelia with the dagger still in his hand. He had a very tense scene with Rosencrantz and Guildenstern, showing that he understood their treachery quite clearly. His high spirits carried through dismissing Polonius and everyone else. Finally, he was alone onstage with the dagger in his hand.

The first five lines were the first beat of the speech. They were given in anticipatory tones, the essential idea in a spooky stage whisper: "Now could I drink HOT BLOOD and do such BITTER BUSINESS." This shocked him into remembering, and he looked down and realized that he was carrying a weapon. He sheathed it as the dialogue turned to his mother. The second beat was a caution to his emotions, as he tamed himself and remembered that he must not harm his mother. Kline sustained the phrases "Let me be cruuu-elll, not unnaturrrrelll" each time. So the first beat was elation and energy, the second a check to action. These were very much metaphors for what Kline saw as Hamlet's continual pattern—a huge vow to a huge task and then caveats restraining him from the ultimate action. He can't quite pull it off.

Thirty-five lines later, Claudius attempted repentance. He concluded his soliloquy, kneeling at the very center of the thrust part of the stage, eyes tightly shut, head bowed. Hamlet entered between the two pillars at the rear and discovered Claudius in an attitude of prayer. He began the soliloquy there, with a stage-whispered "Now might I do it pat, now 'a is a-praying." He then moved behind Claudius, his sword drawn. Kline put as a question to himself the line "And so am I revenged?" [10] He made the crux of the speech a question and gave the answer, "Why, this is *hire and salary*, not *revenge*." From this point forward into the soliloquy, Hamlet made passes at Claudius' head, ear, shoulders, spine with the dagger. He circled in front of him and made stabbing gestures straight down on his head as well. The line "Up, sword, and know thou a more horrid hent" were cut in order for the mimed killing to continue. [11] At "My mother stays," Hamlet roused himself from the evil pantomime and exited on the final couplet. It was obvious that the sin of murder had been committed in thought if not in deed.

Kline explained that the playing space dictated the way this double soliloquy was blocked. Claudius needed to be forward and center for his soliloquy. As Hamlet entered, he needed to take focus from Claudius, but that couldn't be done had the actor remained at the rear of the playing space between two poles: "You cannot stay back between the pillars in that theatre because you are partially blocked and cannot be seen by everyone. It's not as open as it looks—if you stay back, you must move constantly, on every line."

Barry Edelstein added:

Of course, having Hamlet move all around the kneeling body of Claudius violates all notions of "realism." The convention that the kneeling king can't hear Hamlet as he speaks is difficult enough to make believable. But when Hamlet is circling him, stalking him, talking directly to his face, this is even harder to accept. In that tiny playing space, though, we would have had that problem *whatever* we'd done. So we decided to move away from the realm of the naturalistic into something more surreal and expressionistic. Perhaps if we'd had more moments like that (actually, Hamlet clutching his dead father's hand was another such moment), the audience would be better prepared and would more readily accept them. It was my absolute favorite part of the play, essentially and thrillingly theatrical.

Kline felt that trying to demonstrate the convention while doing it— that Claudius does not hear Hamlet, whether he's three feet from him or ten—was too obvious. So he chose a solution which pushed at the sides of the container of the convention, moving the scene into the surreal. He did not contact the audience at any point. He was totally involved *in* the scene and remained so.

The final soliloquy, "How all occasions do inform against me," Kline's favorite, was cut from the production, but the plot event was retained.[12] A tall, blond Fortinbras in military garb entered to the beat of a field drum, stood front and center, and sent his captain to request "conveyance" over the Danish kingdom. Only the first ten lines of IV.iv were spoken. Hamlet had entered at the rear of the playing space, flanked by Rosencrantz and Guildenstern. He watched Fortinbras, who did not see him. Both men watched the Norwegian troops march over Denmark as cadences rolled. The scene sent the message that events outside the castle were inexorably plummeting onward. Kline gave his rationale:

> There were a lot of reasons for our decision. The overriding one was that since I was going to be doing eight performances a week, I felt a need to find places to cut the text in order to get it down to three hours and fifteen minutes, including intermissions (a playing time we did occasionally meet!). So I thought if I cut this speech out, it would set an example for the other actors to donate lines as well. It turns out they weren't as generous as I was [he laughs]. I was looking for as many cuts as I could get and still tell the story. However, I feel that every cut bleeds in *Hamlet*, every cut. I miss them all.

Edelstein reinforced this decision, adding that early in the run there was an intermission after this scene, breaking the production into three discrete movements (I.i–III.i, III.ii–IV.iv, and IV.v–end). However, the first intermission was eventually cut to save time and to keep the production's momentum as high and full as possible. Edelstein also pointed out that the soliloquy was not in either the First Folio or the Bad Quarto of *Hamlet*, so there existed textual authority for omitting it. Finally and decisively, both men felt that this production was not about delay, which is the major burden of the seventh soliloquy, but about the fine line between madness and sanity.

There was, throughout the production, an interesting series of echoes that operated on both the visual and the poetic levels. Hamlet's long fall in the second soliloquy was one of a number that were staged. Kline conceived of Hamlet as a personality who had grandiose plans but never quite achieved what he promised. Horatio's role was to catch Hamlet before he fell; he was obviously very close friends with Hamlet in this production, from the hearty hug in the second scene to the kiss Horatio gave Hamlet after he died. Horatio also caught Hamlet after the play-within-the-play scene was over, when he fell off the platform stage. We remember these falls as Hamlet held Horatio by the wrist to tell his friend that there is a special providence in the fall of a sparrow. Finally, Horatio caught Hamlet as he toppled from the poison at the end of the duel scene.

Another visual echo was the dangling of Ophelia by the arms, which Hamlet did in his rather brutal rebuke in the nunnery scene; later on, Laertes attempted to comfort her in the mad scene and came up with this awkward position again. It seemed to punctuate the horrific insensitivity with which she was treated by Polonius and Claudius at the end of the nunnery scene: she lay on the platform stage emotionally shattered, like a collapsed puppet, while they coldly discussed Hamlet's "madness" over her sobbing body.

There were also a number of arrested swords in the production, all the way from the playful passes Hamlet made at Polonius to the delayed stabbing of Claudius in the sixth soliloquy. Wounds to the ear were initiated in the Ghost's tale of his own death, and these were repeated as gestures throughout, even to the final nick of the envenomed sword on Claudius' ear in the duel scene.

With few exceptions, critics were delighted with this *Hamlet*. One reviewer bubbled over with enthusiasm: "For his major directorial assignment, Kline takes on one of the most difficult plays in the classic canon and solves its problems like a man who has been grappling with Elizabethan drama all his life. . . . Kline's production [is] probably the greatest American *Hamlet*." [13] The *Times* of London printed a long article which praised Kline, commented on the cluster of talents unusually focused in this actor, and bemoaned the dearth of American directors of Shakespeare. [14] All of the reviews commented on the quality of the verse-speaking, the staging of the play, and the way that Kline integrated the madness into an intelligent and witty Hamlet. Kline himself steered clear of reviews:

Critics are the natural enemies of an actor. Aside from their levels of competence or incompetence, people who create theatre can have nothing to do with them in terms of reading reviews. What the critic does is to subvert, stultify, and wound the creative process if it's at all vulnerable. And if it's raw, it's vulnerable. An actor puts himself out there all alone every night and so cannot afford to take a critic too seriously. Imagine, for example, if a reviewer writes, "Ophelia is just unprepossessing. She's kind of pathetic and overweight." And the next night I am acting Hamlet and have to look at her and say, "Soft you now, the fair—slightly overweight and somewhat unprepossessingly pathetic—Ophelia." A critic can poison the audience that reads reviews the night before. So, the long and short of it is that I don't read them.

If Kline treated the critics with a healthy disregard, what forces did affect him during the run of a performance? Here the actor describes each night's performance as an event, as a fluctuating process of give-and-take between himself and the *audience*:

You mentioned the critic who said I spoke the "To be, or not to be" speech more with muted anger than with philosophical contemplation—well, *that night* it was spoken that way, whatever night he was there. Here is this critic writing about it as if it were a fait accompli, something I'd *arrived at* and was destined to repeat itself night after night as "My Interpretation" of that passage. Let me tell you there were nights when an audience would irritate the hell out of me and I would *scream* "To be, or not to be" at them. I've had other audiences moving around so much—face it, you can hear someone adjusting his vertebrae in that theatre because the acoustics are so "live"—that I would take it right to their faces to quiet them down. Or there would be so much rustling and noise that I would do the whole speech with my hands over my ears so I could concentrate. Light spills out into the first couple rows in that theatre and some of those people *think they are in the play with you*. Once when I was holding up the skull of Yorick, I heard someone say loudly, "Yeah, this is a great speech, my favorite," and I thought, "Not tonight it isn't, buddy—you've completely distracted me now." And then there was the man in a white suit and white shoes in the second row who jiggled his foot up and down rapidly. All through the performance, it was bouncing, a *large* distracting movement. And so when I came to the "advice to the players" where I say, "Be not too tame, neither, but *let your discretion be your tutor,*" I just went over and put my hand on his foot and held it until he got the message. It solved the problem.

I know actors are not supposed to be insulted, but sometimes these distractions are a great deal to work against. One night, there was a woman with a hacking cough so consistent that you could set your watch by it—it went off every thirty-five seconds. I got to "The rest is silence" and there it rang out [he demonstrates loudly]. If I had been able to create a smidgin, a soupçon of stillness, she would shatter it. Now if I were playing Richard III, it wouldn't bother me. I would say, "Off with her head," mentally—but Hamlet, in whatever overly-sensitized state of mind I was playing him—takes all these interruptions to *heart.* It works the other way, too—a friend came backstage afterwards one night and I asked him if he'd seen the woman eating Tic Tacs during the Ghost scene. He replied, dazed, "But you've just changed my life with this performance!"

So, many variables can color my "To be, or not to be" on any given night. If I found myself expending too much negative energy denying something that was distracting me, I would just *use it* on "that patient merit of the unworthy takes" because the words were right there for me to use! Other nights, I wouldn't be affected at all because we had an audience that coalesced into a group of intense, concentrated stillness. The point is that a soliloquy is a *process,* not a *result.* There is no one way that I did any given soliloquy during the run.

Likewise, the original "geography" of entrances and exits shifted somewhat when actors found that "traffic control" worked better if they used an entrance or exit other than the original one that had been blocked. The Gravedigger gained and lost a chicken leg during his scene when it became too much to gobble it down and speak the lines simultaneously. Some readings from Quarto crept back in as Kline needed them to help build speeches. One actor sprained a finger and had to catch the falling Hamlet on the back of his arm until he healed. Many such shifts and changes occurred during previews, part of the reason for Joseph Papp's dictum to keep festival productions "in preview" (i.e., off-limits to the press) for about three weeks after opening, which gives the play an opportunity to settle down and find its groove.

Although every effort was made to communicate specific themes to an audience, Kline explained:

> You try to give a certain performance, but there is always a level of resonance out there that you absolutely cannot control as an actor. You try to unite the group, but you may still have three hundred responses. If you can congeal an audience, it's great—but it's only an illusion of community.
>
> There are so many levels of perception in an audience. On one level, "To be, or not to be" is about killing Claudius, and on another level, it is about a state of being. Of course, the actor must never generalize—his task is always to be specific. To me, the soliloquies are not little entr'actes—they're connected to the specific scene that precedes and the one that follows it. Every scene operates on the concrete, story level and on the abstract level as well. There is always *something else* coming off an actor besides plot. It's his reaction to playing that role—that he's really enjoying acting, or he's really troubled. The audience perceives it on an unconscious level. Sometimes the success of a performance comes less from the actor's having a meaningful connection to a given character than from having an intriguing *dis*connection from a character. Maybe because we are encountering the actor at an interesting moment in his or her life. You hear it occasionally in a singer giving an aria or in a performer playing a phrase of Beethoven—there is something in the voice, the contact with that particular musical note—that is so personal and so touching that it lets the perceiver see into the soul of the performer. It usually happens in great works of drama, which are written in verse, already one remove from reality. Poetry puts it onto a level, despite its specificity, where it has connotations and resonations of the universal.

When asked what criteria work to shape the "final" performance—the rehearsed entity that is put forth to an audience—Barry Edelstein answered: "What it really comes down to in the end is what's going to work and what is not. The final arbiter of that is the director—whose vision has been articulated and is strong enough and clever enough to discern when the production is doing what it should."

This, in turn, relates to what Kline meant when he talked about "assuming authorship." An actor assumes full responsibility for his or her own performance within a production. It is shaped and guided by a director, yes, but the freshness and the believability of it are of the actor's forging. In a deeper sense, the director assumes authorship of the production—not of the *play*, which was authored by Shakespeare—but of the *production*, which is a separate entity with its own infrastructure and a great deal of reading and preparation behind it. Actor and director have authored something together that is most certainly *not* the same as "the text." In its mutability and its phenomenality, a good production has an artistic integrity all its own.

This 1990 *Hamlet* seemed to have encountered Kevin Kline at an interesting moment in his life. John Gielgud also took over the direction of his own *Hamlet*,[15] and British newcomer Kenneth Branagh, at the age of twenty-nine, directed himself in *Henry V*. Olivier directed himself in both. The assumption of directorial command by the actor is partly an effort to claim authorship over all the aspects of a production, including the interpretation of the leading role. It is also the next logical step. In any case, Kevin Kline's endeavor is yet another harbinger of actor-centered Shakespeare. Perhaps the days of the director-guru are waning and more actor-directors like Kline will emerge to personify the swing of the pendulum.

10

KENNETH BRANAGH :

Speak, I Am Bound to Hear

Kenneth Branagh's work has epitomized the best of Shakespeare's plays on screen since the 1940s. Early on, chunks of film history like *Birdman of Alcatraz, Rebecca*, and *Dial M for Murder* became part of his practical vocabulary. He stated in 1991: "When I started directing theatre, I would often refer to classic film scenes."[1] He rejected oppressive institutionalism in the Royal Shakespeare Company and successfully segued from his own classical acting ensemble, the Renaissance Theatre Company, to films, including "little movies" like *The Midwinter's Tale* about starving actors and *Dead Again*, a film noir thriller. His early Shakespeares, *Henry V* and *Much Ado About Nothing*, each became blockbusters, the first grossing $1 million in the United Kingdom and $10 million in the United States and the latter grossing $8.5 million in the United Kingdom and $22.5 million in the United States.[2] Branagh's film adaptations of Shakespeare plays have been the most readable by a broad, general audience, true to the populist Shakespeare he espoused in his early Renaissance Theatre Company days.

Branagh came to the 1996 film project described in this chapter with insider credentials. He first played the role of Hamlet in his late teens while a student at the Royal Academy of Dramatic Art. He was Hamlet again in a 1988 production of the Renaissance Theatre Company directed by his mentor Derek Jacobi, whose Hamlet Branagh saw at age sixteen. In 1992, he was directed by Adrian Noble in a production at the Royal

Kenneth Branagh in Hamlet. Hamlet © *1996 Castle Rock Entertainment. All rights reserved.*

Shakespeare Company. He also performed in a BBC radio version of the play. Each of these performances differed substantially from his movie role, the latter of which gives audiences a restless, strategizing prince with an active imagination and a passion for justice as well as for revenge—a performance that makes not only a historical statement, but also one about Branagh's place in the universe at the time of filming this personality role.

Audiences for Shakespeare contain many levels: scholars who have written books about Shakespeare, novice and experienced actors, teenagers awakening to literature, crackerjack graduate students who devour the reading list, secondary school teachers who pass Shakespeare along to a new generation, parents who read Shakespeare in college, the culture-vulture audience of art lovers which emanates from the middle class. Over one hundred summer Shakespeare festivals operating annually (in the United States alone) attest to a continuing interest in Shakespeare. Branagh targets all of these audiences, aiming to be "both traditional and contemporary,"[3] a direction which has the potential for hideous dullness.

But dull Branagh is not. The imitations of Olivier are noticeable in this film version of *Hamlet* (and thus flatter Olivier's tradition): the blonde hair, the whirling-dollying camera, the Waltonesque music. Other productions are quoted as well: Kissing Claudius on the "Farewell, dear mother" speech is straight from the 1980 BBC version of *Hamlet*. These borrowings enhanced the audience's response to the film, reminding the more initiated viewers of the movie's place in a stream of film history and encouraging their appreciation of ironic manipulation of the medium and of theatrical tradition. Branagh's film-making strategies have invited viewers to read the film on a number of different levels, depending on their sophistication as a cineast or theatre buff, providing familiar landmarks for both the initiated and the uninitiated.

Branagh made a very noncommercial decision in using the text of Shakespeare's *Hamlet* in its entirety in his 1996 film, a choice once made by John Gielgud for his stage production, which sparked the waggish complaint about "Hamlet in its eternity." The screenplay is based on the First Folio of 1623, with smaller additions from the Second Quarto (1604–1605) of *Hamlet*.[4] The full text not only reinvigorated the idea of contextualizing the play in a political struggle between Denmark and Norway but also recovered scenes often cut from staged versions. Critics had to confess that in spite of the film's length, Branagh's *Hamlet* had flashes of brilliance.

Critical commentary about the art of acting not only tipped the hat to theatre but also generously nodded to performing artists in both film and theatre, that mix of media common to performers in the twentieth century. These metatheatrical and metacinematic quotations paid tribute to Branagh's fellow actors and to the profession he chose. Acting, particularly acting in a theatre, is an ephemeral art. Once the show is over, there are very few traces of the performance left behind—some costume renderings, a lighting plot, a promptbook if you are lucky, a videotape in extremely rare cases. Since this phenomenal art form provides no finished painting, no bronze statue, no mould of form, not a rack left behind, it is important to honor those who create the two hours' trafficke of the stage. One way to do this, as Branagh divined, was to capture hallmark performances through mass media: "[It is] unrealistic to think that you could eventually reach large numbers of people in the theatre if they [haven't] seen you on television or on film."[5] The resulting *Hamlet* was a film that quoted from high and popular cultural artifacts and created layers of meaning that resonated between medium and audience.

Branagh's 1996 *Hamlet*, which he both starred in and directed, had a veritable arsenal of seasoned classical performers. Derek Jacobi (who played Claudius) had previously performed Hamlet 379 times; one performance was responsible for lighting Branagh's own muse of fire and turning his aspirations toward acting. Jacobi also directed Branagh in a 1988 *Hamlet* in addition to acting over two dozen other Shakespearean roles. Judi Dench (Hecuba) and Rosemary Harris (the Player Queen) both played Ophelia in addition to myriad stage roles.[6] Charlton Heston (the Player King) played in a half dozen stage and screen Shakespeares. Michael Bryant (Priest) performed several Shakespearean leads at the Royal National Theatre. Best known for his film acting, John Mills (Old Norway) played in *Hamlet* and in *A Midsummer Night's Dream*. Of course, Gielgud (Priam) overshadowed them all, having played sixty roles in Shakespeare, including four separate performances of *Hamlet*, two of which he directed and played the lead in as well. By using this panoply of world-class performers, Branagh both commemorates and documents the players' craft on both sides of the Atlantic. One scene showed Heston describing Priam in battle: The camera briefly cut away from America's Moses to Britain's eldest and most famous thespian, Gielgud.

Although the rest of the casting was clearly designed to enhance box-office revenues, these actors, too, were similarly endowed with professional accolades. Neither Julie Christie (Gertrude) nor Gerard Depardieu (Reynaldo) had previously acted Shakespeare, but both turned in creditable performances. Veteran director and actor Richard Attenborough played an English ambassador. Common threads running throughout the meritocracy of performers were knighthoods and dames (also OBEs and CBEs); Tonys, Oscars, Golden Globes and Oliviers; as well as training at the Royal Academy of Dramatic Art.[7]

Branagh also offered parts to a group of up-and-coming British actors whom he admired from his own generation. Simon Russell Beale (Second Gravedigger) had performed several of the title roles at the Royal Shakespeare Company and acted *Hamlet* at the Royal National Theatre in 2000; Rufus Sewell (Fortinbras) and Kate Winslet (Ophelia) were accruing stage and film credentials toward successful international careers. The clowns had few Shakespearean credentials yet provided the acknowledgment that groundlings buy the most tickets and that popular heroes must be included. British comedian Ken Dodd played Yorick;

American Billy Crystal played the First Gravedigger with a Borscht-belt accent; Robin Williams created a subtle and giggling Osric.[8]

An enormously clever audience function was served in selecting this cast. International stars automatically drew a larger audience. With them, Branagh created an immediate identification for a non-Shakespearean audience by overlaying the familiarity of the epic film onto Shakespeare's script. Christie's association with *Dr. Zhivago*, Heston's with *Ten Commandments* and *Ben Hur*, and Attenborough's with *Gandhi* and *Cry Freedom* were all links to the epic concept of the film. While the British theatrical royalty might have been less familiar to an American filmgoing public, these actors added an aura of high-culture respectability to the enterprise.

The movie was set in a loosely defined nineteenth-century era with men in uniforms and women in hoop-skirted ball gowns against the backdrop of Blenheim Castle, the best known of the British stately manors. The 70mm film format afforded not only a wealth of detail on screen but also enhanced the grandiose sweep of the project. The weather was decidedly Zhivago-esque—with wintry effects added by a company called "SnowBusiness"—which justified some of the brandy-snifting habits of Claudius and the other Danes. These were original and unique contrasts to the domestic-tragedy overtones of Olivier's 1948 film version.

Branagh had many discussions with Hugh Cruttwell, former principal of the Royal Academy of Dramatic Art and Branagh's artistic advisor, on the issue of how to present the soliloquies on film. Cruttwell had worked on both *Much Ado* and *Henry V*, films in which Branagh also carried the burden of several functions, including both actor and director. About his trusted friend, Branagh said, "Hugh's an extremely eloquent and frank observer of my work in rehearsal, onstage, and on the film set from take to take."[9] Between the actor and this important "outside eye," there were many deliberations about translating the great speeches to film, particularly about directly addressing the soliloquies into the camera (and thus directly into the film audience's eyes, comparable to breaking through the "fourth wall" in the theatre).

We felt that direct address into the camera seemed too startlingly out of keeping with whatever convention we might have set up for the delivery of those speeches. It always seemed to me to be off-putting and it reduced the impact of what the actor said. We came close to doing it in *Much Ado*, but it was always just off-camera, especially in Benedick's speeches. We had thought occasionally it might be quite funny and useful for comic effect. In the end, we wanted the audience to be able to go to the language rather than being attacked by it or potentially hectored by it.

I decided direct-address was not as effective in communicating the idea of the speech and actually could jerk the audience out of the reality of the film, thus it would ultimately end up being artistically or filmically self-conscious.

It was very important for Branagh to "get it right" for this film because the cultural memory of soliloquies, for most people, was associated with what had been done with them onstage in past productions. In most cases, they were set speeches pronounced in a declamatory way.

Act I, scene i of the film, set in front of Blenheim castle, was a dark and stealthy scene which introduced the sightings of the Ghost of Hamlet's father into conversation between the soldiers on watch and Horatio. Their interaction created a feeling of dis-ease and raised more questions than answers. In I.ii, the audience was transported into a completely contrasting atmosphere, a huge public gathering of Danes celebrating in full royal regalia, seated on bleacher-like seats as Claudius and Gertrude entered, she dressed in a bridal gown. Claudius launched into a very effective public speech, easily achieving the citizens' support for his marriage. His demeanor was that of a very capable politician who proceeded to deal with the nation's business, both civic and private, and then belatedly noticed Hamlet, the mourning son in the background, his attitude toward Claudius stony and yet peevish.

In more private tones, Gertrude attempted to persuade her son that it was time to let go of his sorrow. Claudius joined in with a gentle reprimand, and then returned to public pronouncements, giving notice that young Hamlet would eventually succeed him as king. The scene ended in a magnificent flourish, trumpets and music accompanying a grand exit of showered confetti, petals which left the giant hall drenched in a snow-like cover. The joyous crowds exited noisily, and the doors closed on silence so profound that the petals could be heard falling.

Entirely alone now, Hamlet brushed the petals from his shoulder, as if something unwanted, something he did not wish to deal with, stuck to his garments and his psyche, demanding resolution. He began the first soliloquy (at I.ii.129–59) standing on the raised red dais at one end of the room, supporting himself on the two thrones the monarchs had just vacated. The first syllable was a long groan: "O that this too too solid flesh would melt." [10] His voice was directed inward; this was a discussion with his inner self.

He moved gradually to the opposite end of the room, turning around occasionally, the movement in his body expressing an inner turmoil. On "Heaven and earth, / Must I remember?" he hit an emotional peak and clutched his head. What followed in the speech was less loud and more whispered, filled with pauses and then much slower and more determined on the ending lines as the actor reached a temporary resolution—to give words to his anger while alone, to hold his tongue while his heart was breaking.

Branagh said that a cornerstone of his interpretation of the role was the "trauma of grief":

Although he was clearly distressed by Gertrude's behavior, Hamlet was a man who adored his father. His dilemma was father-linked. One could argue about the ways that relationship might have been— textually you can even read that old Hamlet seemed like a very stern and unloving man—regardless, Hamlet was a man who missed his father very much.

What struck us in filming was that no one got a decent funeral in this play—something that Laertes bemoaned later on for the lack of ostentation in his own family's deaths. The requirement for a period of grieving (never mind the specifics of Hamlet's particular circumstances), to fairly and squarely acknowledge and mourn the departure of a loved one, involved *time*, certainly more time than "A little month." The play seemed to cry out for that.

And also a period of communication. Some might argue that many of the events of this play could have been avoided by a good talk between Hamlet and Gertrude. They don't get to speak until the Closet Scene, and you don't get the feeling that they've talked at any other time during the immediate period after old Hamlet's death.

In so many ways, Claudius is rather a good prospect for the crown—we envisioned him as efficient, capable, authoritative, a perfectly fit king in a court full of sunshine and possiblity. Perhaps even Hamlet could come to that conclusion were it not for the haste. That immense sense of hurt Hamlet carries, especially at the beginning of the play, seems to be emphasized in that empty room which had just been full of everything positive.

That's how we introduced him, feeling his isolation, away from the turrah of everything else. With a certain amount of dignified removal from the center of things (which others might regard as rather petulant), we placed this lone figure amid the marriage tables (no funeral baked meats to be seen). Here he is, a little guy in this vast room, not just raging but hurt, a man in the midst of grief and a deep sense of loss. I wanted that to be placed in one uninterrupted shot.

The second soliloquy, "O all you host of heaven!" (I.v.92–112) took place not as it usually does, on the castle ramparts, but in a haunted wood nearby. Hamlet passed through the castle gates, looking back at the lit edifice, and soon separated himself from Horatio and Marcellus as he sped through the tangled branches and fog. The earth began to crack and break, sending up geysers of flame and spouts of smoke. As a hooded figure appeared, there were cutaway shots which identified the Ghost, old Hamlet on a bier, back in the castle. The blasts and noises continued, trees fell, there was a second shot of the ghostly figure, and finally Hamlet whispered he'd go no farther.

The Ghost's echoing stage whisper told the murderous tale. The figure towered over the son, his ethereally blue eyes bulging as he narrated a story supplemented with cutaway shots of the family, of Claudius and Gertrude playing games in the castle, of a bodice being unlaced. From these shots, the audience could presume relationships, could piece together a story. As the Ghost rendered a graphic account of the actual murder, the crime was illustrated in cutaway shots again—old Hamlet seated in his chair in a snow-filled garden, the pouring of the potion into his ear, Claudius's appalled reaction of horror at himself, old Hamlet falling from the chair. All this high rhetorical working of the pathos of the situation on the son preceded the opening lines of the soliloquy, providing the audience with context for the words.

Finally, the cock crowed, old Hamlet extended his hand to young Hamlet, and Hamlet found himself grasping immaterial air as the Ghost's hand disappeared on "Remember me." On his knees in a patch of snow, Hamlet began his response by bowing his head; shortly thereafter, he fell forward, giving the audience a profile of the son, weeping and choking out his emotions for the first half of the speech.

Then Hamlet stood up quickly in a violent lift of his body on "Yes, by heaven!" and cursed first Gertrude ("O most pernicious woman!"), then Claudius. Anger and resolution replaced the outpouring of pain. On "Now to my word," he lifted a sword and raised it in a frontal view of his face. On "'... Adieu, adieu! remember me.' / I have sworn't," he sealed his vow by kissing the sword.

The flow of the speech was broken by ejaculations in response to the Ghost's remarks and to the situation. Branagh summed up its central idea:

> What do you *do* when you've just heard the Ghost of your father tell you that the Uncle murdered him prior to marrying your mother? Not only is that the case, you are required to revenge your father by killing the King! So, first is the regicide, and then you will be king after that, or perhaps you won't, who knows what will happen— perhaps there will be a revolution in the country! The weight, import, and *massivity* of the information is conveyed fantastically by the sound and music of that speech.

Branagh had a central through-line for his delivery:

> In the choice of language, the choice of words, the way the vowels and the consonants all put themselves together, you get a physical sense of a man trying to hold himself together against circumstances, against physical evidence which is almost beyond the power of any individual to withstand. You get all these aitches: "Host of heaven ... Shall I couple hell." There is a kind of pressing, as if he can barely say those things, as if somehow he is trying *not* to go mad in that moment.

> For me it is not a speech in which he has a nervous breakdown, but in which—in a way that endears us to him immensely—he avoids one.

Kenneth Branagh : 209

I always feel terrific sympathy for Hamlet on those lines. There is a courage to them that is admirable because of the enormity of what he must take in—the unthinkable, the unimaginable in the most concentrated form—has to be dealt with by a human spirit.

He feels profound loss which unsettles his own psyche. He's damaged not only by the loss of his father but by the disappearance of the mother and the removal of the friend Ophelia. We may not, right at that moment, be consciously thinking of those things, but for the actor, you know that this is what the plea is for—he damaged and alone, a mother removed and now, it would seem, complicit.

Branagh detailed the importance of the scene design and underlined his decisions about setting the soliloquy in a unique place:

We wanted to offer a certain kind of thriller atmosphere throughout this sequence, again to take at face value some of the actual mechanics of the storytelling. You have to remember—he was visited *by a ghost!* It's so easy for that to become casual in the context of a classical piece as famous as this is, for that to lose all its innate drama, its capacity for suspense and terror.

We wanted to shock and surprise people, to move the audience around in that wood as a frankly evocatively spooky place where Hamlet was genuinely lost. Thus the soliloquy had a stillness at its center core. He falls to the ground from one shot into another shot. So the setting had a number of practical objectives, one of which was to shake some of the dust off the perpetual imagery that surrounds these key scenes.

The third soliloquy, "O what a rogue and peasant slave am I!" (II.ii.550–605), is a key speech often cited for its metacritical references about theatre and performance. The arrival of the players to the castle set it up, and within the First Player's speech, the cinema audience was treated to seeing a generation of classical actors performing on screen— Charlton Heston speaking the speech, and Judi Dench and John Gielgud appearing in the cutaways, creating a kind of mirror-within-mirror quality for audiences which recalled great actors of the past and celebrated the scope of their talents on both stage and screen.

After the players entered the castle, Branagh's Hamlet escaped from the

State Hall into his apartments. He stood in a book-lined study containing a small toy theatre and theatrical masks on the shelves. Thus, the most histrionic soliloquy was given in the most confined space, a space as circumscribed as a proscenium arch stage, dressed with a number of props which visually suggested past stage performances. Delineating this context was important to the director and demonstrated the kind of invention Branagh attained:

> Here was one scene in which we could see the atmosphere of Hamlet's rooms, the physical representation of the man we were suggesting very clearly was a Renaissance figure, interested in sport and art and a breadth of subjects. We wanted to humanize him, to establish clearly his bookishness, his intellectual curiosity, a sense of what that multifarious intellect and spirit was drawn to. At one point later on, in a scene with Horatio, there is a line about "writing fair," his interest in calligraphy.
>
> We wanted to establish a room of some warmth and interest, untypical from the way the rest of the palace was, different from Claudius's room, different from the hallways and that large central room of the castle, different from the wide open spaces outside. To show that within was a man who would find it difficult to be restrained by Claudius from returning to Wittenberg, so much so that he set up a satellite mode at home in which to pursue all his diversions.
>
> We wanted to provide a notion of a man looking out from this world—the room of a man of some vision, which connected with the references to his popularity in Denmark and to the various predictions that he would have made a terrific king—a room where we see Hamlet's potential.

Branagh often saw a relationship between setting and character. Here, he manipulated the location to make a statement about the interpretation of the persona of Hamlet:

> This is the same process I'm talking about in terms of trying to "lift off" into a whole performance—you're working very very hard to get to the point where magic might occur. I do believe there is a certain kind of mysterious process where, even when you specifically

produce a kind of production vocabulary, you decide on the props for a particular set and discuss in detail with the production designer and the props buyer, and then something can take over. The objects you choose may end up surprising you by being rather apposite and resonant. What are those books in that corner on that shelf? Why did we put that object there? It's a kind of gloss, really, where the prop had some apparently specific reasons but turned out to stimulate in other ways. You hope for that procession of lucky accidents.

There is this fine line between an idea which releases energy and imagery in the play, that has sufficient definition to give you a sense of place and texture, but that is not too confining in terms of historical time. That line between finding an idea which releases the play without being simply two planks and a passion, that speaks a little more loudly and a little more insistently in terms of time and place, but that doesn't become so specific that it has the opposite effect and it reduces. Because you've crammed something capable of simulating large numbers of thought and images into a very clever but small box where, in fact, ideas are *contained* and work only for one or two lines and then have no more resonance. You hope somehow to find a vocabulary which allows you to walk that line.

I think that was a section where there was resonance. We knew once we got into that room, given what the play talked about, that it was bound to suggest things that even we were not consciously aware of.

Once inside this apartment within the castle, Hamlet closed the door, berated himself, and began to refer to the acting performance that the Player King just gave. On "What would he do / Had he the motive and the cue for passion / That I have?" Hamlet slowly opened the tiny doors to the small theatre, completing the gesture by drawing out the phrase, "He would D-R-O-W-W-N-N the stage with tears. . . ." In frustration, the actor then rested his head on a model of a globe, the name of Shakespeare's own theatre and reminder to the audience that all the *world*'s a stage.[11] Then, he angrily knocked over a small table that held a sword, foreshadowing the instrument that subsequently killed him. His anger mounted and he beat on a wardrobe (another of the requisite trappings of stage and screen) and crossed to the casement to deliver the climax of the speech, "O Vengeance!"—an ejaculation from the Second Quarto that was reinserted at Branagh's insistence.

In the final "beat" of the soliloquy, Hamlet moved again to the model theatre and concocted a plot to trap Claudius by the device of adding a speech to the play the players were about to perform. The camera caught him in extreme closeup, his determined eyes looking through the proscenium arch of the toy theatre, a move that put him in the theatre audience's usual position of peering through the fourth wall.

On the assertion "I'll have grounds / More relative than this," he uttered the final phrase of the soliloquy: "—the play's the thing, / Wherein I'll catch the conscience of the king." Instantly, a lone miniature figure onstage dropped through a small trapdoor—an image reminiscent of a body dropping after a hanging—and the film cut to the face of King Claudius. It was a marvelous movie moment, the visual image directly replicating and expanding the text. In fact, the speech was goosed up a bit, opened emotionally when the player was nearer the toy theatre.

Branagh explained the burden of the soliloquy:

> There is much self-disgust in Hamlet here, partly released by this period of inaction of which he is highly conscious, and also the springboard of having just been in front of actors who vent in a therapeutic way. Wouldn't that be a marvelous way to deal with things, if you could just shout a bit! Hamlet is also amazed and rather envies the fact that the First Player had tears in his eyes.
>
> The speech also releases the pitch of excitement within him. He has been alone and not talking to anyone, a period disguised to the world by his having put on an antic disposition. So there is also a sense of relief that some illumination has occurred—not only in terms of what actors can do with extraordinary situations but also in having located a good idea about how to determine if Claudius is really guilty.
>
> It's an explosion of feeling. It takes you through the whole man, and it's very much in the moment. Hugh [Cruttwell] thinks it's the richest speech in all of dramatic literature.

When Branagh reached the vocal climax of the speech, he was literally pounding out the words, anger and fury evident in his outcry:

It's very human, the technique that Shakespeare uses—because we all know it to be the case in our own lives: where you can be in the middle of some extraordinary passion and still some voice in your head asks, "What are you doing!" Interesting human beings are often fascinated by the outer voice that's watching in the middle of some traumatic event. I think that's a very human touch that many people would find appealing in Hamlet: "Why, what an ass am I!" It involves humor and self-awareness and bespeaks a sharply witty and satirical man.

We see these gradations: a man of action, an irrational and almost babbling human being by the time he gets to "treacherous, lecherous, kindless villain": He's almost unable to find the words and when he does, he eats and chews and then spits them out. He does tear a passion but (hopefully) not to tatters.

Branagh articulated the nuances of feeling the actor has to negotiate:

The challenge is to meet all the many layers of it—showing not just the density but also the swiftness of Hamlet's thoughts. It requires so much mental adroitness and vocal dexterity to be both convincingly almost-at-the-point-of-out-of-control yet not so caught up in the passion that the specifics of it do not get conveyed, not being so technically precise as to undermine the genuine sense of the emotion.

Branagh also described how the playwright helped the actor to achieve this volatile combination of effects:

"O Vengeance!" feels like a musical stop to me, a climax or crescendo. The phrase is one of those situations where actors in rehearsal can give you very accurate guestimates about text because they feel the music of it interrupted in a particular way.

The speech comes out at the audience and encourages them to truly experience what he's feeling rather than being consciously reflective as in "To be, or not to be," where a man calmly sits back and considers ideas. The poetry evokes sounds which take us close to the tangible physical effects Hamlet is feeling. There is marvelous music in its structure.

Although delivered as an interiorized speech, it was clearly the most emotionally draining of all the solo speeches. By the time the actor reached the turning beat in the speech—"I have heard / That guilty creatures sitting at a play . . . "—he could almost not stop the flow of angst as it poured forth. He panted his way through the lines about the plot to catch the villain, yet his voice dripped with the hot liquid of the purge that he had just experienced—a truthful, drenching, draining achievement.

Ironically enough, the fourth soliloquy was, according to stage tradition, the central speech in the play. The difficulty in the film was to recognize "To be, or not to be" (III.i.55–89) as the intimidating purple patch that it was and yet "to really make people listen to that speech for the first time." Branagh quipped, "If Shakespeare was a theme park, that would be the ride they'd all want to go on."

It's such a loaded moment in the play in terms of the larger culture, having a weight and baggage that is unique to only this line in literature. Sometimes actors embrace it completely and bring on a book, wearing more conventional Hamlet garb, looking like the image people have seen on a biscuit tin—I swear to god, at that moment half the audience would say it for you after your first intake of breath. I know other actors who have come on and said the line very quickly in order to rid themselves of this phenomenon. I don't think that works either.

There really is a very special feeling in the auditorium, which I felt at both Stratford and at the Barbican when we did it there. When tourists have come to a Shakespearean mecca like that, hearing *Hamlet* live and performing those lines gives something of a lip-smacking relish for it afterwards in a silence that is quite unlike any other. One wants to do it on film without denying the pleasure of all that.

A few audience members will think, "Oh well—that's gone by. That's what we came for." So there is often a little jet lag afterward when you try to pull them back into the experience of the play. For most people, whether they favor Shakespeare or not, some bit of Hamlet—a man with a skull in his hand or a book—has made its way into their consciousness, and they let out a sigh of enjoyment that makes taking them with you a little tricky after the speech is over.

Branagh made it new by *not* making it reflective or contemplative but by underpinning it with suspense. In order to spy on Hamlet, Claudius and Polonius hid themselves behind one of the mirrored doors lining the State Room of the castle—a *reverse* mirror which could be seen through from behind by opening an inside shutter. Hamlet entered the State Room and, after looking at his reflection in precisely the mirror they were hidden behind, delivered the most reflective soliloquy in the play.[12] On "might his quietus make / With a bare bodkin," Hamlet expertly drew a dagger. As he said "And enterprises of great pith[13] and moment / With this regard their currents turn awry, / And lose the name of action," he touched the blade to the mirror. The reaction shot revealed Claudius behind, flinching. The looking glass had simultaneously created a double audience and therefore a double message—one given to Hamlet, who is trying to decide whether or not to kill himself[14] and another message to Claudius, the killer of old Hamlet. A third audience (of course) was in the movie theatre deciphering added layers of meaning. We never knew *for sure* if Hamlet knew that Claudius was stowed behind the mirror, but we very strongly suspected that Hamlet was aware of his presence. Jacobi did a masterful job of reacting in this scene.

Hamlet then glimpsed Ophelia, walked to her, and the nunnery scene ensued. Ophelia signaled several times to him (with glances) that their conversation was being watched, but it was clear that Hamlet was fully suspicious of the situation on "Not I—I never gave you ought." From this point onward in the scene, he knew, and his anger began to build.

After Hamlet said, "Go thy ways to a nunnery," there was a noise behind the wall confirming the presence of eavesdroppers. Hamlet suddenly grabbed Ophelia and dragged her along the wall of doors as he flung each one open in search of the King. He located the correct door, pushed her hard against it, her cheek mashed against the glass. Glaring straight through the door at Claudius, he growled, "Those that are married—all but one—shall live." In the reaction shot, Claudius slammed shut the masking door on the other side as he and Polonius escaped, too quickly for Hamlet to catch the king. The film audience had witnessed a thrilling "smoke and mirrors" trick.

Branagh explained the genesis of this unique idea:

> At the beginning of the sequence on film, we emphasize that Hamlet has been sent for. He comes into that situation a bit furtively, a bit paranoid, his body language saying, "Where are they?" He is a man preoccupied, where any new development could have significant bearing, particularly at the hands of Claudius. A man in that state of mind could be stopped by a mirror. And this opening could defuse the audience expectation of "Oh, here's the famous bit." As he looks around, we are aware from his demeanor that there are many secret doors and mirrors hidden in this hall. The whole scene is charged from the outset.

Branagh's invention actually came from impressions gathered from other times and other performances:

> The idea of doing it into the mirror was suggested by the programme designer of Jonathan Pryce's *Hamlet* in 1980 which had on the cover that image from the Magritte painting where you see the back of the head and then the back of the head ad infinitum, generating the idea that somehow this soliloquy should exist in an enormous landscape where Hamlet should be faced with himself.
>
> The idea also sprang from a trip to Hampton Court I took when I was playing Hamlet at RADA in 1981, and it struck me there that with the number of hidden doors and the sense of corridors interwoven, you could never really be alone, never truthfully say "Now I am alone." Those were the sources of all the secret doors, the physical expression of eavesdropping and politics. With that in mind, you could act in ways that you did not have to hit people over the head with—that Hamlet's been called there, for one—as he looks into the mirror, he realizes that the room might *not* be empty. There is a cautiousness—partly due to his instincts, and partly due to his intellect—so he gets rather caught up in the idea of being watched.
>
> Consequently, the speech is not a case of thoughts recollected in tranquility with Hamlet very clearly knowing where he is going to arrive at the end of the speech. Yet it is reflective, with Hamlet looking deeply into himself to answer the question of whether or not revenge is worth it. He is partly recovering from decisions—he's made

a decision about how to bring revenge about at last, and he's waiting. Into that little space floats a thought: the idea of Claudius being on the other side of that mirror.

The image of Hamlet being in the mirror and Claudius being behind the mirror is an Orson Welles influence from the end of *The Lady of Shanghai* and from some of the shots in *Citizen Kane* where Kane walks by a mirror and there are four of him, images all going on to infinity behind him. It didn't exactly work the way I wanted it to—it would have needed special effects and would've been too obstructive—but that's where the idea began and it got modified to suit our purposes.

Part of the reason he stands there and the camera moves in [at the beginning of the soliloquy] and we only chose to cut away to Jacobi once, is we wanted to hint at the possiblity that Hamlet might kill the king right there and then. Keeping Jacobi alive on the other side of the door kept open what we were going to exploit more directly when Ophelia came in—the sense of danger. It was worth paying the price of distraction from the intellectual meat of the speech in order to provide a keener sense of excitement and interest about the idea of death.

Branagh mused that, in ordinary circumstances, this speech tended to impede the forward motion of the play:

In fact, you could eliminate that speech and it wouldn't interrupt anything in terms of the story of the play. In a way, it's extraneous to the plot. Which is perhaps the reason it has become a marvelous party piece which has had removed from it any real sense that perhaps then or at some point he might actually kill himself.

Branagh talked about effects he did not want:

With both the fourth and the fifth soliloquy, it was important to maintain that people are different in different moments in their lives, but that both speeches *remained in the story* and not divorced from it. Especially with "To be, or not to be," it was not a rhetorical speech to the universe. I was attempting to not make it some arbitrary contemplation taken away from a real man in a real story that the audience has become involved with—as if somehow Shakespeare had decided, "It's time to digress awhile. I'm rather intrigued by putting these thoughts together. Think I'll show off a bit here. This is going to be quite resonant for people!"

The decision to inject danger into the speech, which Branagh said he found "quite useful" in performing it, revitalized and reintegrated the famous fourth soliloquy into the flow of the action. Within the context of the film, the speech was inseparable from the nunnery scene and was one of a series within that arc which began with Claudius's short soliliquy "How smart a lash that speech doth give my conscience," at III.i.50 and ended with Ophelia's soliloquy "O, what a noble mind is here o'erthrown!" (III.i.150–60). This sequence was important in demonstrating the depth of Claudius's treachery as well as initiating the separation of Hamlet and Ophelia, a loss which left him alone and often terrified.

One of the most fascinating aspects of Branagh's filming of this speech is the way in which the visual images pick up on the chief rhetorical device used within the speech—antithesis—where the playwright exploits opposing ideas. One can hear it in the opening lines, of course, "To be, or not to be," and that structural artifice continues throughout the passage. Filmically, we found Hamlet alone in a vast room which once held hundreds of people. The hall was dressed in row upon row of black and white tiles. The major visual image is a mirror which reflects the subject in opposition to himself. Hamlet finally met his "mighty opposite" in Claudius behind the mirrored door.

Because of its ghoulish language, the fifth soliloquy, "'Tis now the very witching time of night" (III.ii.388–99), could have borne the identical setting to the second soliloquy. However, it was simply orchestrated and fairly monotonal in delivery. Hamlet stood flanked by candlesticks, remarking on his bloody thoughts, justifying (and foreshadowing) his cruelty to his mother, and ready to commit the deed which would complete his revenge. The light was dim, the words filled with conviction. The speech was removed from the end of the recorder scene (at III.ii with Rosencrantz and Guildenstern) to a place which immediately prefaced the next important beat, the "double soliloquy" where Hamlet discovered Claudius at what he supposed was the king at prayer.

During the final third of the "witching time" speech, we saw the robe of

Claudius go past and then saw him enter a confessional. A minute re-arrangement of the text provided the opportunity to create much better visual (filmic) continuity.

The double soliloquy was intricately and inventively conceived. Claudius looked around the deserted passageway and then entered the confessional, a large, ornate, wooden cabinet with a place for the confessor and a place for the penitent, divided by a small carved screen at face level. There was a crucifix hanging above his head. Claudius whispered his anguished prayer, beginning "O, my offense is rank, it smells to heaven" (III.iii.36–72), asking forgiveness for a sin for which he still possessed the booty; of this, he was painfully aware. The camera moved in gradually from a waist shot to a close-up of his face on "Help, angels! make assay," the most emotional plea of the performance. The closing line of the speech was a half-line, "All may be well," after which Claudius filled the empty half of the line with the physical gesture of kneeling.

Branagh explained the essentials of Claudius's characterization:

> Two things were important in the approach. At the center of Jacobi's portrayal was, to put the idea crudely, a good man gone bad, even if later behavior—terror and paranoia—involved taking a second position to survival. He was essentially a man who loved Gertrude completely and entirely in a genuine way. When he says, "As the star moves not but in his sphere, I could not but by her," we take that at face value, just as we did with Ophelia when Polonius forces the truth from her about her feelings for Hamlet. His remorse is genuine, not cynical or abstractly considered.
>
> We put that essential persona in a place where he is required to tell the truth, where the act of confession might resolve things for him—a setting that encourages revelation and releases deep feeling. We wanted to offer a genuine moment for Claudius, one which revealed his soul, *not* underpinning it with the notion of a dry intellect resolving his guilt or the trappings of a stage villain. It was not meant to be that.
>
> Nor was it meant to make a statement about Shakespeare's religious views, because he is so careful not to do that. The religious vocabulary in this play is very confused; the playwright uses it where it suits him—it isn't consistently a Protestant play or a Catholic play or whatever.

On "Bow, stubborn knees," Claudius turned and appeared to kneel, continuing his contemplation.

As the soliloquy got handed over to Hamlet, Branagh's face was caught, watchful and plotting, by the camera on the opposite side of the dividing screen in the confessional. "Now might I do it pat" began, and with it, cutaway shots showed a dagger creeping through the screen journeying towards Claudius's bowed head. Shortly followed "And so I am reveng'd," and on "reveng'd," Hamlet knocked the butt of the dagger soundly and it appeared to enter the King's ear, the action accompanied by the sound of gushing blood. One felt a sudden horror, but momentarily Claudius's head appeared again, apparently unharmed, and we realized that this unnerving episode was a fantasy of Hamlet's.[15]

As Hamlet's rationalizations continued (mostly close-up shots) and he justified waiting until yet another time to kill his uncle, the audience saw cutaways of old Hamlet dying, of Claudius drunk and adulterous. The anguish of Hamlet's deliberations was fully rendered in the actor's facial expressions as he finally decided to delay the act of revenge until he could capture his victim on a more damning occasion. The shadow of his raised dagger ("Up, sword, and know thou a more horrid hent") and then the actual weapon was shown crossing his face upon this decision.

The soliloquy closed by handing the final couplet (as did Shakespeare) back to Claudius: "My words fly up, my thoughts remain below. / Words without thoughts never to heaven go." Claudius then looked quickly at the screen near his temple and, although Hamlet had exited by then, we saw in his startled face that he suddenly knew someone had been there. Here was another of those moments when the rather astonishing facial similarity between the two men—the blondish hair, the resemblant beards, and the intelligent eyes always one step ahead of the game, reinforced an illicit and adversarial bond between them. Hamlet's essential persona was cemented as well:

> In my view, he was fundamentally a man of decisive action. The execution of the deed was difficult, but the essential decision had been made, even though he was challenged by later thoughts of the Ghost being a devil. That's why we came up with the idea of a film technique which tricked the audience into thinking Claudius was going to be killed. Anytime you can throw an audience, either familiar

or unfamiliar with the plot, by challenging them—well, the worst price you will pay will be the "Oh, I am so annoyed now! That was so cheap!" Yet, to bring genuine violence into that scene charged with more dramatic currency what followed in Hamlet's soliloquy. Hamlet felt that, "My god, if I kill him in the confessional, he gets off scot-free!" To kill Claudius would have been consistent with Hamlet's being a man of action, but it would have been the wrong way to go about getting revenge. Yet, *he could have done it.*

We were very tight on Hamlet's eyes and hands, so that from a film point of view, you can see them dancing around as he tries to assess what his actions should be. In terms of cuts, it's very busy here.

In a sense, his not doing it fed that frustration with his own in-action, so that when he goes into the closet scene with Gertrude, a murder—not the King's after all—happens very quickly. The impetus to kill arrives there, in the wrong place, and Hamlet commits the revenge through the arras.

The three soliloquies were virtually seamless, beginning with " 'Tis now the very witching time," into which Claudius's body provided a visual transition, then on to "O my offense is rank" abutted against "Now might I do it pat." The camera selected and believeably recorded the reaction shots, and there was not that problem of disbelief that an audience often has with a stage production, where Hamlet stands nearby and speaks (at least loud enough for *them* to hear) while Claudius silently prays and never overhears Hamlet.

Branagh felt that in the theatre, that sense of danger had been re-moved, that people really knew he wasn't going to commit murder there, so the essential tension was gone. He wanted to challenge the audi-ence's familiarity with the story, catch them off guard, and remount the suspense.

The final soliloquy, "How all occasions do inform against me" (IV.iv.32–66), did not appear in the First Folio, which was the master text for this production, but was added from the Second Folio. Actors of Ham-let often make this choice because the speech offers a sense of finality, end-ing all of Hamlet's soliloquizing prior to his departure from Denmark. It is a speech about honor being achieved on the slightest of motives, even when many lives are at stake. Branagh wanted to emphasize the larger consequences of what was essentially a domestic drama until Hamlet became aware of Fortinbras. At that point, the plot began to involve several families in positions of power over entire countries. In this speech, Hamlet was "drawing larger connections with specific behavior and suggesting its consequences, putting himself and his problem in the context of a larger view of the world." [16] Branagh felt that Fortinbras's entrance into the play could seem minimized, but that there should be a connection between Hamlet's anger in "I do not *know* [which he shouts] / Why yet I live to say 'This thing's to do,'" and the family's affairs actually impacting the fate of Denmark.

Since Hamlet was finally putting two and two together and becoming more conscious of the scope of events, Branagh wanted that largeness—suggested by a speech beginning "What is a man"—to be reflected in the filmic expression of the final soliloquy: "It's an enormous question, so it needed an enormous shot."

Here, Branagh broke his usual pattern of the camera starting farther away from the character and coming closer, as if the camera were moving into the subject's mind. Hamlet was foregrounded against a snowy landscape dotted with Fortinbras's Norwegian troops. He was dressed in a black cloak and had just concluded his discussion with the soldier who informed him that Fortinbras was very much in charge of this tiny plot of land—although worthless, it was "already garrison'd." The camera pulled back to reveal the army camp framed by towering mountains. What began as a chest shot became a full body shot as the speech was spoken, moving back until Branagh himself was a tiny speck on the landscape. He eventually looked like an actor in a Greek or Roman (perhaps like Roscius) amphitheater.

At the same time, the actor's voice remained loud, cadenced, and (especially toward the end) emotional. The technique appeared to use Olivier's discovery about filming set speeches in his 1944 *Henry V*—where he felt that the voice should not fade in a "realistic" manner but remain strong while the camera moved *away* from the subject (as opposed to moving *in* for a close-up) in order to create the "full theatrical climax" that matched the heroic proportions of the soliloquizing.[17] Near the end, on "My thoughts be bloody, or be nothing worth!" the voice slowed and inserted pauses on the vocal caesura, Hamlet's arms suddenly rising to a consummational gesture at the end. These choices opened up the closed space in which the scene began to show armed soldiers against a huge mountainous vista. Simultaneously, the sequence acted to distance the audience, bringing them back to reality just before the intermission. Branagh added:

We were shooting in 70 millimeter, and a lot of productions traditionally weighted the first half of a longer film so that there was a certain natural conclusion midway through. The second half of the film moves into a different tempo—we leave Hamlet and go right back into the palace again to pick up more of the domestic details of the story. Hamlet continues to go out into the larger world, toward England. Before, he has lost sight of the full meaning of events that he is being part of and sometimes initiating. Here, he sees that life is no longer a game.

I feel that there is a spiritual heroism in Hamlet there, however stumbling, even if it comes from the words of a murderer [a revenger]. The speech retains our sympathy for a man who, although aware of his own thinking too precisely on the event, feels the irony of what is happening in this little patch of Poland.

There is a martial quality about the language, a call to spiritual arms, a resolve and a command to it. Cinematically, it needed something powerful and appropriate for the import and size of the speech, for the resonance of the ideas in it—it needed vast space. It's about all of Denmark and Norway as well—suddenly, part of northern Europe is changing.

The music under the speech also matched the tone of the moment. Branagh used music quite often under the soliloquies, working with long-time friend and collaborator Patrick Doyle:

We use music where we think it works, where it may help to move the story along and make it easier to listen to. It's always been a subject of debate in the films that we've done—many people are concerned that there is too much music and that it clashes against the verse.

I don't have music on in my house as a kind of "audio fur" for background—I'm a man of silence and when I listen to music, I listen to music. But when I've made a decision in film, I do it because I feel it's right to do so, partly embracing the medium in which we are involved, and partly creating a new medium within it. We're taking plays that were written for a dialogue-based medium and putting them into film, which is mostly about pictures.

In order to avoid simply photographing people talking, music becomes an important thematic element. For instance, repeated preoccupations of Hamlet that emerge across a number of different scenes (or speeches) can be marked musically to indicate developments of thought or to underscore a particular decision you have made if you've made a strong one about the meaning of a scene.

For instance, in the "fall of a sparrow" scene, one might argue that to say it without music is to allow for a myriad of ways to occur in the mind of a particular listener. I wanted to create a certain atmosphere in that scene which music expresses and clarifies, which goes hand in hand with the performance and strikes a particular kind of note. I wished not to offer other possibilities of interpretation for that moment by being more neutral.

Ultimately, there were several consistent principles Branagh followed in this production. Since his major focus was adapting Shakespearean plays to film and, at the same time, capitalizing on a medium which (as several critics have noted) Shakespeare himself would have, Branagh summarized his intentions:

You're always wanting everything. In "To be, or not to be," we wanted audiences to hear the speech anew, to support that with some danger and some sense, to provide stillness and clarity in the shooting. That's why most of the soliloquies were in one shot so that people could follow the dialogue. With a combination of all those requirements in every soliloquy, we were trying to hit all the bull's-eyes. In finding a legitimate way to address the drama of the scene on film, we wanted to exploit all the pictorial opportunities, not simply to shoot people talking.

Another principle, a requisite in performing arts, was variety. Establishing an interesting film rhythm meant seeking ways to change textures in the movie. This was achieved by changing locations (often alternating between public and private, as Shakespeare did), by creating uniquely juxtaposed film shots, and by the use of music. These were *audience considerations*, paramount to a film director's vision:

> There's a limit to the audience's patience and receptivity of thought and power of language. That means you need to allow for rests and breaths and physical space—rationing close-ups, for example. Much of this was reflected in the screenplay and was further adapted and adjusted as we went through rehearsal. It's an immense challenge given the ambition of using a full text—trying to do that without simply being a slave to a predicted short attention span [in the audience].

Another principle, also apparent in every other actor who was interviewed for this book, was the notion of exercising one's creativity and invention, not wanting to do this play in the traditional way, "to break free of conventional Hamlet imagery," i.e., from prior stage conventions. Of course, one must know the performance history of the play and, to a large extent, that implied removing the set-speech delivery often imposed on soliloquies as well as reintegrating the words back into the plot line. This was a tall order and perhaps all the more important because of the size of the project. Clearly, Branagh understood the complexity of the tightrope he walked in designing and preparing his production, yet he took on the challenge with a great deal of energy and optimism: "You hope that surprise and magic and mystery can happen, that that little bit of fairy dust will still come your way."

Branagh is an actor-manager in the mould of David Garrick as well as Laurence Olivier and, lest we forget, John Gielgud. He has accepted this vocation quite naturally, on the strength of his industry and his artistry, taking the torch from his predecessors as he simultaneously honored and acknowledged their accomplishments. This film displays his gifts—a talent for casting, a keen eye for cohering text and character, an independent imagination, and a remarkable instinct about how to clarify text for an audience imbued with film history.

On the final day of filming, Derek Jacobi presented Branagh with a small red book, a copy of *Hamlet* that had been owned by Johnston Forbes-Robertson, Michael Redgrave, and Peter O'Toole. Jacobi explained that it was to be handed on to the finest Hamlet of each generation.[18] It was the supreme accolade to be chosen by another actor for such a gift.

11

SIMON RUSSELL BEALE :

The Motive and the Cue for Passion

It is one thing to be caviar to the general but it is quite another to engender rave reviews from London critics. Simon Russell Beale's 2000–2001 Hamlet received adulation such as has not been heard since Derek Jacobi took on the role of the Prince of Denmark in 1979. No less was heard from reviewers in New York, home to the second group of dangerous theatre critics.

Some critics registered shock and surprise that a nontraditional Hamlet, a man both short and stocky as well as lacking the flowing locks and beautiful profile of the cultural image of the Dane, could so exactly match the persona that Shakespeare presented on the page. To have moved beyond an ideal carefully stored (some might say embedded) in the minds of twentieth-century audiences is a coup of major magnitude, a move forward into the twenty-first century of diversity and opportunity and new talent.

Beale was first lauded for his intelligence, his wit, and the absolute clarity of each spoken phrase in his portrayal of Hamlet. His line readings were not innovative and yet were absolutely crystal clear. Thus was a first trap avoided: Whereas most actors try something different in their attempts to be original in a play that has over four hundred years of stage baggage, Beale was satisfied with simply and lucidly communicating the language of the play to his audience.

To the two qualities of intelligence and clarity must be added the most

Simon Russell Beale in Hamlet, *2000–2001. Photograph by Catherine Ashmore, London.*

necessary of Hamlet qualifications: the creation of a character of finely-tuned sensitivity, a creature who reads motive in every persona he accosts, and who reacts with the vulnerability of a man who wears his heart on his sleeve. Beale performed with immediacy and truth. He was, as other actors say, "always in the moment."

Beale did not burst onto the scene already a phenomenon. His credential was remarkable for a variety and range of roles which would seem to have no particular common thread: Osric, Ariel, Iago, Edgar, the King of Navarre, Mosca, Edward II, Thersites, and Richard III. Few actors traverse far beyond their comfortable line of acting, but Beale has won Olivier awards for his work. Traditionally, Hamlets have been cast for their leading-man status. Beale was an actor who relished being cast against type, enjoying the roles which did not, at superficial glance, seem to fit his physical appearance. His gift was his ability to wrap the role around himself so expertly that audiences were drawn into his self-belief, his absorption of the part.

This *Hamlet* production alternated between previews in London and tours to the provinces during the summer of 2000 before officially opening in London in August. It also played in Glasgow, Aberdeen, Stockholm, Dublin, Elsinore, Belgrade, Boston, Minneapolis, Tucson, Phoenix, and New York before returning to London a year after its opening. Elsinore was unique for the cast because they played inside the courtyard (which hadn't been done since the late 1970s) as the seagulls, the dying light, and the bitter cold and wet atmosphere re-created the natural setting of the play. Beale recounted: "We had to go to the toilet outside [during the performance], and during a gap in the play I went out and had a pee. When I walked back behind the courtyard dressed as Hamlet, there was a spooky feeling in being Hamlet and yet hearing it going on all around me." [1]

Belgrade presented an even more extraordinary experience because the Royal National Theatre tour was the first visit of a major Western national theatre company since the bombing had stopped. It was here, Beale said, that he was "reminded of the importance of live performance in Belgrade. It was the fact that we were there to touch and talk to and smell each other. The fact of the bombing was out in the open and you couldn't hide. The theatre was full, packed to the rafters. They welcomed us with tremendous generosity of spirit."

Beale also told a reporter:

> In Belgrade . . . I stopped to look in a window, and a woman came out of the shop. She recognized me from the posters of the show, and said, "Hamlet. Hamlet." Then she said, "To be or not to be"—about

fourteen times! It was the only English she knew, that single little phrase. That's bizarre, isn't it—and terribly moving.

The visit was also the subject of speeches in the House of Lords, extolling the company for the importance of the diplomatic mission.

The mise-en-scène of the production was designed to emphasize the cultural climate of postmedieval Christianity as well as to provide some practical answers to taking a large production on tour. The back wall was covered with windowless panels. Ornate lighted lamps resembling brass censers hung from the flies and were raised and lowered during scene changes, even swinging sanctimoniously as actors jarred them. A number of large trunk-like boxes were used for a variety of effects—heaped high as a parapet for the Ghost's appearance to Hamlet, for Gertrude to open as she regarded souvenirs of her marriages, to hide Polonius in Gertrude's closet, to become the Gravedigger's[2] grave.

The background and transitional music of Lasso motets resembled Gregorian chants, sacred dirges which punctuated the action and set the mood for pendulous scenes. Often side-lighting the action, the lighting was golden, melancholy, always filled with floating dust motes such as would trouble the mind's eye. Costumes were heavy and rich, reminiscent of Italian Rennaisance paintings.

The full cast shared the bustle of the famous opening scene, "Who's there?" "Nay, answer me; stand and unfold yourself" and then the conversation high on the castle with the soldiers and Horatio magically recombined into a full-blown scene. The stage was now set for the solo entrance of the man playing the title role.

Beale had made some sweeping statements about this play to an interviewer who wanted to know why the play had lived so long in the annals of literature. He replied:

> It asks the big questions: What happens after death? What's the value of my life? Other plays—*Lear*, for instance, ask these questions indirectly. In *Hamlet*, they're direct.
>
> Millions of other people have asked the same questions, but *Hamlet* is like a glass of white wine; it's done with such delicacy for such big questions. With such humor and irony.[3]

Prior to the play's opening, Beale spent long hours in rehearsals and in concentrated individual work with the director and the company. Beale described the director's methods:

> When I began, I didn't have a notion of Hamlet. The director John Caird and I read the play together and discussed it, just us two, for about a month beforehand, an act a week.
>
> John Caird's lovely; he's very, very sharp, very clever. He gave me confidence that Hamlet was a good role for me to take. Hamlet was, as we set forth, gentler than I imagined he would be.
>
> John gave the characters the benefit of the doubt, which was wonderful. His view of the play was very loving. For example, at the beginning of the play, one feels that things could work out fine— Hamlet's just got a feeling that something's wrong, but that's all, and he's on his way back to Wittenberg. In this view, Claudius is a man who has done one terrible, terrible thing, as Hamlet himself says, "Some vicious mole of nature" that carries "the stamp of one defect." A rather optimistic view of human nature, John has.

Such openness in the director, already known for his prize-winning *Nicholas Nickleby* and *Les Misérables*, increased the company's collaboration on the production and created a valuable sense of teamwork and family once the tour was on the road:

> By the time I arrived in rehearsal, I thought John would come in with a fully edited text. Instead, he spent two weeks with the whole company cutting the play. Which is a long time. We all did it together, which is a fantastically good way to get to know the play because every line has to be argued and supported or dismissed. He would say, "Couldn't we lose that line, what do you think?" That made it the actor's burden to cut. Everyone agreed on things. It was a very gentle process, people were generally willing to lose lines. There were a couple of cases where an actor would say, "I really do need this line in," and John would say "fine."
>
> We originally tried to get the production down to three hours but we soon knew we couldn't do that, so we settled on three and a half. By the end of two weeks, everyone knew the play backwards

and forwards. This was a much better process of cutting the play, doing it with the entire company.

John is very open to ideas, from whatever source. The idea of Rosencrantz and Guildenstern making their entrance over the boxes came from our stage manager. John would always, always listen to other people's ideas and never dismiss them. He was fantastically generous.

There was a free blocking period. I don't remember ever really setting blocking. We played around with the boxes and shifted them around and generated ideas until things got solidified.

In an odd sort of way, though, the role of Hamlet is never solidified, never totally conquered. Beale described his own avenue into it:

He's a mystery. I think it is more accurate to say that I am in love with him and that is slightly different. It would be presumptuous to say that I understand him well, because there is so much there that I don't do in our version. Also, he's complex and changing all the time.

I would *not* be in love with Iago, who is an extraordinary character and great fun to play, but, my god, you couldn't love the man! I wanted Hamlet to be a sweet prince. As I began the rehearsals, I gradually realized he was becoming that. He is a gentle man despite all his violence and arrogance. But to play him so soft is a bit of a risk—something I don't normally do. I'm much more inclined to give a character exactly the opposite of the benefit of the doubt. I often place them in the worst light, Thersites or Richard or Iago or whomever. But I'm actually in love with Hamlet—with his soul and with his noble heart.

Beale had looked closely at what he thought of as Hamlet's shortcomings, those beyond his killing of Polonius later in the play:

Obviously, I find bits that are puzzling. For example, when he attacks Laertes over the grave, which he later apologizes for and admits was a mistake—it's like a sudden reappearance of the madness he thought he'd got over. Also, his attitude to women is entirely received wisdom. Perhaps that's a twenty-first century perspective. However, given the Hamlet that I do, to a serious divinity student, his outlook would be traditional. I still think, "Come on, you don't have to give us that stuff about vessels of sin, Hamlet—you can do better than that."

The part that worries me is that the violence is hedged with something that is perfectly explainable, but unattractive. Since his mother behaved badly, he assumes that is how all women behave. I don't think he can have a decent human relationship once his father has given him the commission to kill Claudius. After that, all human relationships are gone, including the one with Horatio, which has been a remote relationship anyway, a gentlemenly one, not a fully fledged one.

In a way, he's got to get rid of Ophelia because he realizes that, consciously or unconsciously, she will be destroyed along with him. The "to a nunnery" comment is a very particular way of saying it: "This is a serious gesture. Get out of here."

At first Hamlet does not know that Polonius and Claudius are present in the nunnery scene (it's a great mistake to assume that Hamlet knows everything just because he is who he is). It also highlights her lie, if he doesn't know they're being watched. The only person who *directly* lies to him is Ophelia, and this devastates him. She's caught up in this hideous world—she's already sold her soul. And yet her position is impossible. She's not in a position to refuse her father, but that doesn't make any difference to Hamlet. To him, she's compromised herself, and the lie she tells him breaks his heart.

It also means the scene has somewhere to go. It's a hugely important scene because so much of the play is about love betrayed. It starts with his mother, then Rosencrantz and Guildenstern, then Ophelia— a series of betrayals.

Then there's only the audience left, waiting there.

Beale explained, bit by bit, how he created his reading of the character, which was both intellectual and emotional, by making his own links, building a web of logic and connections for himself:

The glory of the part is that it is so enormous that you'll never get it right, you'll never understand it all. It's similar to Iago, because you have to build it up step by step. Whereas Richard III is partly a physical thing, where you have to make a very grand first silhouette of the character that's sexy and witty and clever yet has this terrible physical burden.

With Hamlet it's a series of little decisions.

One major decision, however, was most certainly out of Beale's hands. His own mother died after he began rehearsals on the play that they both had desperately wished she could witness. He indicated that the entire play was a tribute to her and added, "Not much good about it, is there? In God's plan." Her loss deepened and informed his very real sense of grief, and perhaps subconsciously his interpretation of the prince, a character that he wanted his mother to be able to love.

The soliloquies in Hamlet are, of course, a challenge most actors relish, and a theatrical construct that affects the entire play: "The exciting thing about Hamlet is [being able to] determine the pace. Sometimes he speeds through; sometimes he stops the show on the soliloquies." Beale cut his teeth on acting the great soliloquizers, having performed Iago, Richard III, Thersites, and even Pangloss, so he had considerable experience with audience address in his credentials. Not many actors do, unless they train or perform in musical theatre:

> I don't know how or when when I made the decision to do them direct-address—sometime during the rehearsals. Now, it's absolutely deliberate to do them that way. The director is very important in allowing this.
>
> Richard III's soliloquies were audience-addressed—he's leader of the gang—up to the Bosworth speech, where it's desperate and internal. It's always fascinating to find that wonderful moment when characters stop soliloquizing: Richard stops, of course, when he gets the crown; Iago stops when the plot becomes too busy and he doesn't have time to contact the audience anymore; and Hamlet stops when he returns from the boat trip.

There were moments, within the larger context of the direct-address mode, when Hamlet retreated into himself. They were moments of extreme isolation, when Hamlet realized that his only friends were not onstage. Beale explained it this way: "He is saying to the audience, 'I've got to go through with this and I need to make a decision.' So that in the third soliloquy when he says, 'Am I a coward?' he is saying, 'tell me,' to the audience. What he's after is, 'Tell me, and then we can move on from there.'"

John Caird's opinions coincided with Beale's point of view:

There's a well-known axiom that the audience is the missing character in any play you're doing. In a Shakespeare play, that's probably more true than in others, because the story is so full of soliloquy. So many characters have a relationship with the missing character, that when you get an audience for the first time you complete the circle of communication, and find what the play needs in order to have a meaning. Consciously or otherwise, actors learn a tremendous amount from a live audience about attention, about timing, about tension.[4]

The director made these remarks during the first previews, and then made them more specific about Beale:

In a positive and creative way he's fallen in love with the audience. I think it's a necessary part of his journey. To arrive in front of an audience and have them so manifestly and audibly appreciative must have been music to his ears. He's bound to be seduced by their response, but he's an honest player so he won't be corrupted by it. Over the next few weeks he'll continue to play with the audience, but he'll become more rigorous in the way he does so. The great risk in the first few previews in a big, romantic part is self-indulgence. But Simon is an extremely self-denying actor, so I don't think he'll ever be guilty of that.[5]

In the collaborative spirit of the enterprise, understudy Simon Day offered thoughts about how the soliloquies operate within the play: "I think the soliloquies are the key, because they're Hamlet stripped bare, talking through his thoughts and feelings. They provide stepping stones, and if you can get them right, then everything falls into place."[6] Beale's summation was more overarching: "The play is unquestionably Hamlet's debate with God, and where that leads him in the final act is probably to a good place."[7] Consequently, there is a primary burden to these speeches, as Beale noted:

I think the most important thing is *to make the argument clear.* One way of doing this is to play down any sense of hysteria that

Hamlet might feel. You must convey rationally, carefully, to the audience what is going on in your head. In moments of hyper-emotion, you shouldn't cloud the argument.

There is this thing in the back of my mind where I remember hearing a director say, "I don't care how *you* feel. I want you to make *me* feel." But if you don't get the argument across, there is no foundation for any emotional life at all (especially within the audience) if they don't understand what I am saying.

The first soliloquy was performed downstage left, with Beale kneeling in front of one of the trunks. He was alone until Horatio entered near the end of the speech. He began the opening lines, "O that this too too solid flesh would melt" (I.ii.129), motivating them from the examination that he does of his own hands held in front of him, a recognizable, pure, and natural choice. He also employed a two-fingered pinch on "In a little month," a phrase which was repeated throughout the soliloquy. Beale talked about his actor's perspective on the speech:

> With all those sub-clauses coming into the flow of it, the soliloquy is a hellish technical nightmare. I suddenly realized that it is also a very accurate portrayal of the panic of grief. I think Shakspeare obviously knew about those moments in life. Hamlet cannot breathe properly. He cannot *settle*. The other soliloquies have a very logical progression, but this one doesn't. It's a stream of consciousness soliloquy, and he's saying, "I don't want to remember the details, but I cannot help it. Yet I will remember this one central thing."

Beale expanded on his choice of "solid" from the other choices offered in editions of the play, i.e., "sallied," and "sullied":

> We decided on "solid" because it was not overly complicated. Now is the time to be talking about the flesh being *solid*, to talk about melting away and killing yourself. Now is not the time to be talking about original sin [sullied flesh]. He does that later. That's *my* decision, *my* taste.
>
> John Caird did a rather dangerous game late in rehearsals, where a character's name would be shouted out, and you had to go to the front of the room and everyone else imitated you. When it was my

turn, everyone stuck their hands up in the air in the same way that I did at those moments.

Funnily enough, I have a link with that gesture which I've only just noticed. Right at the end, after I've killed Claudius and Horatio takes the cup from me, I look at my hands in a very similar way.

After the first soliloquy, the Ghost lured Hamlet away from his companions to a remote place on the castle ramparts. Hamlet reacted with great consternation to the Ghost's long and gory narrative. Just before the illusion wafted away, he handed Hamlet a dagger, directly commissioning his son to the deed of vengeance. The second soliloquy, "O all you host of heaven," was spoken from a piled-up parapet created from the boxes onstage, which represented a distant location atop the castle, and the words were an extended reaction to the vivid details of old Hamlet's murder. The performance of the speech was not overly physicalized because the actor was keeping his balance on top of about twelve feet of stage furniture.

During the last third of the speech, Hamlet referred to his "tables": "My tables—meet it is I set it down. . . . " The actor has a choice to produce these or not. Beale and Caird liked the idea of using this prop, which had first appeared during Claudius's speech in I.ii, where he attempted to persuade Hamlet to break off excessive shows of grief. He remarked:

> It's such an odd moment, and I was a bit skeptical about using the notebook.[8] Hamlet has just seen the Ghost and he thinks—Well, I'd better write it down. Why does he do this? Because it can be a lovely insight into Hamlet being a scholar.[9]
>
> I did not want it to be so odd that the audience had never seen it before, which would be a really out-of-the-blue and strange thing. So, we established the book earlier on in the production as a thing that Hamlet does—jots down his pensées, so to speak.
>
> The speech has been at a dangerous level recently, and I would like to take it down a bit. It can become a one-note rant. The soliloquies are very difficult if you are trying to change something in them, because you don't have the stimulus of the other actors to respond to. You also have a muscle memory about how the rhythm of the speech goes—what you have settled on in rehearsal; once you have this, you

like to fulfill it each time or you feel you are cheating the audience! My great weakness is that I pause too often, and I have to keep reminding myself that I need to tighten it up a bit.

Beale also had reservations about the Ghost handing over the dagger, but he felt the gesture was supported by the text:

> The Ghost was "Armed at point exactly, cap-a-pe" as he was sighted by the soldiers in I.i, and this detail has been emphasized in the dialogue, but we didn't want him clanking around in a huge armor. I've never met a ghost, but I presume perhaps this is a ghost you can touch as you would a real human being. So this is why he has the dagger and why he gives it to Hamlet.
>
> It's like Excalibur, a precious object. That also helped me to be more devastated after I'd murdered Polonius—I'd not only killed the wrong man, but I'd done it with the sword Dad gave me. Later on, I also have great despair when I am forced to hand the sword over to Claudius: That was a real abdication of responsibility and dignity.

The use of properties first introduced, seen, and then reappearing was one of the superb achievements of this production. Not only did the objects have a kind of continuity, but they also took on a more freighted symbolic value. Gertrude took what we assume to be her original wedding veil out of a trunk—it reappeared at Ophelia's grave, the bride-to-have-been, punctuating the uselessness of her death.

The next major soliloquy, "O what a rogue and peasant slave am I," also made use of a prop. After Hamlet recited the lines from the "rugged Pyrrhus" speech just after greeting the players to Elsinore, he gave over gracefully to the First Player. From these visitors, he took a very toy-looking sword and used it in his next scene, which was the soliloquy. The speech was beautifully managed, with Beale about five feet from the edge of the apron, looking directly into the audience's eyes when posing questions:

> This sequence demonstrates what I was talking about when I mentioned the "panic" of grief. A friend of mine said, "It's like being mugged." One goes on perfectly normally long after a personal tragedy, and then suddenly, Wham. It is like that with the players. At first Hamlet is having such a good time with them, and then all of a sud-

den, the Player does that speech about Pyrrhus and his not being able to act, "his sword, seemed i' the air to stick,"—and Hamlet's father's death all floods back to him and then leads him to this soliloquy which really started, as it were, a page or two before.

In the first part of this soliloquy Hamlet castigated himself for not acting when he had more motive to do so than the Player did, and at the end there was a very active plotting sequence. Beale said:

> "Rogue and peasant slave" is fantastic. I used to think it was a rather ordinary argument—isn't that awful, in my arrogance—because you think—Well, he doesn't say anything here you don't know already. But there is something about committing this long passage to memory that does something to your insides, your bowels. It is so bloody long. It has a definite story—a beginning, a middle and an end. An absolute shape. Plus it is the most direct of the direct-addresses that I do. Right into people's eyes.
>
> The prop sword, which he was given by the Players as a joke, he happens to be holding in his hand. I don't use it at the beginning of the speech, but I suddenly realize I have it and I use it to gesture toward "this player here" who has just exited. I also use it to hit on a trunk at "Fie upon't, foh!" in anger. And then I use it to motivate "I have heard that guilty creatures sitting at a play. . . ."
>
> I quite like the idea that he is holding it and just talking. It tickles me—the fakeness of the sword, which is on a fake stage set already.

Early on in rehearsals, Beale experimented with a number of ways of handling this gargantuan speech:

> I'm not so sure what to do about "O, what a rogue and peasant slave." It's very long, with three or four sections, and halfway through I think I'm boring people to death. I don't know where Hamlet's brain is, so I'm trying it in different ways. Is this a man who can't feel anything, in which case you can play it as self-mocking throughout, or does he really feel something, then pulls back and says "Why what an ass am I?" It's a really tricky one.[10]

By the end of the American tour, Beale was saying:

I've changed just a bit on "About my brains!" [II.ii.588, about two-thirds of the way through this third soliloquy.] I used to do it internally, but now I pound my head as if to say "Think, think! Come on, crank it up, let's throw some ideas around!" which gets him on to the plot to watch Claudius sitting at a play.

Beale made some interesting textual choices, one of which was nontraditional: He omitted the "O Vengeance" line—which appears in the First Folio of the play but not in the First or Second Quarto—after "Bloody, bawdy villain! Remorseless, treacherous, lecherous, kindless villain." He explained:

> I cannot do it. I felt embarrassed by it. Dennis Quilley [who played Polonius and the Gravedigger during the first part of the run] was very upset that I didn't do it. I tried and tried and tried, and then I felt there was no point in beating against a locked door. I can just about manage "treacherous, lecherous, kindless." So I took the coward's way out.
>
> And, you know, I do have the support of the *Hamlet* editions that say there are other options.
>
> But using the phrase didn't suit my Hamlet. He's so gentle. . . . I suppose that every actor does cut the cloth to suit himself.

The most famous soliloquy of all took on weight and resonance for Beale: "This speech is now my favorite. 'Rogue and peasant slave' used to be my favorite but 'To be, or not to be' crept up alongside it." The "tables" came out on this speech as well, as reported in Jonathan Croall's *Hamlet Observed*, which closely documented the rehearsals in June 2000:

> Simon speaks the soliloquy with great simplicity, sustaining its argument very clearly. John suggests that the first line is simply a repetition of what Hamlet has already concluded, and the idea emerges of Simon writing it down in his notebook before he starts the speech. John stresses that it begins casually—"There's always the suicide option"—but then it becomes more serious: "It's not just about himself, it's not just about suicide, it's about existence." [11]

Beale described the speech as a single arc. Despite his enormously modest and unadorned delivery very directly into the eyes of the audience from the front apron of the stage, the speech was not without its technical traps. Beale explained:

> As for "To be or not to be," it's wonderful when it works, but that's quite rare. Although it's a stopping soliloquy, it mustn't grind to a halt. It's a delicate balance, and I tend to slow down far too much. The sentences are oddly constructed, and you can lose the main verb. "Puzzles the will" comes at a very odd place, and if you slow down too much before that on "the undiscover'd country," you have a problem.[12]

But for Beale, many of the internal images recalled his personal situation concerning the loss of his mother.

> She died about a month before I started work on *Hamlet*, late in 2000. There were about five months of really grim decline. Pancreatic cancer. It presents itself very late. By the time she found out, she was pretty far gone. It's a really horrible one, and she was a doctor so she must have known that it would be. She knew I was going to do Hamlet and she really wanted to see it. She would say, "I will see it. I will see it." And she just couldn't make it.
>
> She comes to mind on "Adieu, adieu, adieu! Remember me," when the Ghost departs, and also on "O all you host of heaven!" The description of "The undiscover'd country from whose bourn / No traveller returns" is self-referencing. It always seemed quite an odd line because the Ghost, my father, returned. It's one of those slightly illogical things that Shakespeare does that doesn't really matter. I did a little twist in it last night. I coined it a bit, making it clear that it was "undiscover'd," which gave the line a freshness and a slightly more proactive meaning.[13]

Beale performed at the Lyttleton on the first night with a framed picture of his mother placed on the prop table: "It meant so much to me. . . . Every time I came off she was there."[14]

The next soliloquy, "'Tis now the very witching time of night," had a definite place in the sequential arc of the play-within-the play scene:

> That's all linked with where John put the interval.
>
> It is a bit fascinating that Hamlet's reaction to the play-within-the-play, the revelation that Claudius is guilty, is further *inaction*.

Calling for music, calling for the recorders, is another delaying tactic. Part of this is Hamlet's passivity as well: He's waiting for how the courtiers are going to react. Hamlet waits for that summons after the play is over, waits for Rosencrantz and Guildenstern (who are sent by the King). He doesn't charge right after the King when the play is broken off.

This highlights John's decision to hold the interval there. When Hamlet finally gets the proof he wants, that Claudius killed King Hamlet, it's devastating.

He breaks down, he needs time to think. *The interval.* In that time —he summons up this rebellious mode which leads to "Now might I drink hot blood," that soliloquy.

The speech is, I think, slightly fake, slightly horror fiction. I mean, he sort of believes it.

It also ends with, to the modern ear, an incomprehensible rhyming couplet that we simply couldn't cut (incomprehensibility being the yardstick for which we decided whether or not to make cuts—the audience had to be able to at least understand the lines): "How in my words somever she be shent, / To give them seals never, my soul, consent" (III.iii.402). It's almost impossible for me to understand it even now! You can't cut it because it's a bloody rhyming couplet. It is an odd soliloquy.

The next speech took place very soon afterward. Claudius attempted to pray for forgiveness without much success, "O my offense is rank, it smells to heaven!" which the audience perceived, but Hamlet did not. The King knelt in front of a large trunk, and he finally put his head down on the top of the trunk in despair. Beale maintained that Hamlet was so wrapped up in his next objective that the turmoil of it saved Claudius's life:

Hamlet knows he has to go to his mother, and the prospect frightens him to death because he's not very good at confrontation, and now all the cards are on the table. He *has* to face the major problem, which is his relationship with his mother. She's a powerful woman, and he's put it off already by telling Polonius, "I will come by and by,"—I'll come when I am ready. Even over Claudius's praying body, he says, "Now to my mother," still slightly putting it off.

The tension that apprehension engenders in him leads to the death of Polonius eventually. He's in such a state of fear that has been accumulating during that walk across the castle, via the chapel, which is frightening, cold, dark, lonely.

The speech is the most perfect example of a genuine logical problem. It's like a syllogism, A is B and B is C and so on. Funnily enough, it gets a laugh on "this is hire and salary, not revenge." There is passion toward the end, when it's "Then trip him, that his heels may kick at heaven, / And that his soul may be as damn'd and black as hell, whereto it goes."

Of course, certain soliloquies often clarify other parts of the play:

I couldn't see doing this play in a godless universe—it has to have a strong Christian Renaissance basis. Even Claudius saying to Laertes's boast to cut Hamlet's throat in the church, "No place, indeed, should murder sanctuarize,"—that is firmly canon law. Equally, Hamlet is not going to kill Claudius in the chapel because he really does believe in purgatory, and he does believe in hell. That is absolutely Catholic, straight down the line.

When Hamlet reached Gertrude's closet, and once the murder of Polonius was over, the Ghost reappeared. Caird staged a beatific moment where Hamlet stood still while both Gertrude and Hamlet's father each stroked him in a suspended choreographic moment which was the only confirmation of its kind before the duel: "You suddenly realize that's all Hamlet wants is a return to the status quo. His body relaxes from the grief. That moment of quiet was John's idea."

"Now might I do it, pat" was the final soliloquy for this production since much of the political side of the play, including Fortinbras and his exploits, was omitted. "How all occasions do inform against me," (IV.iv.32–66, the seventh soliloquy) was one of the cuts made.

For all the naturalness and comprehensibility in Beale's verse-speaking, he held decided opinions about the art form:

At Cambridge, I had a colleague who taught me about simplicity in presentation. Steven Unwin was artistic director of a small touring theatre. I was introduced to a sort of Puritan clarity about these things.

He didn't want any fat on the language, he wanted it presented clearly and well and accurately.

I suppose my English teacher at school taught me the rules of verse early. I was at Cambridge for three years and the Guildhall School of Music and Drama for a year, and I left before we got on to the Shakespeare class, so I learned most of my verse-speaking at the Royal Shakespeare Company on the floor. It's quite a dangerous thing to do and I made a lot of mistakes (such as over-elaboration). But I think I know the rules now. Sort of.

I still do count the iambic pentameter. I am very strict, in fact. Sam Mendes taught me that, that you can actually do the dadum-dadumdadumdadumdadum the whole time. If you really can't make it work, then you are safe to reverse the stress or whatever. I am tempted to do lovely things like "O THAT this TOO too SOLid FLESH would MELT" rather than "OH thet-this TOO too SOLid FLESH would MELT," and also "But THAT the DREAD of SOMEthing AFter DEATH," rather than "BUT thet-the DREAD of SOMEthing AFter death." It has a lovely softness in my mind [not making a syncopated trimeter at the beginning of the line but rather saying it strictly iambically]. I prefer it. It's slightly less logical but it has a slightly better rhythm. I can be very strict about meter and a bit bossy about it sometimes to other people.

My big weaknesses, from the purist point of view, are big gaps [long pauses]. Also not necessarily replying on cue to the half-line. I sometimes do that, but very often I don't.

I don't care so much about the structure of the verse as I do about *being clear*. If that means I break up the verse more than I should, well, sometimes that is clearer to the modern ear. Frankly, I don't mind that. If you obey the rules strictly, sometimes certain lines become incomprehensible.

It's a vexed question, of course. It has to do with *taste*, not with *rules*.

Beale's standards most certainly paid off in terms of critical assessments. John Goss, reviewing the production in the *Sunday Telegraph* on October 9, 2000, made this comment:

This is a Hamlet who has earned the right to lecture the players on how verse (or highly charged prose) should be spoken. He is a master, for example, of the slight emphasis which focuses feeling in a single word without drawing undue attention to the fact. . . . But he is equally responsive to the general shape of a speech—what Gielgud called "the whole span of the arc"—and to the forward movement of thought.

One of the reasons that Beale's Hamlet was so successful was that he showed so many of the colors in the Hamlet spectrum. This prince was touchingly emotional, putting his head in his hands to weep after Ophelia left the play scene, convincing us that the two of them could have, under different circumstances, become a couple. The jokes were played full-out with a sardonic wit made effective by enormously skilled comic timing. His sense of princeliness not only moved the action along as people scurried to obey his commands but also projected a sense of what Denmark could and should have been had he been crowned.

The director offered his summation of Beale's work early on in rehearsal:

> Simon is becoming more and more impressive. The way he holds the whole play together in his imagination is quite extraordinary. His fascination for the development of the character, his appetite for experiment, and his daring as an actor are constantly astonishing. He lives on the experience of driving the play through with his will and passion and fire. He's like a racehorse at the start of the Grand National: every time we go into a single scene or a run of the play, he can't wait to get at it.[15]

Beale assessed this role against the many he had already played:

> The part just adapts itself to you; it's one of the most hospitable an actor can play. It says, Come and get me, I've got everything here, just pick what you want. But it does demand that you strip everything away. . . . As an actor, the part enables you to say, I don't need to do any tricks, I don't need to show off in any way. You're able to stand onstage and allow people to have faith in you, to see that you

are interesting as a human being—that of course applies to everyone onstage, but particularly to Hamlet. It's a most liberating experience, if you can get anywhere near that. You think, This is it, this is the Holy Grail of acting.[16]

Obviously Simon Russell Beale's particular cup runneth over.

NOTES

INTRODUCTION

1. Laurence Olivier, *On Acting* (London: Hodder and Stoughton, Sceptre edition, 1987), 52.

2. Glenn Collins, "Kevin Kline Dons Another Crown," *New York Times*, July 1, 1984.

3. Only a few major theatres keep promptbooks. The Royal Shakespeare Company does, the Royal National Theatre keeps some, and the New York Shakespeare Festival has begun to document major productions with videotapes. The practice is by no means uniform in the United States or Great Britain.

4. See E. W. Roessler, *The Soliloquy in German Drama* (New York: Columbia University Press, 1915), 3.

5. An actor can use apostrophe to address the speech to gods, absent persons, natural forces, or parts of the body, as Bernard Beckerman explained in *Shakespeare at the Globe* (New York: Collier-Macmillan, 1962), 84. The performance energies are thus sent "outward," however, not necessarily to spectators.

6. I must hasten to state that Derek Jacobi's Hamlet on tour is an exception to this. Furthermore, Jacobi's soliloquies on the 1980 BBC *Hamlet* were different from his stage performance of them. See chapter 5.

7. Michael Goldman, "The Future of Performance Criticism," presentation at the Shakespeare Association of America meeting, Seattle, Washington, April 11, 1987.

8. In this book I have excluded the shorter solo "asides," (speeches of two to eight lines). They reinforce the character's soliloquizing tendencies rather than define them and rarely offer more than one "beat" of meaning or emotion, whereas soliloquies develop several thoughts and offer more meat for the actor. See Maurice Charney, "Asides, Soliloquies, and Offstage Speech in *Hamlet*: Implications for Staging," in *Shakespeare and the Sense of Performance*, ed. Marvin Thompson and Ruth Thompson (London: Associated University Presses, 1989).

9. For consistency, all line citations are taken from G. Blakemore Evans, ed.,

The Riverside Shakespeare (Boston: Houghton Mifflin, 1974). If a given production changed the order of the soliloquies (most productions use the Second Quarto and First Folio sequencing of "O, what a rogue," shortly preceding "To be, or not to be") or the wording in them ("sullied" or "solid" instead of "sallied"), that choice was noted. If a soliloquy was excluded, the omission is usually discussed in the chapter.

10. See, for example, Wolfgang Clemen's *Shakespeare's Soliloquies* (London: Methuen, 1987). Clemen mentions performance in the introduction to his book (1–12), but the discussion is neither thorough nor convincing. He does present several literary readings of selected soliloquies in nonspecific and nontheatrical contexts. See also William E. McDonnell, "The Shakespearean Soliloquy: A Problem of Focus," *Text and Performance Quarterly* 10 (1990): 227–34. McDonnell decrees which soliloquies are direct-addressed, inwardly addressed, or "debatable," offering for evidence videotaped versions of plays and his own close reading. He quite accurately clarifies that his conclusions are his opinions as opposed to being based on stage practice.

11. Peter Brook, *The Empty Space* (New York: Avon, 1969), 16.

12. See John Barton, "Set Speeches and Soliloquies," in *Playing Shakespeare* (London: Methuen, 1984), 94. In a workshop at the Jerusalem Theatre Conference on June 1, 1988, Barton demonstrated with Royal Shakespeare Company actors Estelle Kohler and Harriet Walters that what are technically "monologues" (i.e., Katherine's banquet speech in *The Taming of the Shrew*) should be largely shared with an audience. He said, "It [the set speech delivered to oneself] can go on for a few lines and then there is a law of diminishing returns." Barton clearly saw monologues and soliloquies as requiring the same performance mode.

13. A six-year endeavor, from 1979 to 1985, the series used grants from the Exxon Corporation, the Metropolitan Life Insurance Company, and Morgan Guaranty Trust Company of New York.

14. An entire journal, *Shakespeare Bulletin*, devotes pages to these "academic reviews," productions evaluated by university professors.

15. Tyrone Guthrie, *A Life in the Theatre* (London: Columbus Books, 1960), 187.

16. Sally Beauman, *The Royal Shakespeare Company: A History of Ten Decades* (Oxford: Oxford University Press, 1982), 239.

17. See Beauman, chapters 10 and 11, 236–87.

18. Guthrie, 124.

19. Ralph Berry, "Hamlet and the Audience," in *Shakespeare and the Sense of Performance*, ed. Marvin Thompson and Ruth Thompson (London: Associated University Presses, 1989), 24.

20. Laurence Olivier, quoted in an article by Michael Billington, *Manchester Guardian Weekly*, July 23, 1989.

21. John A. Mills, *Hamlet Onstage* (London: Greenwood Press, 1985), 180.

22. Guthrie, 184–88.

23. Brook, 96ff.

24. During this time, there were upwards of twenty summer or year-round Shakespeare festivals operating in various parts of the United States, many planted in vacation spots.

25. Glenn Loney and Patricia Mackay, *The Shakespeare Complex: A Guide to Summer Festivals and Year-Round Repertory in North America* (New York: Drama Book Specialists, 1975).

26. This book is a production diary, complete with undertext, rehearsal and performance notes, compiled over a period of two years of playing the role (New York: Grove Weidenfeld, 1989), vii–viii.

27. John Russell Brown, "The Nature of Speech in Shakespeare's Plays," in *Shakespeare and the Sense of Performance*, ed. Marvin Thompson and Ruth Thompson (London: Associated University Presses, 1989), 56.

28. There are six lines which are structured as questions, plus the section at II.ii.571–75, which includes a series of them.

29. Arthur Colby Sprague and J. C. Trewin, *Shakespeare's Plays Today* (Columbia: University of South Carolina Press, 1971), 36.

30. Fortinbras in Polish productions is, of course, a special case in and of itself.

HAMLET'S SOLILOQUIES

1. [Oh Vengeance!] This line appears in the First Folio of the play, but not in the First or Second Quarto. G. Blakemore Evans' *Riverside Shakespeare* (used as a reference here) includes the phrase only in the "Textual Notes" (an extended list of variants in First Folio, First Quarto, and Second Quarto) to *The Tragedy of Hamlet, Prince of Denmark*, specifically on p. 1190. I include the phrase in brackets, since most actors elect to use it in performance. It offers a vocal and emotional climax to the speech when it is acted. It can be numbered as line 581-b.

1. JOHN GIELGUD: THE GLASS OF FASHION

1. Gyles Brandreth, *John Gielgud: A Celebration* (Boston: Little, Brown, 1984), 64.

2. This was the production documented by Rosamond Gilder in *John Gielgud's Hamlet: A Record of Performance* (New York: Oxford University Press, 1937).

3. Richard Burton's soliloquies are discussed in a later chapter.

4. Bernard Grebanier, *Then Came Each Actor* (New York: David McKay, 1975), 488. The italics are mine.

5. John Miller, narrator for "John Gielgud: An Actor's Life," a "Great Performances" series program produced in association with WNET, Channel 13, Executive Producer, Jac Venza, copyright TVS, 1988.

6. Gielgud, quoted in Gilder, 165–69.

7. Gielgud added this list of *Hamlet*s he had viewed to the quotation cited here when he was reviewing this chapter.

8. Hal Burton, *Great Acting* (New York: Bonanza Books, Crown, 1967), 140.

9. See the discussion in Frances Teague, "Hamlet in the Thirties," *Theatre Survey* (May 1985): 71–75.

10. John Gielgud, *An Actor and His Time* (London: Sidgwick and Jackson, 1979), 85.

11. See Brooks Atkinson, review of *Hamlet, New York Times*, October 9, 1930, and also "A Sensitive, Restrained *Hamlet*," review in *Literary Digest* (October 24, 1981): 24.

12. Gilder, 14.

13. Gilder, 165–69.

14. Gilder, 213.

15. Gilder, 6.

16. The promptbook is housed in the Billy Rose Theatre Collection at the New York Public Library's Performing Arts Research Center, item no. *NCP 1937.

17. Gilder, 81.

18. Gilder, 13–20.

19. In Gilder, Gielgud explains: "In this speech I very much wished to use the word 'sullied' for 'solid.' It is now agreed upon by most of the commentators as the correct reading, but fearing I should be accused either of altering the line because I am thin [i.e., not terribly "solid"], or else of pronouncing 'solid' with an Oxford accent, I gave up the idea" (138). Line numberings are from G. Blakemore Evans, ed., *The Riverside Shakespeare* (Boston: Houghton Mifflin, 1974).

20. Gilder, 95.

21. Gilder, 95.

22. Gilder, 41.

23. Gilder, 39.

24. Gilder, 39.

25. Gilder, 38.

26. This comment from Gielgud in no. 5 in a series of BBC interviews titled "*Hamlet*: The Actor's View," recorded April 6, 1954, and now located at the National Archives of Sound, London, item DSUB-PC 10107W, X20424.

27. Gilder, 107.

28. Gilder, 115.

29. Gilder, 49.

30. Gilder, 146.

31. Gilder, 146–47.

32. Gilder, 147.

33. Italics, denoting emphasis, are Gilder's, on 147.

34. Gilder, 148.

35. Gilder, 148. Gielgud attributed the business of writing to Irving.

36. Gilder, 53.

37. Gilder, 53.

38. Gilder, 55.

39. Gilder, 151.

40. Gilder, 152. Gielgud added in a personal note that "Shakespeare seems to echo this agony in the murder scene of Macbeth."

41. Gilder, 153.

42. Gilder, 55.

43. Note added to chapter by Gielgud.

44. Gilder, 55.

45. Gilder, 55.

46. Note added to chapter by Gielgud.

47. Gilder, 173.

48. Gielgud adds in a note: "By 'frankly Elizabethan,' I meant the theory of killing in cold blood forfeiting forgiveness in Heaven for the victim."

49. Gilder, 59.

50. Gilder, 175.

51. Gilder, 175.

52. Gilder, 175.

53. This bit of business was subsequently dubbed "The Theft of the King's Sword" by A. C. Sprague and J. C. Trewin in *Shakespeare's Plays Today* (Columbia: University of South Carolina Press, 1971), 32. It began in this 1936 production and became popular with actors. Burton used it in the 1964 production directed by Gielgud.

54. Note added to chapter by Gielgud.

55. Gilder, 59.

56. Gilder, 195.

57. Gilder, 195.

58. Gilder, 197.

59. Gilder, 197.

60. BBC interview, "*Hamlet*: The Actor's View." Gielgud also mentions that it was often left out in early twentieth-century productions and that Forbes-Robertson restored it to performances.

61. BBC interview, "*Hamlet*: The Actor's View."

62. G. B. Shaw, "A Letter to John Barrymore," *Ladies' Home Journal*, February 1926.

63. Gilder, 30.

64. Gilder, 33–34.

65. Note added to chapter by Gielgud.

66. Note added to chapter by Gielgud.

67. Gilder, 65.

68. Note added to chapter by Gielgud.

2. GUINNESS, OLIVIER, AND BURTON: THE MOULD OF FORM

1. The letter was received by Mary Maher on May 4, 1988, as a response to her letter of April 18, 1988. The relevant parts of the letter are reprinted here.

2. Alec Guinness, "My Idea of Hamlet," *Spectator* 187 (July 1951): 8.

3. From a television documentary about Alec Guinness on the BRAVO channel titled "Biography," recorded in 1985 and aired on March 15, 1987.

4. From the BRAVO "Biography" documentary, 1987.

5. From the BRAVO "Biography" documentary.

6. Guinness explained in an article that a book titled *On "Hamlet,"* by Salvador de Madariaga (1948), persuaded him of the idea that Spain was just as influential to England in Shakespeare's time as America was to England in 1951. This resulted in his hiring a Spanish designer for the production. See "My Idea of Hamlet." Written by Guinness, the brief editorial functions as an apologia for the production, giving reasons for its overall lack of success.

7. Indeed, Guthrie directed Olivier's Old Vic *Hamlet* in 1937, and although the performance was designed to emphasize Hamlet's attraction to his mother, the audience barely noticed. See John A. Mills, *Hamlet on Stage* (London: Greenwood Press, 1985), 234–35.

8. Guinness, 8.

9. Robert Tanitch, *Guinness* (New York: Applause Theatre Books, 1989), 30.

10. From the BRAVO "Biography" documentary.

11. Robert Helpmann used this gesture in his 1944 production of *Hamlet*, but it appears to be original with Guinness. In the 1951 *Hamlet*, Guinness refrained, on reading Granville Barker, from dropping the curtain after this soliloquy. See Guinness, "My Idea of Hamlet."

12. Tynan certainly had an insider's point of view, having played the First Player in the production. He later wrote a book titled *Alec Guinness* (London: Camelot Press, 1953).

13. Tanitch, 68.

14. In his book *On Acting* (London: Hodder and Stoughton, Sceptre edition, 1987), Olivier said: "In those days there was a way of doing things. They wanted their verse spoken beautifully, and if that was not how you delivered it, you were considered an upstart, an outsider. So I was the outsider and John was the jewel; and a shining one too, deservedly so. John still has the most beautiful voice, but I felt in those days he allowed it to dominate his performances and, if he was lost but for a moment, he would dive straight back into its honey" (50).

15. For a full discussion of the early Olivier *Hamlet*, see Mills, 233–37.

16. The Two Cities film was produced by the J. Arthur Rank Organization.

17. Jack Jorgens, *Shakespeare on Film* (Bloomington: Indiana University Press, 1977), 214.

18. Allegedly, the horse had a distracting expression. See Dale Silviria, *Laurence Olivier and the Art of Film-Making* (London: Associated University Presses, 1985), 143.

19. John A. Mills says that Olivier "used the Q2 reading, 'sallied' (emended to 'sullied'), and as he spoke it wiped his mother's parting kiss from his face as though defiled by it." Mills hints that this might have been the "first step in the revelation of an Oedipus complex" (236).

20. The usual placement (Second Quarto and First Folio) is before the nunnery scene.

21. Roger Furse, "Design and Costumes," in Brenda Cross, *The Film "Hamlet": A Record of Its Production* (London: Saturn, 1948), says: "We attempted to work out sets to the timing of the script. For example, we knew how many stairs went to fourteen lines of dialogue" (47).

22. He was directed by Michael Benthall, and the production ran for 101 performances. See Mills, 251–52.

23. Mills, 261.

24. Kenneth S. Rothwell and Annabelle Henkin Melzer, *Shakespeare on Screen* (New York: Neal Schumann, 1990), 70.

25. Bernice Kliman, *"Hamlet": Film, Television, and Audio Performance*

(London: Associated University Presses, 1988), 289. Fortuitously, three copies are still extant (but not available for viewing by the general public) at the Folger Shakespeare Library, the New York Public Library Performing Arts Research Center, and the Library of Congress Motion Picture Division.

26. See pp. ix–x of the Redfield book, which is somewhat anecdotal and certainly less reportorial than Sterne's.

27. William Redfield, *Letters from an Actor* (New York: Viking, 1966), 12.

28. Richard Sterne, *John Gielgud Directs Richard Burton in "Hamlet": A Journal of Rehearsals* (New York: Random, 1967), 42ff.

29. Redfield, 39.

30. In fact, the Sterne and Redfield accounts are enormously valuable primers for actors.

31. Redfield, 84.

32. Sterne, 324.

33. Philip Burton was quoted by Melvyn Bragg in *Richard Burton: A Life* (Boston: Warner Books, 1990), 185.

34. See Bragg, 185–86. Burton seems to have suffered a crisis of confidence, and Elizabeth Taylor asked for Philip's help. See also Bragg, 92–96, which discusses how Philip Burton mentored him during the 1953 production. Bragg here mentions the marked differences between Burton's and Olivier's Hamlets.

35. Both Redfield and Sterne explain that this changed from day to day. At one point, Gielgud outfitted the principals in capes, only to discard them later.

36. Sterne, 43.

37. John McClain, "Powerful Effort Made by Burton," review of *Hamlet*, *New York Journal American*, April 10, 1964.

38. Richard Watts, Jr., "Richard Burton Scores as Hamlet," review of *Hamlet*, *New York Post*, April 10, 1964.

39. Edward Sothern Hipp, "Burton in High Gear," review of *Hamlet*, *Newark Evening News*, April 10, 1964.

40. Norman Nadel, review of *Hamlet*, *New York World Telegram and Sun*, April 17, 1964.

41. Michael Smith, "Burton's *Hamlet*," review of *Hamlet*, *Village Voice*, April 23, 1964.

42. Walter Kerr, "Burton's *Hamlet*," review of *Hamlet*, *New York Herald Tribune*, April 10, 1964.

43. "*Hamlet*," review of *Hamlet*, *Women's Wear Daily*, April 10, 1964.

44. George Oppenheimer, "Burton Opens on Broadway in *Hamlet*," review of *Hamlet*, *Newsday*, April 10, 1964.

45. Sterne, 69.

46. Redfield, 80.

47. Sterne, 325.

48. Sterne, 71.

49. Sterne, 326.

50. Kerr, *New York Herald Tribune*.

51. Sterne, 329.

52. Hipp, *Newark Evening News*.

53. Sterne, 36.

54. Sterne, 93.

55. Sterne, 73.

56. Cronyn won a Tony for his performance.

57. Gielgud aimed much of his direction at killing the applause, but he was completely unsuccessful.

58. Bragg, 198.

59. Bragg, 305.

3. DAVID WARNER: THE ROGUE AND PEASANT SLAVE

1. Recounted by David Warner in an interview taken by Mary Maher on January 30, 1987, in Tucson, Arizona. Unless otherwise noted, subsequent Warner quotations come from this interview.

2. Ralph Berry, *Changing Styles in Shakespeare* (London: Allen, 1981), 84–87.

3. Review of *Hamlet*, *The Times*, August 20, 1965.

4. Ronald Bryden, review of *Hamlet*, *New Statesman* (August 27, 1965): 295.

5. Don Chapman, review of *Hamlet*, *Oxford Mail*, August 20, 1965.

6. David Benedictus, review of *Hamlet*, *Spectator*, August 27, 1965.

7. Berry, 84–87.

8. Bryden, 295.

9. Penelope Gilliat, "Ophelia, Prince of Stratford," review of *Hamlet*, *Observer*, August 22, 1965.

10. "*Hamlet*," condensed from a talk by Peter Hall to the company, in *Theatre at Work: Playwrights and Productions in the Modern British Theatre*, ed. Charles Marowitz and Simon Trussler (Great Britain: Cox, 1967), 160–63. The original and complete text of the speech appears to be lost.

11. Marowitz and Trussler, 160.

12. Marowitz and Trussler, 161.

13. Marowitz and Trussler, 162.

14. Marowitz and Trussler, 162.

15. Marowitz and Trussler, 162.

16. Recounted by Tony Church in an interview taken by Mary Maher on June 6, 1988, in London. Unless otherwise noted, subsequent Church quotations come from this interview.

17. Norman Cockin, "Post-war Productions of *Hamlet* at Stratford-upon-Avon, 1948–1970" (M.A. thesis, University of Birmingham, 1980), 111–12.

18. Stanley Wells, *Royal Shakespeare: Four Major Productions at Stratford-upon-Avon* (Manchester: Manchester University Press, 1977), 27.

19. Bryden, 295.

20. Cockin, 116.

21. Berry, 96.

22. W. A. Darlington, "Hamlet of Vigour but Lacking in Poetry," review of *Hamlet, Daily Telegraph*, August 20, 1965.

23. Robert Speaight, "Shakespeare in Britain," *Shakespeare Quarterly* 26 (1965): 319–20.

24. Bryden.

25. Geoffrey Lane, "David Equal to the Test," review of *Hamlet, Wolverhampton Express and Star*, August 20, 1965.

26. Benedictus.

27. J. C. Trewin, "*Hamlet*," review of *Hamlet, Birmingham Post*, August 20, 1965.

28. John Gardner, "Hamlet, Child of Our Times," review of *Hamlet, Stratford-upon-Avon Herald*, August 27, 1965.

29. "—And an Actor Says They're Pathetic, Harmless Creatures," *Stratford-upon-Avon Herald*, August 27, 1965.

30. Hugh Leonard, "Fireworks," review of *Hamlet, Plays and Players* 13, no. 1 (October 1965): 32–33.

31. Speaight, 321.

32. Charles Marowitz, "Hall's Hamlet," *Plays and Players* 13, no. 5 (February 1966): 14.

33. "Youthful Hamlet Commands Part," review of *Hamlet, Nottingham Evening Post*, August 20, 1965.

34. Fred Norris, "The Loneliness of a Long Distance Hamlet," review of *Hamlet, Birmingham Mail*, August 20, 1965.

35. S. M. Friar, "Youthful Hamlet," letter, *Birmingham Post*, August 24, 1965.

36. Herbert Kretzmer, "Was This Squatting Really Necessary?" review of *Hamlet, Daily Express*, August 20, 1965.

37. Bryden, 295. The emphasis is mine.

38. *Nottingham Evening Post*, August 20, 1965.

39. David Nathan, "This Hamlet Hardly Needs a Ghost," review of *Hamlet*, *Sun*, August 20, 1965.

40. Julian Holland, "Nothing Princely about This Hamlet," review of *Hamlet*, *Daily Mail*, August 20, 1965.

41. Gardner, *Stratford-upon-Avon Herald*.

42. Lane, *Wolverhampton Express*.

43. Anthony Merryn, "Immature But Full of Promise," review of *Hamlet*, *Liverpool Post*, August 20, 1965.

44. W.H.W., "Unconditional Surrender to a Memorable Prince," review of *Hamlet*, *Birmingham Mail*, August 20, 1965.

45. Harold Hobson, "The Offbeat Hamlet," review of *Hamlet*, *Sunday Times*, August 22, 1965.

46. Alan Brien, "The Boy's Own Prince," review of *Hamlet*, *Sunday Telegraph*, August 22, 1965.

47. R. B. Marriott, "The Peter Hall and David Warner *Hamlet* is Fresh and Free," review of *Hamlet*, *Stage and Television Today* 4402 (August 26, 1965): 13.

48. Mervyn Jones, "Without the Prince," review of *Hamlet*, *Tribune*, August 27, 1965.

49. Jack Bentley, "Curtain Up," review of *Hamlet*, *Sunday Mirror*, August 22, 1965.

50. What Elizabethan actors *actually* did with the soliloquy in performance remains very much a point of speculation.

51. Cockin, 124–25.

52. I am interpreting here from responses heard on a sound recording taken at the Aldwych on March 9, 1966, during a live performance. The recording is housed at the National Sound Archives in London, David Warner's *Hamlet*, no. LP29930.

53. Movements about the stage and exits and entrances are from the most thorough and best kept of the promptbooks, the 1965 version, housed at the Nuffield Library, Shakespeare Birthplace Trust, Stratford-upon-Avon.

54. Warner changed the line reading from "sallied" (Riverside) to "solid," which is preferred in the Signet Classic Shakespeare used for the production.

55. Speaight, 320.

56. From the Tony Church interview: "The actual contraption was a mind-boggling thing to live with because we had to have more than one of them to be able to do the lines "'tis here" and "'tis here." The person controlling the thing stood on this ramp about halfway up the machine and held a walkie-talkie because he couldn't see except through tiny hollows in the armor. It was originally

supposed to come out of a trap door. I remember that rehearsal—this monstrous thing couldn't get in and out!"

57. Gilliat, *Observer*.

58. There were three Ophelias. The first and harshest was Glenda Jackson. Janet Suzman replaced her, and Estelle Kohler finished the run. Warner says that each sparked a different performance from him in their scenes together, but that Jackson received the roughest treatment.

59. Fredson Bowers argues just this point in "Hamlet's Fifth Soliloquy," in *Essays on Shakespeare and Elizabethan Drama*, ed. Richard Hosley (Columbia: University of Missouri Press, 1962), 213–22. He feels that Shakespeare includes this soliloquy to make sure that the audience knows that Gertrude has been chosen for later redemption and Hamlet intends no harm whatever to her in the upcoming closet scene.

60. Robert Speaight, "Shakespeare in Britain," *Shakespeare Quarterly* 27 (1966): 396.

61. See Sally Beauman, *The Royal Shakespeare Company: A History of Ten Decades* (Oxford: Oxford University Press, 1982), 239. In Peter Hall's initial years at Stratford (by 1960), the stage was redesigned with a rake, a new false proscenium arch, and an apron stage that jutted fourteen feet into the auditorium. The Aldwych was redesigned to match the Stratford stage. It could not be described as three-quarters thrust, but the alterations made the actors and the play more accessible to the audience.

62. See Alan Sinfield, "Royal Shakespeare: Theatre and the Making of Ideology," in *Political Shakespeare*, ed. Jonathan Dollimore and Alan Sinfield (Manchester: Manchester University Press, 1985), 178.

63. Cockin, 118–19.

64. Beauman, 283ff.

4. BEN KINGSLEY: IN MY MIND'S EYE

1. Ben Kingsley was interviewed by Mary Maher at the Lyric Hammersmith in London on March 18, 1989. Unless otherwise indicated, all subsequent comments are from that interview.

2. Dick Murray, "A New *Hamlet*," review of *Hamlet*, *Northampton Chronicle and Echo*, May 19, 1975.

3. Michael Coveney, "*Hamlet*," review of *Hamlet*, *Plays and Players* 20, no. 10 (July 1975): 37.

4. J. W. Lambert, "Plays in Performance," review of *Hamlet*, *Drama, the Quarterly Review of the Theatre* 120 (Spring 1976): 49–50.

5. "She Was a First at RST," *Stratford-upon-Avon Herald*, May 18, 1975.

6. In 1990–91, the original hut was torn down and replaced by a permanent brick structure, also called The Other Place.

7. The number of performances was calculated by Marian Pringle at the Nuffield Library, Shakespeare Birthplace Trust, Stratford-upon-Avon.

8. Lambert, 49.

9. Richard David, "The Problem of Hamlet," in *Shakespeare in the Theatre* (Cambridge: Cambridge University Press, 1978), 68–69.

10. "Artifact," *Time Out* (January 29, 1976): 49.

11. Irving Wardle, "Variety in a Personal Statement," review of *Hamlet*, *The Times*, February 5, 1976.

12. Vicki Dalton, "A Fitting Tribute to Buzz," review of *Hamlet*, *Hereford Evening News*, May 16, 1975.

13. Wardle, *The Times*.

14. Coveney, *Plays and Players*.

15. John Barber, "Hamlet of Clarity, Speed, and Immediacy," review of *Hamlet*, *Daily Telegraph*, February 5, 1976.

16. Murray, *Northampton Chronicle*.

17. David, 69.

18. Nicholas de Jongh, "*Hamlet*," review of *Hamlet*, *Guardian*, May 19, 1975.

19. Wardle, *The Times*.

20. Michael Coveney, "Hamlet," review of *Hamlet*, *Financial Times*, May 19, 1975.

21. De Jongh, *Guardian*.

22. Murray, *Northampton Chronicle*.

23. Barber, *Daily Telegraph*.

24. De Jongh, *Guardian*.

25. Barber, *Daily Telegraph*.

26. Benedict Nightingale, "Bubbles," review of *Hamlet*, *New Statesman* (February 20, 1976): 237.

27. M.A.M., "Roundhouse Downstairs *Hamlet*," review of *Hamlet*, *Stage and Television Today* 4947 (February 12, 1976): 20.

28. Wardle, *Times*.

29. Nightingale, *New Statesman*.

30. Murray, *Northampton Chronicle*.

31. De Jongh, *Guardian*.

32. David, 70.

33. From the RSC promptbook at the Nuffield Library, Stratford-upon-Avon: RSC Other Place 1975, *The Tragedy of Hamlet, Prince of Denmark*, Signet Classic Edition, 71.21/HAM, S. 1907-i (vol. i).

34. M.A.M., *Stage and Television*.

35. From the National Archives of Sound recording of the production of *Hamlet*, taken at the Roundhouse on March 3, 1976. Kingsley confirms that the production did not change when it moved into London.

36. The readings of the text here are from the Royal Shakespeare Company's *The Other Place 1975* promptbook, which indicates that the cast used *The Signet Classic Shakespeare*, edited by Edward Hubler, so text and line numberings are cited from it.

37. From the National Archives of Sound recording, March 3, 1976.

38. David, 66–67.

39. From the National Archives of Sound recording, March 3, 1976.

40. Nightingale, *New Statesman*.

41. "Stallion" is crossed out in the promptbook, and Kingsley opted for "scullion," the Folio reading.

42. Lambert, 50.

43. David, 68.

44. M.A.M., *Stage and Television*.

45. Nightingale, *New Statesman*.

46. David, 72.

47. Lambert, 50. The speeches could have varied slightly from night to night.

48. These moves are described in the promptbook, 6–8.

49. See *The Arden Shakespeare*, ed. Harold Jenkins (London: Methuen, 1982), 343.

50. From the promptbook and the National Archives of Sound recording.

51. Lambert, 50.

52. Clare Colvin, review of *Hamlet, Spare Rib* (February 1976): 39.

5. DEREK JACOBI: THE COURTIER, SOLDIER, SCHOLAR

1. Dale White, "An Actor Compares Stage and Film—Derek Jacobi: The Motive and the Cue for Passion," *Shakespeare Newsletter* (Spring 1983): 9.

2. Sally Beauman, "Hamlet Now," *Dial*, WNET-TV newsmagazine (November 1980): 25.

3. Derek Jacobi was interviewed by Mary Maher at his home in London on July 5, 1988. Unless otherwise noted, his commentary is from that interview.

4. Now the Royal National Theatre.

5. The major changes were in Claudius, the Ghost, and Ophelia.

6. Irving Wardle, "*Hamlet*: Old Vic," review of *Hamlet*, *The Times*, May 31, 1977.

7. Michael Coveney, review of *Hamlet*, *Financial Times*, January 24, 1978.

8. Eric Shorter, "*Hamlet* Revival is the Best All-round," review of *Hamlet*, *Daily Telegraph*, January 24, 1978.

9. Ned Chaillet, "*Hamlet*," review of *Hamlet*, *The Times*, January 24, 1978.

10. Chaillet, *The Times*.

11. Wardle, *The Times*.

12. Julian Glover joined the production as part of the first touring company in 1977 and then joined the second touring company in 1979. He was interviewed by Mary Maher on November 7, 1985, in Tucson, Arizona. Unless otherwise noted, his comments are from that interview.

13. From the press release advertising the BBC *Hamlet* via PBS, WNET-TV, May 1980.

14. British expression describing one who follows a strict set of rules.

15. For a fuller discussion of the Time-Life *Hamlet*, see Mary Z. Maher, "Hamlet's BBC Soliloquies," *Shakespeare Quarterly* 26, no. 4 (Winter 1985): 417–26.

16. The recording was released on Argo SAY 35 in 1982. Argo is a subsidiary company of Decca.

17. Jacobi had just completed this enterprise when he was interviewed.

18. Ned Sherrin, "Directing Debs Have a Bash at the Bard," *Sunday Times*, August 28, 1988.

19. Jacobi prefers "solid," as noted.

20. Geoff Brown, "Shakespeare on the Straight and Narrow," *Plays and Players* 24, no. 11 (August 1977): 29.

21. From a BBC program titled "Shakespeare's Heroes," for which Jacobi was interviewed by Michael Billington on August 2, 1979. Audiotape located at the National Archives of Sound, London, item no. LP39270.

22. John Barber, "Hamlet Strays from the Bard," review of *Hamlet*, *Daily Telegraph*, May 31, 1977.

23. "Shakespeare's Heroes," BBC interview, August 2, 1979.

24. Beauman, 28.

25. Brown, 29.

26. Review of *Hamlet*, *Financial Times*, May 31, 1977.

27. May 31, 1977, issue.

28. May 31, 1977, issue.

29. January 24, 1977, issue.

30. Beauman, 29.

31. "A *TPQ* Interview: Clyde Vinson Talks with Derek Jacobi," *Text and Performance Quarterly* 9, no. 1 (January 1989): 69–70.

32. "*TPQ* Interview," 71–72.

33. Sherrin, *Sunday Times*, August 28, 1988.

34. From a BBC program called "The Arts Worldwide." Derek Jacobi was interviewed by Ossia Trilling about the Old Vic production of *Hamlet* at Kronberg Castle, Elsinore, during the company's world tour on September 11, 1979. Audiotape located at the National Archives of Sound, London, item no. LP39346.

6. ANTON LESSER: A NOBLE MIND

1. Miller was an executive producer in "The Shakespeare Plays" series as well as artistic director for the Old Vic in the late eighties, but neither endeavor continued beyond three years. His book *Subsequent Performances* (London: Faber and Faber) was finished in 1986.

2. A review from *The Guardian* in *London Theatre Record* 2, no. 17 (August 12–25, 1982): 457.

3. Miller, 111.

4. Jack Tinker quoted in a review from *Daily Mail*, in *London Theatre Record* 2, no. 17 (August 12–25, 1982): 452.

5. Rosalie Horner in a review from *Daily Express*, in *London Theatre Record* 2, no. 17 (August 12–25, 1982): 452.

6. John Elson in a review from the Sunday *Daily Mail*, in *London Theatre Record* 2, no. 17 (August 12–25, 1982): 452.

7. Clemen says, "This direct address of the audience is important for the understanding of Shakespeare's soliloquies. The open stage protruding right into the pit, with the audience on three sides, favoured close contact, even intimacy, and a secret understanding between the audience and the soliloquizing actor who was able to project his emotions by means of gestures, physiognomy, and stage business"(*Shakespeare's Soliloquies* [London: Methuen, 1987], 4).

7. DAVID RINTOUL: TH' OBSERV'D OF ALL OBSERVERS

1. The name has been shortened to A Center for Theatre Education and Research, retaining the ACTER acronym.

2. The Second or "Good" Quarto is referred to here.

3. The largest theatre in the Royal National Theatre complex in London.

4. The Second Quarto uses "stallyon," which meant a male prostitute. Many actors use the Folio's "scullion" (a kitchen wench), since "stallyon" has lost its original meaning. "Scullion" retains a hint of lowliness.

8. RANDALL DUK KIM: SIR, A WHOLE HISTORY

1. Randall Duk Kim was interviewed by Mary Maher on August 1, 1987, shortly after he had finished a performance of *Hamlet* at the American Players Theatre. He was interviewed again in Phoenix on April 15, 1991.

2. Morris Carnovsky's book *The Eye of the Actor* and later the man himself were powerful influences in Kim's acting career.

3. Chappell was the director of Kim's first *Hamlet*, with the Honolulu Theatre for Youth.

4. "Shakespeare in Minneapolis," *Shakespeare Quarterly* 30 (1979): 219.

5. She played Ophelia.

6. See Hamlet and Osric's conversation about Laertes' choice of weapons at V.ii.142–55.

7. Tyrone Guthrie states in *A Life in the Theatre* (London: Columbus Books, 1960): "An important thing to learn in the course of rehearsal is where and how to rest, how to eke out limited resources of energy so that there will still be enough in reserve for the critical last lap" (111).

9. KEVIN KLINE: IN ACTION HOW LIKE AN ANGEL

1. Linda Winer, "Not Just Another Leading Man," *Newsday*, Weekend section, January 27, 1989.

2. Kevin Kline was interviewed by Mary Maher in New York on June 7, 1990. Unless otherwise noted, his remarks are from this interview.

3. Diane Venora was directed in *Hamlet* by Joseph Papp in a 1982–83 production at the New York Shakespeare Festival.

4. Barry Edelstein was interviewed in New York on June 8, 1990. Unless otherwise noted, his commentary is from this interview.

5. Malcolm L. Johnson, "Kevin Kline Stages a Great *Hamlet*," review of *Hamlet*, *Des Moines Register*, June 3, 1990.

6. Kline chose "solid" because he felt that more of the audience would understand it. It was also the reading used in the First Folio.

7. It took me three viewings of this piece of business to figure out how it was accomplished.

8. Not in Folio, this phrase was reinserted.

9. He also did it in II.ii between the Polonius section and the Rosencrantz and Guildenstern section.

10. There is no question mark at the end of this phrase in First or Second Quarto or Folio.

11. Also, Kline used a dagger, not a sword.

12. The seventh soliloquy was, however, reinserted in the PBS/WNET-TV production of this *Hamlet*, aired on November 2, 1990.

13. Johnson, *Des Moines Register*.

14. John Peter, "Why the Play's the Thing to Bring Stars Back to Earth," *Sunday Times*, May 13, 1990.

15. Out of six productions of *Hamlet*, Gielgud directed himself three times—in 1934, 1939, and in the troop performances in 1944.

10. KENNETH BRANAGH: "SPEAK, I AM BOUND TO HEAR"

1. Martin Booe, "Ken Again," *Premiere* (September 1991): 78.

2. Zeffirelli's *Hamlet* cost twice as much to film and made $1.6 million in the United States and $20.7 million in the United Kingdom. See Rupert Widdicombe's "Shakespeare on Film," in the [London] *Sunday Times* November 19, 1995, 10.5.

3. Judith Weinraub, "The Man Who Would Be Boffo," *Washington Post*, January 11, 1990.

4. See the explanation in Kenneth Branagh's *Hamlet, by William Shakespeare, Screenplay and Introduction* (New York: W. W. Norton, 1996), 174.

5. Kenneth Branagh, *Beginning* (London: Chatto, 1989), 178.

6. Dench had played in (or directed) nearly three dozen Shakespeares and Harris upwards of fifteen.

7. Richard Attenborough was formerly chairman at RADA.

8. Osric was mysteriously stabbed by a woolly-coated sleeve during the duel scene, possibly by one of Fortinbras's henchmen.

9. Branagh was interviewed by Mary Maher in London on September 4, 2000. Unless otherwise indicated, all subsequent comments are from that interview.

10. I am here quoting from the screenplay published by Kenneth Branagh, *Hamlet, by William Shakespeare, Screenplay and Introduction* (New York: W. W. Norton, 1996), 17. Although the Riverside edition uses "sallied," Branagh does not.

11. I am indebted to my student Cameron North, from my "Shakespeare in Performance" class, for this shrewd observation.

12. On screen there is a chest shot of Hamlet to the left of the mirror and a full body shot of him reflected at the right of the mirror's image.

13. Both the First Folio and the Second Quarto use "pitch" instead of "pith."

14. Or possibly Claudius.

15. It is only a brief second later, during a flashback of old Hamlet's death, that one remembers that the old king also died from poison administered in the ear.

16. Kenneth Branagh, personal interview, September 4, 2000.

17. Laurence Olivier, *On Acting* (London: Sceptre, 1987), 175.

18. Branagh, *Screenplay*, 206.

11. SIMON RUSSELL BEALE: THE MOTIVE AND THE CUE FOR PASSION

1. Simon Russell Beale was interviewed by Mary Maher on May 18 and 19, 2001, in Tucson, Arizona. Unless otherwise indicated, his remarks in this chapter are from that interview.

2. There was only one Gravedigger in this production.

3. Jennifer Lee Carrell, "Quintessential Prince Reflects 'Hamlet' and Its Reach," review of *Hamlet*, *Arizona Daily Star*, June 3, 2001, E1.

4. Jonathan Croall, *Hamlet Observed* (London: NT Publications, 2001), 41.

5. Croall, 41.

6. Croall, 32.

7. Croall, 68.

8. The prop was a tiny book-like object with a small writing utensil chained to it.

9. I thought it an odd choice as well, until I looked down at my own notes, carefully taken during the intermissions of the times I had seen this particular *Hamlet*, crowded among other observations in my own journal. Mr. Beale was certainly correct.

10. Croall, 29.

11. Croall, 28.

12. Croall, 79.

13. Beale is here talking about changes which often strike the actor in performance, this one during the tour to Tucson in May, 2001.

14. Croall, 73.

15. Croall, 33.

16. Croall, 79.

STUDIES IN THEATRE HISTORY AND CULTURE

Actors and American Culture,
1880–1920
By Benjamin McArthur

The Age and Stage of
George L. Fox, 1825–1877:
An Expanded Edition
By Laurence Senelick

Classical Greek Theatre:
New Views of an Old Subject
By Clifford Ashby

Embodied Memory: The Theatre
of George Tabori
By Anat Feinberg

Fangs of Malice: Hypocrisy,
Sincerity, and Acting
By Matthew H. Wikander

Marginal Sights: Staging the
Chinese in America
By James S. Moy

Melodramatic Formations:
American Theatre and Society,
1820–1870
By Bruce A. McConachie

Meyerhold: A Revolution
in Theatre
By Edward Braun

Modern Czech Theatre:
Reflector and Conscience
of a Nation
By Jarka M. Burian

Modern Hamlets and
Their Soliloquies: An
Expanded Edition
By Mary Z. Maher

"Othello" and Interpretive
Traditions
By Edward Pechter

Our Moonlight Revels:
"A Midsummer Night's Dream"
in the Theatre
By Gary Jay Williams

The Performance of Power:
Theatrical Discourse and Politics
Edited by Sue-Ellen Case and
Janelle Reinelt

Performing History: Theatrical
Representations of the Past
in Contemporary Theatre
By Freddie Rokem

The Recurrence of Fate:
Theatre and Memory in
Twentieth-Century Russia
By Spencer Golub

Reflecting the Audience: London Theatregoing, 1840–1880
By Jim Davis and Victor Emeljanow

The Roots of Theatre: Rethinking Ritual and Other Theories of Origin
By Eli Rozik

Shakespeare on the American Yiddish Stage
By Joel Berkowitz

The Show and the Gaze of Theatre: A European Perspective
By Erika Fischer-Lichte

Textual and Theatrical Shakespeare: Questions of Evidence
Edited by Edward Pechter

The Theatrical Event: Dynamics of Performance and Perception
By Willmar Sauter

The Trick of Singularity: "Twelfth Night" and the Performance Editions
By Laurie E. Osborne

Wandering Stars: Russian Emigré Theatre, 1905–1940
Edited by Laurence Senelick

7/16 D